FREUDIAN SLIP

FREUDIAN SLIP: PSYCHOANALYSIS AND TEXTUAL CRITICISM

SEBASTIANO TIMPANARO

VERSO

London • New York

This edition first published by NLB 1976
© NLB 1976
First published as *Il Lapsus Freudiano*
© La Nuova Italia 1974
Verso paperback edition first published 1985

3 5 7 9 10 8 6 4 2

Verso
UK: 6 Meard Street, London W1F 0EG
US: 20 Jay Street, Suite 1010, Brooklyn, NY 11201
www.versobooks.com

Verso is the imprint of New Left Books

ISBN-13: 978-1-84467-674-3

British Library Cataloguing in Publication Data
A catalogue record for this book is available from the British Library

Library of Congress Cataloging-in-Publication Data
A catalog record for this book is available from the Library of Congress

Typeset by Hewer Text UK Ltd, Edinburgh
Printed by in the US by Maple Vail

Contents

The Italian word *'lapsus'* covers all forms of 'slip' referred to by Freud ('slip of the tongue', 'slip of the pen', misprint and so on), and is sometimes used in a general way to refer to what are properly speaking 'parapraxes' (Italian: *'atti mancati'*). I have nearly always translated 'lapsus' as 'slip', but occasionally given the more precise form 'slip of the tongue', or 'slip of the pen', when it seemed particularly apt in the context.

The Italian *'amnesia'* has generally been rendered as 'instance of forgetting'. In Chapter 10, Timpanaro seeks to provide a more precise formulation of the differences between the strictly 'Freudian' instance of forgetting (*'amnesia'*) and other, 'non-Freudian' types of forgetting (*'dimenticanza'*). Here I have retained the term 'amnesia' to specify the former, and translated the latter as 'forgetting'.

The Italian term *'banalizzazione'*, which designates the form of textual corruption that consists in the substitution of more recondite, difficult and unfamiliar words or linguistic forms by others which are more colloquial or stylistically easier, has been anglicized to 'banalization'. [The specialist term for this phenomenon in textual criticism has traditionally been 'trivialization', from the German *Trivialisierung*.]

Timpanaro uses the work *'rimozione'* wherever the reference is to the technical Freudian term for repression (German *Verdrängung*). This has been rendered throughout in English as 'repression'. He employs the word *'repressione'* in a more general sense of social and political repression, equivalent to the German *Unterdrückung*. This has been rendered in English as 'suppression' or 'oppression'.

Translator

Note

Works cited in abbreviated form

In references given in the form 'p. 99 = 76', the first page number refers to the German edition of *The Psychopathology of Everyday Life (Zur Psychopathologie des Alltagslebens)* in Freud, *Gesammelte Werke*, vol. IV. The second page number refers to vol. VI of the *Standard Edition of the Complete Psychological Works of S. Freud*, published in London under the editorship of J. Strachey.

In references to other works by Freud, I have consistently given first the volume and page number in the *Gesammelte Werke* (indicated by *GW*), and then the volume and page number of the *Standard Edition*, edited by Strachey (indicated by *SE*).

The following works are referred to in the abbreviated forms:

Dain = A. Dain, *Les manuscrits* (Paris, 1964²).

Fornari = Bianca Fornari and Franco Fornari, *Psicoanalisi e ricerca letteraria* (Milan, 1974).

Fränkel = H. Fränkel, *Testo critico e critica del testo*, trans. by L. Canfora with a note by C. F. Russo (Florence, 1969). (This contains the most important methodological section of *Einleitung zur kritischen Ausgabe der Argonautika des Apollonios* (Göttingen, 1964).

Havet = L. Havet, *Manuel de critique verbale* (Paris, 1911).

Hook = *Psychoanalysis, Scientific Method and Philosophy*, a symposium, edited by S. Hook (New York, 1959).

Jones, *Life* = E. Jones, *Sigmund Freud: Life and Work*, in 3 volumes (London, 1957).

Musatti, *Trattato* = C. L. Musatti, *Trattato di psicoanalisi*, new ed. (Turin, 1962, 1966²).

Pasquali = G. Pasquali, *Storia della tradizione e critica del testo* (Florence, 1952²). (Anastatic reprint, Milan, 1974).

Rapaport, *Structure* = D. Rapaport, *The Structure of Psychoanalytic Theory. A Systematizing Attempt*, Monograph 6 of 'Psychological Issues' Vol. II, no. 2 (New York, 1960).

Reich Speaks of Freud = *Reich Speaks of Freud*, edited by M. Higgins and C. M. Raphael (London, 1972).

Roazen, *Broth. Anim.* = P. Roazen, *Brother Animal. The Story of Freud and Tausk* (New York, 1969).

Roazen, *Freud: Pol. and Soc.* = P. Roazen, *Freud: Political and Social Thought* (New York, 1970).

Robert = Marthe Robert, *The Psychoanalytic Revolution* (London, 1966).

West = M. L. West, *Textual Criticism and Editorial Technique* (Stuttgart, 1973).

Willis = J. Willis, *Latin Textual Criticism* (Urbana, 1972).

There are equally or more important works which are not included in the above list, but which I have preferred to cite in full in the footnotes, since I happen to refer to them less frequently.

Preliminary Remarks

This work discusses, at times quite forcefully, many of the explanations of 'slips' and instances of forgetting which Freud provides in *The Psychopathology of Everyday Life,* and some of the methodological principles he expounds in the same work. There is a danger that the forcefulness will be taken for presumptuous folly, and that an ambition to 'refute psychoanalysis' will be attributed to the present work, that is out of all proportion to its character and limits. Yet the very idea that a major movement of thought, which has had, and will for long continue to have, such a strong impact on the whole of modern culture, can be 'refuted' by the exposure of a certain number of its errors, is a petty academic illusion. We all know how many times Marxism has been 'refuted' in that way! I do not believe, of course, that psychoanalysis is comparable to Marxism either in its content of objective truth or in its power of liberation. I am not among those who advocate a fusion or integration on equal terms of these two movements. On the other hand, a serious critical attitude towards psychoanalysis is obviously not to be confused with a mere hunt for errors. So much the less can a work such as this, which (apart from certain necessary digressions) examines only one part of Freud's doctrine, have any general pretensions to refute it.

All the same, I am bound to follow this first declaration, which is not one of false modesty, with a somewhat more arrogant claim. I believe that the discussions of Freudian explanations of the 'slips of the tongue' and other parapraxes *(Fehlleistungen)* to be found on the pages below are pertinent to any overall judgement of psychoanalysis. For I think that they help to demystify a mode of reasoning which is also to be found in other of Freud's works – in particular, *The Interpretation of Dreams* and in general, all those writings which are dominated by the work of 'interpretation', which belongs to the anti-scientific aspect of psychoanalysis. I deliberately use the word 'anti-scientific', although aware that it is vague and apt to arouse suspicions, rather than 'ideological', because I regard it as (at any rate provisionally) the more appropriate to designate the *ensemble of diverse* objections to be made against psychoanalysis – objections which are interrelated, but not immediately identical.

One of these is the Marxist objection that psychoanalysis is a bourgeois doctrine, and to that extent incapable of seeing beyond an 'ideological' horizon delimited precisely by the class interests of the bourgeoisie: a doctrine which undoubtedly expresses a profound crisis of this class, but seeks to resolve it within the framework of the bourgeois social order, and confuses (except in a few moments of lucidity) the 'discontents' of *a particular* form of civilization, based on historically and socially determinate class divisions and forms of oppression, with the 'discontents' of civilization *as such* – which allegedly cannot be eliminated except at the too high price of a regression to a state of nature. This objection has often been vigorously formulated in recent years by Marxist psychologists and psychiatrists. It is, in my opinion, wholly just, but it does not exhaust the reservations inspired by psychoanalysis. Moreover, taken in isolation, it is open to polemical retort by more or less orthodox Freudians: for they can reply, with some reason, that the problem of illness (including that of mental illness and neuroses) cannot be reduced without residue to a social problem, since man is also possessed of an animal and biological nature, which is remoulded but not annulled by that 'second nature' instituted by labour and social relations of production.

It is precisely in this respect that the materialist – as opposed to pragmatic or voluntarist – Marxist encounters a second objection to psychoanalysis, apparently opposite in character to the first. This is that psychoanalysis has deleteriously widened the gap between psychology and neurophysiology. I say '*apparently* opposite' because I believe that there is an intrinsic contradiction in psychoanalysis which renders it liable to both criticisms. On the one hand, it eternalizes situations which are historically specific.

For example, it abstracts what truth there is in the notion of 'hatred of the father' from an authoritarian structure of the family, which remains transient even if it is slow to pass away, and transforms it into a sort of eternal destiny of mankind.[1] In this sense, then, psycho-analysis is too 'naturalistic'. Yet, in another sense, it remains suspended in a limbo between the 'biological' and the 'social', rejecting contact with the one no less than with the other. No doubt, some Freudian will tell us that Freud's initial training was strictly anatomical and physiological, and that to the end he regarded the gap between psychology and neurophysiology as merely provisional. But it is a fact that he did not feel, at least in those works written after the *Three Essays on the Theory of Sexuality,* any real pressure to make even a small move towards closing this gap. On the contrary, as psychoanalysis was gradually transformed into a general theory of humanity and civilization with a distinctly Schopenhauerian and metaphysical hue, the gap became ever wider. Wilhelm Reich's life and work, even in its best period before his exile in America, has more of the character of a dramatic and suggestive personal experience, a series of extraordinary intuitions and attempts at theoretical and practical innovation, than a success-ful surpassal of the limits of psychoanalysis; while his project to biologize psychoanalysis issued in a confused vitalism lacking any serious experimental basis. Yet none the less Reich was profoundly correct in seeking to recall psychoanalysis to its hedonistic origins (confused by opposite impulses from the start, and thereafter ever more attenuated), and in wanting to use this hedonistic nucleus to extend the limits of psychoanalysis in a *two-fold* direction, towards the politico-social and the biological, thereby transforming it from an agent of 'consolation' into one of liberation.[2]

[1] That the Oedipus Complex must be taken as a historical and relative formation has been demonstrated time and time again. It is well-known that study of non-monogamous and non-patriarchal family structures, past or present, has made a decisive contribution in this respect. Freud's mistake in taking a psychological situation associated with monogamy and paternal authority as an absolute condition is strikingly similar to the error made by classical bourgeois economics and its successors in their eternalization of capitalist relations of production.

[2] The extent to which the 'Reich case' remains an embarrassment for the Freudian Marxists is clearly revealed in the Proceedings of the recent Milan conference which are published in *Psicanalisi e politica* (Milan 1973): see in

Finally, there is a third objection to psychoanalysis which does not relate directly (though it does so indirectly, as I shall try to show) either to its class position or to its anti-materialist inspiration. This concerns the captious and sophistical method, resistant to any verification, quick to force interpretations to secure pre-ordained proofs, employed by Freud and Freudians in their explanations of slips, dreams and neurotic symptoms. This is no new criticism either. In fact, it has constantly accompanied the development and diffusion of psychoanalysis, during Freud's life and after his death. All the same, I think it serves some purpose to corroborate its justice with a series of concrete examples taken from a work which, to the best of my knowledge, has hitherto been very little criticized from this standpoint – indeed has always been regarded as the ideal expository text to overcome resistances to psychoanalysis: namely,

---

particular G. Jervis's excellent paper and the discussion of it (pp. 81 sq., 99 sq.) and the perceptive, but to my mind too narrowly and 'passionately' Freudian contributions of E. Morpurgo (pp. 184 sq., 191 sq.). Just as Marx and Engels found that at a certain point it was more useful to try their strength directly against the old Hegel, leaving Feuerbach in abeyance as a mere moment (although an important one) in their earlier formation, and thereby preferring – for serious reasons, yet whose consequences were not entirely positive – the richly articulated idealism of the former to the impoverished and simplistic materialism of the latter, so too there is a tendency today to by-pass Reich for a direct confrontation with the 'great bourgeois intellectual', Freud. I have already said that Reich does not represent, even for me, a successful attempt at synthesis between a psychoanalysis of the left and Marxism, and it would be altogether too easy to show that, even in his better period, his Marxism suffered in many respects from impatience and lack of rigour. It is this which also explains his later abandonment of Marxism and his brief illusion that a 'sexual revolution' could be achieved in the United States, that would be a-political and peaceful in character, yet none the less profoundly regenerate society as a whole (cf. especially the preface to the 1949 edition of *The Sexual Revolution*). All the same, at least in one respect, the Reich of the better period was truly Marxist: in his belief that even in the case of the neuroses of sexual origin, it was not so much a question of 'interpreting' reality as of radically changing it (which taken to its extreme implied the extinction of the family). He was a Marxist, too, in his opposition to Freud's social and familial conservatism, and to the oppressive, pseudo-socialist puritanism which gained ever increasing ground in Stalinist Russia. In this he developed, if in a unilateral fashion, a Fourieresque line of thought which had already found powerful expression in Engels's *Origins of the Family*. Moreover, his legal persecution in the United States, and his death in prison, suggest that even in Reich's late work there persisted, perhaps to a greater extent than he himself believed, an element that was incompatible with bourgeois society, whose subversive potential was not confined to sexual ethics.

The Psychopathology of Everyday Life.[3] The propadeutic character of this work was stressed by Freud himself in his *Lectures* of 1915–16: the three lectures (II–IV) which follow immediately after the first introductory chapter are devoted to the theory of 'parapraxes' – that is, to a summary (with certain new additions) of the content of his earlier work. It is reaffirmed today by Cesare Musatti* in his introduction to the Italian edition of *The Psychopathology*: 'If the technique works in simple situations that can be understood by everyone, it is plausible that it should also work for situations that are much more complex: whereby the reader of this book is destined to become an adherent of analytic theory.'[4] Musatti's

---

* Cesare Musatti (1897): professor of psychology at the University of Milan, and most notable Italian authority on psychoanalysis; a militant anti-fascist and left socialist, who has always considered Marxism and psychoanalysis two distinct systems, each valid in its own domain.

[3] For the exceptionally favourable reception accorded this work right from the start, and the paucity or absence of criticism which it has enjoyed ever since, see Jones, *Life*, Vol. II, p. 375: 'The book had more favourable reviews than most of Freud's, and even the *Neue Freie Presse* found the ideas interesting. It has probably been the most popular of Freud's writings.' See the similar comments in J. Strachey, Introd. to Vol. VI of the *Standard Edition*, p. x; and the bibliographical note at the end of Boringhieri's edition of 1965, p. 255: 'While being one of the most widely read of Freud's works, *The Psychopathology of Everyday Life* is also one of the least discussed: its theory was already fully expounded in the first edition, and critics have provided only additions and clarifications, contributing to it rather than correcting it.' Among such contributions deserving particular mention are: A. Maeder, *Contributions à la psychopathologie de la vie quotidienne*, 'Archives de Psychol.' 6 (1907), p. 148 sqq., and *Nouvelles contributions à la psychopathologie de la vie quotidienne*, idem 7 (1908), p. 283 sqq.; E. Jones, *The Psychopathology of Everyday Life*, 'American Journal of Psychol.' 22 (1911), p. 477 sqq.; Musatti, *Trattato*, p. 333 sqq. The work of Maeder and Jones was used by Freud himself in the subsequent editions of his work. So far as the arbitrariness of explanations is concerned, Maeder's work is more detrimental than Freud's. Jones and Musatti, on the other hand, despite their substantial acceptance of the entire Freudian theory of the 'slip', reveal a somewhat greater caution of formulation and an effort to cite only those examples whose Freudian explanation has a certain verisimilitude. For further bibliographical material see Strachey's bibliography in Vol. II of the *Standard Edition*. Even today the Freudian theory of the 'slip' is considered to be 'above suspicion' by J. A. Arlow, in Hook, p. 114 sq., even more so, if anything, by Robert, Chap. 12 and passim, and Fornari, p. 58 sq. For the genesis and composition of *The Psychopathology* see Jones, *Life*, Vol. II, p. 372 sqq., and Strachey, Introd. to vol. cit., p. xii sq.

[4] Boringhieri's edition of 1965, p. xi.

authority is deservedly great, and even one who does not subscribe to his 'Freudian orthodoxy' must acknowledge that – in contrast to the faith of so many other orthodox Freudians – this is in his case not a dogmatic allegiance to the Master, but a deliberate choice in favour of everything which is enlightened and rational in Freud's work, with a particular emphasis on the experimental instance. (Musatti himself has stressed this many times.)[5] Yet the experimental method precisely demands that we can submit our findings to verification; it demands a 'differential diagnosis' that does not privilege the explanation of those symptoms most suited to a prior theoretical construction. It is these criteria, in my opinion, which make it impossible to assent to Musatti's verdict. Indeed it seems to me that the very simplicity and accessibility of the cases considered by Freud in *The Psychopathology* demonstrate in a particularly clear and direct way (even more so, for example, than those in *The Interpretation of Dreams*) the fragility of most of his explanations of them, and the basic defects of the method by which he arrived at these.

In any case, what Freud understood by the propaedeutic value of his work was not that it sweetened a theoretical pill to capture the benevolence of a hostile public, nor that it represented a sort of 'entertainment' which the author had allowed himself in the margin of his more important works. In 1930 A. A. Roback, in one of his books, included Freud among the three 'great Jews' of the twentieth century along with Einstein and Bergson (the latter, in fact, hardly so great!), but expressed perplexity over his theory of 'slips'. Even at this late date, Freud declared in reply that he considered this theory an 'indispensable' part of psychoanalysis: 'In the chapter on the doctrine of lapses you express disbelief concerning just that part of psychoanalysis that has most readily found general recognition. How then are you likely to judge our other less attractive discoveries? My impression is that if your objections to the conception of lapses are justified I have very little claim to be named besides Bergson and Einstein among the intellectual sovereigns. . . .'[6]

[5] In a particularly effective and persuasive fashion in the introduction to the *Trattato*, p. xviii sqq.
[6] In Jones, *Life*, Vol. III, p. 480, and in Robert, p. 371. Cf. S. Blanton, *My Analysis with Freud* (New York, 1971)

Freud's reaction doubtless went too far in claiming an indissoluble linkage between all the elements of psychoanalysis; we do not believe that the entire edifice collapses if the theory of 'slips' falls or is largely disproved. But Freud's statement does remain an index of the enormous importance which he never ceased to attach to *The Psychopathology of Everyday Life*.

Finally, it goes without saying that a charge of anti-scientificity of the kind in question here has meaning (whether it is accepted or rejected) only for those Freudians who, like Freud himself, are convinced that psychoanalysis is a science. It has neither significance nor interest for those who, as Giovanni Jervis★ put it critically in an article some years ago,[7] seek 'to absolve Freudian theory from any concern with scientificity in the traditional sense'. Anyone who has transformed psychoanalysis into a pastiche of Husserl or Heidegger, orienting it towards a mysticism that evokes Jung much more than Freud; or conversely anyone who has falsified Marxism by interpreting it not as a critique of the ideological, capitalist use of a false scientific 'neutrality', but as a critique of science *tout court* – all science being identified with this false neutrality – will take no interest in discussions of the sort with which this book is concerned. Indeed, such trends may try to manipulate them to the greater glory of psychoanalysis, and effect a marriage between an 'obscurantist Marxism' which has regressed from science to metaphysics (or to a mere pragmatism) and a psychoanalysis subjected to an analogous regression (more easily achieved in the case of psychoanalysis, since 'regressive' elements which have to be invented in Marx and Engels by wholly arbitrary 'readings' of their works, are all too present in Freud himself, especially in his later works). There are, of course, also dangers in a

★ Giovanni Jervis: Italian Marxist psychiatrist and psychologist, who has made a particular study of psychoanalysis, while developing political and social criticisms of it; author of a recent *Manual of Psychiatry* in Italy.

[7] *Quaderni Piacentini* 28 (September 1966), p. 101. Jervis observed that 'psychoanalysts the world over show an extraordinary capacity for dissociating themselves from the objections advanced against them in the name of scientific method' (idem). Jervis has subsequently emphasized the extent of his distance from psychoanalysis, founded primarily on political considerations: see, for example, his contribution to *L'Erba Voglio* 3, no. 11 (May–June 1973), p. 16 sqq.; and in *Psicanalisi e politica* cit., p. 74 sqq.

stress on the need for scientificity. The most serious of these is the risk of separation between those engaged in a field of work and those outside it, and the formation or re-formation of closed castes with their own esoteric idiom and their own privileged interests. All the same, this danger is not to be eliminated by a utopian flight from science, but by the establishment of a continuous and correct relationship between practice and science – a science in which the experimental instance is accorded its due rights, and in which objective reality is registered and known in order to be transformed, rather than voluntaristically denied or manipulated. It is to readers who accept this premise (itself, of course, provisional and in need of serious development) that the present work may be of some interest, at least as a basis for discussion.

2

Freudians and Textual Critics: an Overdue Encounter

I have not yet explained the subtitle and specific theme of this work: why psychoanalysis and textual criticism? While the last decade has witnessed a fairly intense exchange of experiences between psychoanalysis and linguistics, issuing at times in a union that has exercised a strong influence even of late on Marxism, it would seem at first glance that a branch of philology can contribute little or nothing to a discussion on psychoanalysis. For textual criticism is a science, which though it possesses clearly defined affinities with linguistics, has remained much more 'traditional' than the latter – and so more exempt from methodological anxieties and impulses of innovation.

Yet, in the particular case of the 'psychopathology of everyday life', it might be said that psychoanalysts and textual critics have to a large extent studied the same phenomena – though their methods and purposes in doing so have been very different. The task of the textual critic is to inquire into the origin of alterations undergone by a text in the course of its successive transcriptions, so as to be able to correct those errors persuasively or to establish which of two or more variants deriving from different sources is the original, or approximates most closely to it.

Among the various types of errors of transcription, there are at least two which have nothing to do with a 'slip of the pen'. On the one hand, there are those mistakes which are inaccurately termed 'palaeographic'; these consist of misunderstandings of signs in the written text which the copyist had before him – for every kind of writing, ancient or modern, contains signs that resemble each other and are therefore liable to confusion. On the other hand, there are those alterations which have been *consciously* made in the transmitted text. These are due either to a deliberate intention to change, amplify, abridge or gloss what the author wrote, or, even more frequently, to the copyist's illusion that he is restoring the original when he corrects what, from the standpoint of his own culture, seems deficient in sense and which he thus takes to be a mistake of an earlier copyist or an oversight on the part of the author. In the latter cases, the text is not in fact defective – or perhaps sometimes it is, but ought to have been emended along quite different lines. Of course, these conscious modifications may themselves tell us much, not only about the copyist's level of culture, but also about his psychology as an individual, and above all that of his social milieu. One need only think of the suppression or euphemistic evasion of 'dirty words' not only by mediaeval monks but even sometimes by philologists of the last century in their publication of ancient texts,[1] not to mention editions expressly designed to be used in schools, which are still, in many cases, expurgated *ad usum Delphini* ['for the use of the King's son']. However, none of these textual manipulations have the involuntary character (at the level of the conscious Ego) which marks the 'slip'.

But it has long been realized that the majority of mistakes in transcription and quotation do not belong to either of the two categories just mentioned. They are, on the contrary, 'errors due to distraction' (let us adopt, for the moment, this extremely imprecise formula), to which anyone transcribing or citing a text may be subject – whether scholar or lay man, mediaeval monk or modern typist or student. Indeed even the errors of the first two categories, which in themselves have nothing in common with the

---

[1] For examples of alterations of mediaeval codices due to prudery, see Pasquali, pp. 119, 416; D. Comparetti, *Virgilio nel medio evo,* new ed. (Florence, 1943) I, p. 105 note 1, also note 2; V. Tandoi in 'Studi ital. filol. class.' 36 (1964), p. 173 note 2. Another example is Planude's correction to Callimachus, epigr. 25, 5 Pfeiffer, which seeks to eliminate the reference to a homosexual love affair. In modern times – apart from the scholastic texts, to which we shall shortly refer – modifications of this kind were made by Angelo Mai to the editions of the Mitografi Vaticani (*Classici auctores,* III; see Giuseppina Barabino in 'Mythos, scripta in honorem Marii Untersteiner', Genoa, 1st Fil. Class., 1970, p. 61) and to the *Geta* of Vitale of Blois (*Classici auctores,* V; see R. Avesani in 'Italia medioevale e humanistica' 2, 1959, pp. 531 and note 4, 535; idem 3 1960, p. 395).

'slip', hardly ever occur 'in a pure state'. The palaeographic error, it is true, has its origin in a misunderstanding of a written sign. However, a psychological (or psycho-cultural) mistake is very often grafted onto this, so that what is produced is an erroneous word which resembles the correct word in its written aspect, but also is determined by the influence either of its context or of words sounding like it which are more familiar to the copyist, closer to his everyday experience.[2] Similar considerations obtain for the second category of errors, where it is sometimes difficult to distinguish the truly and genuinely conscious alteration from the unconscious effects of 'banalization' – that is, the substitution of one word by another whose meaning is actually or apparently the same, but whose usage is more familiar to the copyist. We shall have frequent occasion to refer to the phenomenon of banalization.

It may be objected that a mistake made in copying a text that one has before one's eyes is very different from a mistake made in attempting to remember a word or phrase registered a long time before. The majority of the cases examined by Freud are, as is well known, of the latter type. The difference is certainly not negligible, and we shall keep it in mind whenever necessary; but it is not as important as it might seem. For it has long been established[3] that a copyist, whether ancient or modern, does not as a rule transcribe a text word for word, still less letter for letter (at least not unless he is transcribing a text written in a language or a script of which he is wholly ignorant), but reads a more or less lengthy section of it and then, without looking back at the original at each point, writes it down 'from memory'. He is therefore liable, if only in

[2] For the rarity of *exclusively* palaeographic errors see, e.g. Pasquali, p. 471; Willis, pp. 55–57.

[3] The basic studies are still those of E. Bruhn, *Lucubrationum Euripidearum capita selecta*, 'Jahrbücher für class. Philol.' Suppl. 15 (1887), p. 227 sqq. See also Pasquali, pp. 113 sqq., 471 sq., 483 sq.; J. Andrieu, *L'explication psychologique des fautes de copiste*, 'Rev. Ét. Lat.' 28 (1950), p. 279 sqq. It is obviously possible to refer here only to a tiny part of the huge bibliography on these problems. On the subject of the various elements comprised in the process of transcription, see, besides the authors already cited, Dain, p. 41 sqq. (who refers to his personal instruction from A.-M. Desrousseaux); Fränkel, p. 72 sq. Probably the act of copying is even more complex than would appear from these accounts, but for our purposes it is not necessary to dwell on the more recondite distinctions. See also Froger (cit. below, note 14), p. 11 sq.

the brief interval between the reading, or, as the case may be, the dictation, and the actual transcription of the passage, to commit errors which are not substantially different from those examined by Freud and (though with other methods) by psychologists who were his predecessors and contemporaries. Moreover, the attention can wander in the course of reading itself, thus producing 'slips' even at that stage in the proceedings. This occurs all the more so because our reading, and to a greater or lesser extent that of classical and mediaeval copyists also, is nearly always synthetic: we do not look at all the letters of a word one after the other, but when we have recognized some letters and glanced at the word as a whole we mentally 'integrate' the rest of its letters. At least as far as alphabetical scripts are concerned, we tend to read them as if each word was a unique 'design', an ideogram. (This is the reason why misprints can so easily escape us when we correct proofs. Because we are intolerant of an analytic reading we believe we have read the right word even when there is a mistake in one of its letters; in the same way we can fall into the opposite error of reading, in place of the correctly written word, another which is different in one or two letters.)

Furthermore, a textual critic often has to deal with what is called an indirect tradition – that is, with quotations, often from memory, of complete texts by other authors. Quintilian frequently commits such errors in quoting Virgil; Francesco De Sanctis in citing Dante or Petrarch, Leopardi or Berchet. Finally, he must consider oversights which are much more likely to be those of the author himself than of his copyists. Thus Cicero in a moment of distraction once wrote, instead of the name of Aristophanes, that of Eupolis – another great Athenian writer of comedies; on another occasion he confused the name of Ulysses' nurse, Euriclea, with that of his mother, Anticlea.[4] Here we are manifestly concerned

4 The first case (*Orator*, 29), Cicero assures us on his own testimony (*ad Att.* XII 6, 3), concerns an error of his own, and not one on the part of the copyist: Cicero realized it in time to correct the error before the work was made public, and it is true that the codices that have come down to us have *Aristophanem* and not *Eupolin*. In the second case (*Tuscul.* V 46) the Ciceronian correspondence has not preserved any evidence of 'self-criticism', and the codices have *Anticlea*. Since Cicero does not refer directly to the famous episode in the *Odyssey* (where Euriclea, washing Odysseus' feet, recognizes him by a scar), but to Pacuvius'

with 'slips of the pen' analogous to those studied by Freud. (We abstain for the moment from any explanation of them.) Moreover, Freud himself also devotes a section of his book (Chap. VI) to errors of reading and transcription, and points to the 'internal similarity' between forgetting and making slips in reading, speaking and writing (*vergessen, verlesen, versprechen, verschreiben*).[5] Nor, indeed, were these phenomena overlooked by previous or contemporary textual critics, or by psychologists of the 'traditional' school, who for the most part followed Wundt. They had already noticed such a similarity, even if they had interpreted phenomena of this kind in a very different way from Freud. We have only to recall *Versprechen und Verlesen*, the work of Rudolf Meringer (a linguist) and Karl Mayer (a psychologist), which was published in Stuttgart in 1895 – that is, a few years before the appearance of the first edition of Freud's work (in the *Monatsschrift für Psychiatrie und Neurologie* of 1901). This is a book that Freud cites and discusses many times.[6]

---

staging of the scene in his tragedy *Niptra*, which is no longer extant, one cannot wholly exclude the possibility that Pacuvius was deliberately departing from Homer's account, and that he had substituted Odysseus' mother (who, according to the *Odyssey*, was already dead by the time he returned home) for his nurse. The latter hypothesis is maintained by I. Mariotti, *Introduzione a Pacuvio* (Urbino, 1960, p. 39). Nevertheless, given the similarity between the two names, reinforced by the conceptual affinity between mother and nurse, the hypothesis of a 'slip of the pen' on Cicero's part still seems to me to be more likely: see W. Zillinger, *Cicero und die altrömischen Dichter* (Würzburg, 1911) p. 71 sq., which cites various other slips made by Cicero in his quotations from memory of ancient Latin poets. See also the analogous examples of slips which are cited later, Chap. VI.

[5] See *The Psychopathology*, p. 268 = 239 sq. Freud adds: 'Language points to the internal similarity between most of these phenomena; they are compounded alike [in German] with the prefix "*ver-*".' In saying this, he paid his tribute to an ancient prejudice – one of Greek origin but perpetuated throughout mediaeval and modern times, and given a final and spasmodic lease of life by Heidegger – that languages (and above all certain languages: Greek and German) are the depositories of a sort of original wisdom, and that etymology, in the Greek sense of the term, discloses the 'true' significance of words which lies beneath a veil of later distortion. In reality *ver-* does give a pejorative connotation to many words, but very frequently this has nothing in common with the errors due to 'repression'; and in very many other cases, in conformity with its original sense, it has no pejorative connotation whatsoever.

[6] See especially p. 61 sqq. = 53 sqq., and the many other references cited in the index of the German and English editions.

Yet not one of these traditional linguists and psycholinguists ever replied to Freud. Neither Meringer in a subsequent book, nor Marbe and his pupils, nor Havers, nor anyone else, so far as I have been able to ascertain, deigned even to mention, let alone confute, *The Psychopathology of Everyday Life*.[7] Did they lack arguments? Perhaps so, to some extent: their work was too flatly classificatory, and when they posed the problem of 'explanation' they had recourse to neurophysiological hypotheses of insufficient rigour and specificity (Wundt, as we shall see, had something better to supply in this respect). Their absence of response also had to do with the fact that these authors were linguists with a certain interest in psychology, or psychologists with a certain interest in linguistics, but *not philologists*: they had virtually no experience of the kind of errors of transcription and quotation just considered. But despite these limitations, they should have been in a position, to my mind, to confront Freud successfully at least on some points. Their failure to do so, therefore, can only be explained as a 'conspiracy of silence' towards a doctrine which still created a scandal in reactionary academic circles. It was only later – for the most part after Freud's death – that linguistic studies drew closer to psychoanalysis. But structuralist linguists, and even more so, structuralists who are not linguists, have been attracted by other aspects of Freud's work,

---

[7] See R. Meringer, *Aus dem Leben der Sprache: Versprechen, Kindersprachen, Nachahmungstrieb* (Berlin, 1908); K. Marbe, *Die Bedeutung der Psychologie für die übrigen Wissenschaften und die Praxis*, in 'Fortschritte der Psychologie und ihrer Anwendungen' 1 (1913), p. 5 sqq., especially 32 sqq.; J. Stoll, *Zur Psychologie der Schreibfehler*, idem 2 (1914), p. 1 sqq.; W. Havers, *Sprachwissenschaft und Fehlerforschung*, in 'Donum natalicium Schrijnen' (Nijmegen-Utrecht, 1929), p. 27 sqq., (which pays particular attention to the role of error as a possible source of general linguistic innovation: Havers cites many other works by psycholinguists – unfortunately not all of them available to me. But neither he, nor so far as I have been able to see the authors cited by him, refer to Freud, even polemically). Havers' *Handbuch der erklärender Syntax* (Heidelberg, 1931) is useful if laborious reading (especially the chapter on 'Syntaktische Fehler und ihre psychischen Bedingungen', p. 54 sqq.). See also A. Thumb, *Psychologische Studien über die sprachlichen Analogiebildungen*, in 'Indogermanische Forschungen' 22 (1907–8), p. 1 sqq., who adopts a position very close to that of Havers, but gives special attention to errors responsible for morphological and lexical, rather than syntactical, innovations: M. Leumann, *Zum Mechanismus des Bedeutungswandels* (1927), now in his *Kleine Schriften* (Zürich-Stuttgart, 1949), p. 286 sqq.

and little concerned with his explanations of 'slips';[8] while now that a conspiracy of silence or a reactionary hostility has been replaced by a vogue for psychoanalysis, one can only suppose that Freud's explanations of the latter appear to them to be perfectly correct.

What then of the textual critics? Here, too, there has been scarcely any contact. Naturally something, or more than something, could have escaped my attention here. Yet it is a fact that even scholars who are quite convinced of the frequency and importance of psychological errors in the transmission of texts (from Eduard Schwartz, the editor of Eusebius' *Historia ecclesiastica,* to Louis Havet, the author of that extensive treatise on the 'pathology and therapy of errors', the *Manuel de critique verbale*; from Alphonse Dain and Jean Andrieu, intelligent followers of the Havet tradition,[9] to Hermann Fränkel, whose long experience as editor of Apollonius Rhodius was responsible for lively and non-conformist developments in methodology[10]) do not make so much as a polemical mention of *The Psychopathology of Everyday Life*, although their works appeared at a time when Freud's book was already known and when there was much talk of psychoanalysis even among laymen. Even recent works inspired to a greater or lesser

[8] Roman Jakobson, who of all the major structuralist linguists is most aware of the need for interdisciplinary studies, tends to concentrate his attention on Freud's work on aphasia, which is closest to his interests (see Jakobson, *Selected Writings,* I, s'Gravenhage 1962, under 'Freud' in the name index). The developments – or involutions – that certain Freudian terms have undergone at the hands of structuralists who are not linguists, and of phenomenologists wavering between religion and revolution, although interesting in other respects, are not relevant to our present theme.

[9] Andrieu – a very gifted scholar who died prematurely – was of all textual critics perhaps the most aware of the need to provide 'individualizing' psychological explanations of errors in transcription; and in the article cited above (note 3) he pursued with much finesse, perhaps even undue subtlety, some of the clues in Havet's work. But not even Andrieu names Freud, while his explanations, though a response to partially similar problems, take a direction quite different to those of Freud, and tend rather to converge with some of Wundt's remarks on the way in which a word in thought precedes a word on the page, and on the errors that derive from this disjuncture.

[10] See the work cited in the list of titles, p.7.

extent by the structuralism of Contini,* which are innovatory in theory but also lavish in their interdisciplinary coquetry and ambition to *épater les philologues*, do not contain, if I am right, any appeal to Freud's work. For their part, the Freudians, if they have shown (as we have said) a growing interest in linguistics, seem wholly unaware of any need for an exchange of methods and experiences with textual criticism.

So far as I can tell, the first philologist to read *The Psychopathology of Everyday Life* with any interest, or at least a polemical curiosity, was Giorgio Pasquali.* In an article entitled *Congettura e probabilità diplomatica* ('Annali della Scuola Normale' 1948, p. 220 sq., reprinted in the second edition of the *Storia della tradizione e critica del testo*, p. 483 and note 1) he deplored the fact that in explanations of errors made in transmitting texts, far too little importance was attached to the slips of the copyist; and in citing the work of psychologists and psycholinguists of potential use to textual critics, he included (alongside the more traditional Meringer, Mayer and Havers) Freud's book in a translation of 1948, adding: 'I have only this Italian translation at my disposal, which is not good, but adequate for my purposes; the cases referred to are fairly instructive, the explanations seem to me, as they do to many psychiatrists, to be for the most part far-fetched.' He returned to this theme in a review of *Les manuscrits* by A. Dain:[11] 'I have

* Giancarlo Contini (1910): professor of romance philology at the Universities of Fribourg (Switzerland), Florence and now Pisa, who has written on literature, linguistics and philology, with particular reference to past and present Italian poetry, and formed a large school of disciples in Italy.

* Giorgio Pasquali (1885–1952): one of the best classical philologists of this century, who was professor at the University of Florence; a pupil of Wilamowitz, Leo and Wackernagel in Germany; author of works on Horace, archaic Latin metre, Plato's correspondence and other books; innovator in textual criticism with his *Storia della tradizione e critica del testo*, to which scholars like M. L. West and E. J. Kenny in England are indebted.

[11] In 'Gnomon' (1951), p. 235: I quote from the Ital. trans. in *Storia della tradiz.*², p. 472. There is also the brief allusion in a short note written in 1948, and now included in *Lingua nuova e antica*, edited by G. Folena (Florence, 1964), p. 294: 'The examples are splendid and ample, while their explanation seems to me for the most part puerile.' But 'puerile' is scarcely the appropriate word: what is wrong in the worst of Freud's explanations is something quite different – their captiousness and lack of verifiability, and their claim to discover a case of 'repression' behind every instance of a 'slip'.

briefly dealt with this type of error, which is still too little studied, in *Annali della Scuola Normale di Pisa* (. . .), and made use in doing so of the work of Meringer, K. Mayer, Havers and also of the psychiatrist Freud (though rigorously expunging all Freudianism, that is to say pansexuality).'

I believe – as I have already said, and as I shall try to show – that we are justified in passing a negative judgement on most of the explanations of 'slips' given by Freud. Nonetheless, Pasquali's judgement needs to be verified: it would be imprudent, and above all anti-Pasqualian, *iurare in verba magistri* ['to swear by the master's word']. It is true that Pasquali belonged to a Central European culture (one that was much more Germanic, however, than Austrian – and the difference is not unimportant if one thinks of how many of the most sophisticated currents of 20th century bourgeois culture, from logical empiricism to psychoanalysis, from marginalist economics to Austro-Marxism and dodecaphonic music, emerged in the course of the last decade of existence of the multinational Austrian Empire, and of how much more traditional German culture remained, despite the shocks administered to it by Nietzsche).[12] It is equally true that Pasquali was interested in medicine and biology, and was free from the moralistic and racist prejudices which had made the right wing of the bourgeoisie hostile to psychoanalysis for so long. Nonetheless, it is clear from his remarks that his contact with psychoanalysis was not only belated, but very fleeting. This is confirmed, I would say, by his use of the term 'the psychiatrist Freud', at a time when Freud's work had already acquired world renown and embraced a far larger field than that of psychiatry alone. An advocate of psychoanalysis might also legitimately point to the fact that the 'many psychiatrists' whose authority Pasquali invoked would have been,

---

[12] In Germany during the years 1908–14, when Pasquali's intellectual formation was determined, psychoanalysis still encountered the most intense hostility: see Freud, *Selbstdarstellung*, *GW* XVI 75 sq. = *An Autobiographical Study*, *SE* XX 50 sq. There is also a note in *GW* XIII 103 = *Group Psychology and the Analysis of the Ego*, *SE* XVIII 90 sq. It is likely that in his youth Pasquali acquired only a superficial and indirect (possibly distorted) knowledge of psychoanalysis, and that later he made no effort to improve it; this is all the more likely in that during the worst years of Nazi and Fascist tyranny, psychoanalysis was banned from German and Italian culture.

in all probability, traditionalist and 'right-wing' opponents of psychoanalysis; and he would certainly protest (for many good reasons, even if not for quite so many as he believes) against the identification of Freudianism with pansexualism – all the more so in that *The Psychopathology of Everyday Life* by no means lacks explanations of 'slips' in which sexuality plays no part; indeed these are far more frequently to be found in it than in *The Interpretation of Dreams.*

As early as 1949, Lanfranco Caretti,* a Pasqualian who was sensitive to the new ferments in European culture which were circulating in Italy after the long slumbers of fascist dogma and anti-semitic persecution, provided an explanation of a 'political slip'. It was hardly – as we shall see – an orthodox Freudian one'. Nevertheless, it implied a much less hasty and negative verdict on Freud's work.[13] More recently, Luigi Enrico Rossi, in a review of Hermann Fränkel's *Testo critico e critica del testo,* has drawn attention to the need for textual critics to reflect on *The Psychopathology of Everyday Life.*[14] Thus the kind of analysis we shall attempt in the following pages may be of some utility – even if it inevitably runs a risk of seeming excessively meticulous, and if the aim of presenting it in a form that facilitates its reading and criticism by psychoanalysts and others of alternative cultural background obliges me to provide explanations of certain concepts and procedures of textual criticism which will appear superfluous to philologists.

* Lanfranco Caretti (1913): professor of Italian literature at the University of Florence, and author of important critical and philological studies of Ariosto, Tasso, Parini, Alfieri and Manzoni.

[13] L. Caretti, *Lingua e Sport* (Florence, 1973), p. 91 sq. Some interesting remarks are also to be found in another of Caretti's works, *Casi di filologia eterodossa,* now included in: *Il 'fidato' Elia e altre note alferiane* (Padua, 1961), p. 127 sqq.

[14] In the Book Supplement of *Paese Sera,* 30 January 1970. R. Marichal adopts a highly individual position in the collection by various authors entitled *L'Histoire et ses Méthodes* (Paris, 1961), p. 1257: he readily admits the 'psychoanalytic' character of every error of transcription, but at the same time maintains that the philologist of today, since he is not able 'to psychoanalyse an unknown subject who has been dead for two thousand years' must abandon any attempt at a Freudian explanation of such errors. See also J. Froger, *La critique des textes et son automatisation* (Paris, 1968), p. 14, who also admits, however, that there are errors of a non-psychoanalytic nature.

3

Pedestrian (but True) Explanation of an Incomplete Quotation

At the beginning of *The Psychopathology of Everyday Life* – before the treatise breaks up into a host of examples, discussed often very briefly and interspersed with methodological considerations to be taken up and expanded in the last chapter – there are two extended examinations of specific 'slips of the tongue', with a whole chapter devoted to each. It seems certain that the book owes this structure not to external circumstances, to the disjointed manner in which it was written, but to Freud's intention of making these two examples arouse in the no doubt incredulous or reluctant reader an initial conviction in the justice and fertility of his method. For this reason we believe we too should devote more time to these examples than to later ones. We shall begin with the second, because certain methodological defects which are particularly apparent in Freud's explanation here will help us understand better the weakness of his explanation also of the first case and the others examined in the rest of the work.

A young Austrian Jew, with whom Freud strikes up a conversation while travelling, bemoans the position of inferiority in which Jews are held in Austria-Hungary. His generation, he says, is 'destined to grow crippled, not being able to develop its talents nor gratify its desires'. He becomes heated in discussing this problem, and tries to conclude his 'passionately felt speech' (as Freud, with a pinch of good-natured irony, calls it) with the line that Virgil puts in the mouth of Dido abandoned by Aeneas and on the point of suicide: *Exoriare aliquis nostris ex ossibus ultor* (*Aeneid*, IV 625). ('Let someone arise from my bones as an Avenger' or 'Arise from my bones, o Avenger, whoever you may be'.)

But his memory is imperfect, and all he succeeds in saying is *Exoriare ex nostris ossibus ultor*: i.e. he omits *aliquis* and inverts the words *nostris ex*.

What is the explanation for this double error? The most mediocre of philologists would have no difficulty in giving one. As we have already mentioned, anyone who has anything to do with the written or oral transmission of texts (including quotations learnt by heart) knows that they are exposed to the constant danger of banalization. Forms which have a more archaic, more high-flown, more unusual stylistic expression, and which are therefore more removed from the cultural-linguistic heritage of the person who is transcribing or reciting, tend to be replaced by forms in more common use. This process of banalization can affect many aspects of a word. For instance, it can affect its spelling: forms like *studj, havere* easily turn into *studi* and *avere* in texts transcribed today or even more so in quotations written down from memory. It can affect its phonetic character: one so often reads or hears someone recite the famous line from Ariosto: 'O gran bontà de' cavalieri *antiqui*!' with the *antiqui* replaced by *antichi*, even though the rhyme between the third and fifth lines of that octet favours the more archaic form. It can affect its morphology: '*enno* dannati i peccatori carnali', wrote Dante, *Inferno*, V 38; but in various manuscripts of the *Commedia* one finds *sono* or *eran*, or some similar banalization (see Petrocchi's critical edition). It can affect its lexical character: again in Dante the archaic form *aguglia* was nearly always replaced by the more usual *aquila* in certain manuscripts – and still is today in quotations loosely made by modern authors. Finally, it can affect its syntactic or stylistic-syntactic character: in the sub-title to Ruggiero Bonghi's *Lettere critiche, Perché la letteratura italiana non sia populare in Italia* ('Why Italian literature is not popular in Italy'), the subjunctive *sia* is itself not popular enough in Italy, so that when the sub-title is quoted from memory one frequently finds it replaced by the indicative mood *è*. We have deliberately cited extremely elementary examples. But frequently banalizations take on a more complex character, and involve the whole context and not just a single word. It is frequently difficult and sometimes impossible to establish whether what is involved is unconscious banalization or deliberate alteration; but certainly in a great number of cases one

can exclude this latter possibility. We have all had the experience
of checking a text we have quoted from memory or even transcribed ourselves and finding we have made a certain number of
slips – consisting for the most part, precisely of banalizations.[1]
For a long time, ever since I was a boy, I believed that in the sonnet
In morte del fratello Giovanni, Foscolo had written: '. . . mi vedrai

---

[1] The most frequently quoted examples in the manuals on textual criticism
have to do with orthographic, lexical, morphological and word-order banalizations. Less common, in general, is the case of syntactic banalization. Thus it
might be useful at this stage to cite a few examples of these from Latin texts
because, as we shall find, these are precisely the sort of corruption we shall be
dealing with in the case of the line from Virgil quoted by the young Austrian.
Cicero, *De div.* I 65, quoting from memory Plautus *Aulul,* 178, writes *praesagibat
animus frustra me ira, cum exirem domo,* instead of *praesagibat mi animus (. . .) cum
exibam domo*: the conjunctive, in a construction like this, was more common
in the syntax of Cicero's era, and in addition corresponds to an individual stylistic
preference on the part of Cicero (regarding such omissions as that of *mi* after
praesagibat, see below). Cicero again, *Tusc.* III 30, quoting Terence *Phorm.* 245,
unconsciously simplifies the archaic and superfluous construction *ut ne* into a
simple *ne.* Of the two branches of the manuscript tradition which have kept
alive for us the comedies of Terence, one of them (the so-called Calliopean
edition) when compared to the other (the Bembino codex) is rich in syntactic
banalizations, which sometimes go so far as to destroy the metre: e.g. in *Eun.* 17,
the impersonal *quae nunc condonabitur* (with *quae* as direct object) becomes *quae
nunc condonabuntur,* which is syntactically simpler but metrically impossible;
ibid. 622, *illa cum illo sermonem illico* undergoes a substitution of *incipit* for *illico*
(whereas Terence had implied the verb). Other examples are in G. Jachmann,
Gesch. des Terenztextes im Altertum, Basel 1924, p. 116. In Virgil, *Aen.* VIII 662,
scutis protectis corpora longis, the Greek accusative was not understood by the
scholiast from Juvenal 8, 251 (or his copyists) and was replaced by the corrupt
form *corpore.* In *Aen.* X 154 the stylized 'relative genitive' *libera fati* was replaced,
perhaps as early as Servius, and certainly in a mediaeval Virgil codex, by the
more common form *libera fatis.* In Ovid, *Heroid.* II 53, *quid iam tot pignora nobis?,*
part of the manuscript tradition has *prosunt* (which Ovid had implied) instead
of *nobis*; see the commentary by H. Dörrie, Berlin 1971. It would be just as easy
to quote examples from mediaeval or even contemporary texts. In connection
with Boccaccio, A. E. Quagli has brought to light a rich crop of syntactic corruptions (see especially 'Prime correzioni al "Filocolo"', in *Studi sul Boccaccio* I,
1963, p. 127). It hardly needs saying that the impulse to commit a syntactic
corruption leads one at times to omit words, at others to add them or modify
them in various ways: the aim being always to end up with a construction that
sounds better to the person copying or quoting from memory. As we noted
above, unconscious banalization cannot always be distinguished from the
conscious sort; but even if we remain sceptical, in several cases the second
possibility must be excluded. One cannot believe, for example, that Cicero
deliberately banalized the syntax of the archaic poets he quoted, bearing in mind
the fact that when he wrote verses he freely imitated the ancients.

seduto/su la tua *tomba,* o fratel mio', ('. . . you will see me seated/upon your *tomb,* o my brother'), instead of 'su la tua *pietra*'; this was an obvious corruption (*pietra* in the sense of tombstone does not occur in common speech) perpetrated unconsciously, perhaps from the very first time I tried to commit that sonnet to memory.

Now, in the line from Virgil quoted by Freud's young travelling companion, the construction *exoriare aliquis . . . ultor* – whether *aliquis* is to be understood as subject and *ultor* as its predicate ('Let someone arise from my bones as an Avenger') or whether *ultor* is to be understood as subject and *aliquis* as its attribute ('Let some Avenger arise from my bones')[2] – is highly anomalous. The anomaly consists in the coexistence in the line of the second person singular with the indefinite pronoun *aliquis*: Dido uses the familiar *tu* form of address to the future Avenger, as if she saw him standing in front of her, prophetically, already clearly outlined; while at the same time she expresses with the *aliquis* (and also, a little later, in line 627: *nunc, olim, quocumque dabunt se tempore vires,* 'Soon or in after-time, whenever the strength is given') his indeterminate identity. Dido's expression is at one and the same time an augury, vague as all auguries are ('Come, sooner or later, someone to avenge me'), as well as an implicit prophecy of the coming of Hannibal, the Avenger whom Virgil, writing *post eventum,* certainly had in mind, and of whom the ancient readers of the Aeneid would immediately think ('He is alluding to Hannibal', explains Servius in his commentary which dates from antiquity).

In German, i.e. the language spoken by Freud's young interlocutor, such a construction is virtually untranslatable literally; the same difficulty occurs, for that matter, in Italian, French and English. Something has to be sacrificed: either one wishes to bring out the character of a mysteriously indeterminate augury, which means rendering *exoriare* by the third person singular rather than the second person ('. . . let some Avenger arise'); or one prefers to conserve the immediacy and directly evocative power of the second person singular, which means modifying somewhat, if not suppressing outright, the *aliquis* ('Arise, o Avenger, whoever you may

[2] The distinction between the two interpretations probably stems more from our need for logico-grammatical rationalization than from any real necessity to choose imposed on us by Virgil's text.

be . . .'; 'Arise, unknown Avenger . . .'). The first solution, for example, was chosen by Wilhelm von Hertzberg, a philologist and translator who achieved a certain fame in the second part of the 19th century: 'Mög' aus meinem Gebein sich einst ein Rächer erheben'.[3] Earlier, the poet and authentic translator Johann Heinrich Voss had opted for the second solution, suppressing the *aliquis* altogether: 'Aufstehn mögest du doch aus unserer Asche, du Rächer'.[4] Translating yet more freely, but still renouncing the stylistic-passionate effect of the Latin text, Friedrich Schiller, in a free rendering of the Fourth Book of the *Aeneid,* had written: 'Ein Rächer wird aus meinem Staub erstehn'.[5] Here both the character of augury and the direct invocation to the Avenger are lost. This same aspect of the expression's uniqueness and intractability to translation is underscored by the comments of German philologists: '*Exoriare aliquis* . . . pro: *exoriatur aliquis,* sed longe vividius et confidentius dictum: exoriare tu, quem video ultorem fore, etsi nescio, quis futurus sis' (Forbiger); '*Exoriare aliquis,* Sprache der wildesten Leidenschaft. Die Dido sieht im Geist das Bild des Hannibal und redet ihn an, ohne ihn jedochweiter zu kennen' (Ladewig); and so on.[6]

But while philologists and translators, in direct contact with the text, were aware of the untranslatability of this expression from Virgil, a young Austrian of average culture, for whom Dido's words were no doubt little more than a distant memory from grammar school, was led unconsciously to banalize the text, i.e. to assimilate it to his own linguistic sensibility. The unconscious elimination of *aliquis* corresponds precisely to this tendency: *exoriare ex nostris ossibus ultor* is a sentence which can be transposed

---

[3] *Die Gedichte des P. Virgilius Maro,* III, Stuttgart 1857, p. 98. On Hertzberg (1831–79) see C. Bulle in *Allgemeine Deutsche Biographie* XII, pp. 249ff.

[4] J. H. Voss, *Des P. Virgilius Maro Werke,* II, Reutlingen 1824, p. 87.

[5] *Schiller's Sämtliche Werke,* I, Stuttgart-Tübingen 1835, p. 222, St. 113, 2. Not very differently, but with greater emphasis on *aliquis,* W. Binder, *P. Virgilius Maro's Werke,* II, Stuttgart 1857, p. 93: 'Aufersteh'n soll Einer aus unsern Gebeinen, ein Rächer'.

[6] Among Italian translators, whom I shall ignore here because they have no direct bearing on our problem, only Giuseppe Albini, to my knowledge, translated the expression literally, knowing that the price to be paid for this, here as on other occasions, was a certain stylistic rigidity: 'Sorgi un da l'ossa mie vendicatore' (IV, line 817, of his several times republished version).

perfectly into German without any need to strain the order of words. It was no accident that the young Austrian's 'simplified' quotation corresponded to the rendering given by Voss, reproduced above.

If we were to stop here, however, we would still leave ourselves open to a legitimate objection. Every one who knows a foreign language, however superficially, is capable of remembering elements of that language (words, morphological structures, syntactic structures) which have no counterpart in his or her mother tongue. The Greek absolute genitive, for instance, or the extensive use of infinitive clauses in Greek and even more in Latin, certainly sound strange to a German – and one could cite analogous constructions in the case of an Italian. Yet an Italian or German lawyer, doctor or man of letters could, and in fact until a few decades ago actually did, quote word perfectly famous passages from ancient authors containing those very constructions, without running the risk of transforming them into dog-Greek or Latin.

Very true. But *exoriare aliquis . . . ultor* is a strange and isolated expression not just from the point of view of German, but also within the context of Latin (even if, as one can read in any worthwhile aesthetic commentary on the Fourth Book of the *Aeneid,* it has a powerful and efficacious 'strangeness' about it). Certain 'parallel passages' have been sought and found in other Latin authors, but in part these are what Eduard Fraenkel would have called 'pseudo-parallels', and in part they are archaic constructions which may have exercised some influence over Virgil's expression, without in any way detracting from its originality. With justification, A. S. Pease, in his commentary on the Fourth Book of the *Aeneid* (Cambridge Mass. 1935, republished Darmstadt 1967), maintains that these comparisons count for very little, and the qualification of 'unique case' (*singulär*) given to our passage in Hoffmann-Szantyr's *Lateinische Syntax* (p. 430) is substantially correct. Servius himself, glossing *exoriare* with *exoriatur,* makes it clear that the appearance of the indefinite *aliquis* with the direct appeal to the Avenger would have come as a surprise even to the Latin reader.

How much more isolated must this expression have been in the ragbag of items of information on Latin syntax and readings of

Latin authors (among whom the ancient poets would have occupied a relatively minor position) that our young man – a 'young man of academic education', says Freud: certainly not a Latinist by profession – carried with him from his schooldays. The examples we mentioned above – Greek absolute genitive, infinitive clauses, etc. – serve precisely to clarify the point that here we are dealing with a completely different sort of case. In the case of the Greek absolute genitive, etc. we have to do with Greek or Latin constructions which are extremely common and are the subject of *specific instruction* at school; they remain in the memory as the elements which distinguish the classical languages from our mother tongues. In the case of Virgil's expression, on the other hand, we have to do with a construction which the young man had come across only in that single passage from the *Aeneid,* which was given no emphasis whatsoever – if it was mentioned at all – in any school textbook on Latin syntax, nor (we may suppose with a great deal of certainty) given any emphasis in the 'serious' if rather antiquated textbooks the young Austrian would have studied in his later years at his city's grammar school. Thus it came about that the uniqueness of the construction in Latin combined with its odd sound to a German, to make the young Austrian commit a stylistic and syntactic banalization.

We can go further. While banalization is sometimes effected by substituting a simpler expression for a more difficult one, or by adding clarifying words where they were merely implied in the original text, in our case the banalization is concretized in a reduction of the original text, viz. in the unconscious suppression of *aliquis.* Now *aliquis* was exposed to the danger of being omitted for a more general reason, namely that of all the words in Virgil's line (leaving to one side the preposition *ex* to which we shall return), it is the only one that is not strictly necessary to the line's meaning. If we suppress *exoriare,* or *nostris ossibus* or *ultor,* the line loses all its sense: if we suppress *aliquis,* however, the line is certainly damaged both metrically and aesthetically, but it still has a meaning, particularly in regard to the polemical use that the young Jew wanted to make of it. Now an examination of the most frequently encountered involuntary omissions in manuscript traditions demonstrates the prevalence of *two* types of omission.

The first is due to genuine 'oversights': it may happen that the copyist skips a whole line of the text before him, or his gaze may jump from one group of letters, usually at the beginning or end of words, to a similar group of letters in a contiguous or neighbouring word (the so-called *saut du même au même*). Such omissions are of no interest to us here, because even though they may in some sense be considered as psychological errors, they almost always spring from the *reading* of the text (or from the copyist's searching in the text for the point at which he left off transcribing the previous line and from which he must now begin again) and not from *memorizing* it once read. A second category, which is of more immediate interest to us, consists in omissions of relatively superfluous words, i.e. words whose absence certainly impoverishes the text from the stylistic and even conceptual point of view, but does not render it meaningless.

Let us take as an example the first ten pages of J. Willis's edition of the *Saturnalia* by Macrobius (Leipzig 1963, 1970). In the critical apparatus, let us observe the omissions of words encountered in one codex or another. We shall see that seven omissions belong to the first category (pp. 3, 5; 5, 24; 6, 19; 8, 16; 9, 3; 9, 9; 10, 24). One (p. 9, 18), concerning the words *nihil ex omnibus,* is not explicable with full certainty (*saut du même au même* with the last letters of the following *quae veteribus?* would put this one as well in the first category). The remaining eleven omissions belong instead to the second category, i.e. they concern words which are 'superfluous' in the sense defined above (p. 1, 15 *omnis*; ibid. *per* – the Z codex copyist will have understood *promoveas* as transitive and *haec sola* as complement object; 3, 23 *nos*; 3, 25 *ista*; 4, 13, *id*; 7, 24 *in cena*; 7, 26 *mihi*; 8, 5 the first of the two *vel*; 8, 18 *se*; 8, 20 *etiam*; 10, 26 *sequentam*); to these one last omission should probably be added, that of *visum* on p. 6, 20. It will be observed that, among the omissions belonging to this second category, many are monosyllabic. The evidence of other manuscript traditions shows that this is a general phenomenon: the very smallness of such words (made even smaller in Latin and Greek codices by being abbreviated), their frequent, if not universal use simply as 'link words', in many cases also their weak accentuation (in Greek and Latin they are often enclitics or so-called proclitics) – these are all factors which contribute towards making them less visible or more easily forgotten by the copyist. But even if we leave the monosyllables to one side, we are still left with a considerable number of words whose omission can only be explained by a tendency for the memory to discard anything superfluous and retain whatever is indispensable to a text. The example of the Macrobius codex we quote here is far from being isolated: essays devoted to many other Greek and Latin manuscript traditions give analogous results.[7]

---

[7] Marbe ('Die Bedeutung der Psychologie für die übrigen Wissenschaften und die Praxis', in *Fortschritte der Psychologie und ihrer Anmendungen* I, 1913, pp. 5ff. and esp. 32ff.) observed that in copying 'words are omitted only in cases where they have no particular importance for the meaning of the sentence'; Stoll ('Zur Psychologie der Schreibfehler', ibid. II, 1914, pp. 1ff.) said much the same. The two psychologists – who were perhaps basing their statements on too few experiments – did tend to exaggerate. On the other hand, this type of omission has not yet received an adequate treatment in the manuals on textual criticism, and indeed is seldom mentioned at all. But if we scan the critical apparatus of classical editions, and leave to one side all omissions due to *saut du même au même* as well as the extremely frequent omission of monosyllables (to be on the safe side), then we are left with a considerable number of omissions which, in the great majority of cases, can only be explained by the tendency to leave out anything which is not strictly necessary to meaning and grammar. Such omissions do not always concern individual words, but can also involve parenthetic clauses. See, for example, what W. D. Ross (*Aristotle's Metaphysics,* I, Oxford 1924, p. clxi) has to say concerning omissions in one or other of the branches of the *Metaphysics* manuscript tradition: for the most part what are omitted are 'clauses not essential to the grammar. The copyists have evidently paid attention to the grammar, and been thereby saved from making more omissions than they have made' (apart from this rather curious consolation, prompted by the thought of all those other omissions the copyists might have made had they not paid so much attention to grammar, it should be realized that this 'attention' was always, or nearly always, of an unconscious or semiconscious variety). See also the list of omissions in the Andocides Q and A codices – and those for other Greek orators – in Umberto Albini's Introduction to Andocides, *De pace,* Florence 1964, pp. 29ff.: Albini notes that in codex Q there is a tendency to omit 'particular superfluities', to omit elements in a phrase or even whole sentences 'without the whole suffering from it'. How frequently this is due to a deliberate intent to 'scholastically clarify and shorten', and how frequently to unconscious simplifying processes during transcription, should perhaps be re-examined. Albini, in so far as Andocides is concerned, opts for the former possibility (and in certain cases he is undoubtedly correct), yet he does not exclude the latter: particularly since the other, unquestionably superior, branch of the manuscript tradition, codex A, contains omissions of this type (Albini, ibid.). For that matter, the critical editions of Demosthenes, Cicero and nearly all Greek and Latin writers in prose (also of those poets who employed metres which were barely intelligible to mediaeval copyists) record

Nor, obviously is the phenomenon limited to ancient manuscript traditions.

Alfieri wrote in a letter: 'Fin adesso sempre sono stato in dubbio' ('Until now I have always been in doubt'). This is the authentic version, as established by Lanfranco Caretti. But Mazzatinti's older edition of Alfieri omits 'sempre'.[8] Was this a case of deliberate omission, hinging on Mazzatinti's pedantic desire to rid the text of what he saw as a disturbing pleonasm? We cannot exclude this possibility since, as we know from Caretti's investigations, Mazzatinti's edition contains both negligent oversights and cases of arbitrary interference. However, it seems likely to me that the 'sempre' was omitted involuntarily, precisely because it was super-fluous. An example taken from Leopardi's *Zibaldone* (p. 1794 in the author's manuscript) is even clearer. Leopardi had written: 'Non solo il fanciullo non ha nessun' idea del bello umano e ha bisogno dell'assuefazione per acquistarla, ma, per perfezionarla e gustare tutti i piaceri che puo dar la sua vista, e bisogno un'assue-fazione lunga. . . .' ('Not only does the child have no idea of human beauty and need familiarization to acquire it, but in order to perfect it and taste all the pleasures that the sight of it can give, a lengthy familiarization is necessary . . .'). This is the correct version, as published in Flora's edition; but the first Lemonnier edition, published by a commission under the chairmanship of Carducci, omitted 'tutti'.[9] Here the omission is clearly involuntary, and is explained by the fact that the adjective is not indispensable.

If then we leave transcriptions and concentrate on quotations from memory, as in the case narrated by Freud, it is clear that we will come across virtually no omissions of the first category (linked as they are to reading errors, as we noted above) and the over-whelming majority of omissions will belong to the second cate-

---

numerous omissions of this kind. I promise to return to this subject at greater length elsewhere.

[8] L. Caretti, *Studi e ricerche di letteratura italiana,* Florence 1951, p. 161. An analogous case is quoted by Caretti on p. 159: 'Non me ne far sapere nessuna affatto' has become 'Non me ne far sapere affatto'.

[9] Flora's edition in its turn is not exempt from omissions of this type, as will be seen when Giuseppe Pacella's new critical edition is published shortly.

gory. So from this point of view as well, *aliquis* (together with *ex*)[10] was the most easily forgettable word in that line from Virgil. But the principal reason why it was forgotten remains the one I expounded first, namely the tendency to banalize a highly irregular syntactic structure. Moreover in other cases, e.g. in the passage from Terence quoted above in note 1, the two motives reinforce each other: *ne* in place of *ut ne* is at one and the same time a syntactic banalization and an elimination of the superfluous.

The young Austrian, as we saw, also made another mistake: he quoted *ex nostris ossibus* instead of *nostris ex ossibus*. This too is a banalization. It is a banalization in terms of Latin usage, since the word-order adjective-preposition-noun, although occurring frequently in Latin, was nevertheless not so common as the order preposition-adjective-noun (or preposition-noun-adjective), and was particularly rare in prose.[11] It is also a banalization with respect to the German word-order, in which, in a phrase corresponding to *nostris ex ossibus,* the attachment of the proposition in front of the whole complement it governs is precisely the rule. However, as Freud himself remarks ('he attempted to conceal the open gap in his memory by transposing the words'), this second error could

---

[10] It was no accident that *ex* was also vulnerable in the young Austrian's memorized quotation. In fact he told Freud later that 'at first he had felt a temptation to introduce an *ab* into the line' in place of *ex* (*The Psychopathology of Everyday Life*, p. 18 n 1 = 12 note 2). Freud comments: 'Perhaps the detached portion of *a-liquis*'. But *ab* for *ex* is again a banalization, and this must have been the main reason behind the error the young man was about to commit. Whether his remembering the initial vowel of the forgotten word *aliquis* might have contributed something as an accessory reason seems highly doubtful to me. In any case there seems to be no need for this highly extravagant hypothesis.

[11] Cf. J. Marouzeau, *L'ordre des mots dans la phrase latine,* III, Paris 1949, pp. 60ff. I have also noticed a passage in *Rhetorica ad Herennium* (I 5, p. 191, 17 in F. Marx's major edition, Leipzig 1894) in which the correct reading *qua de agitur,* as transmitted by various codices, is found to be banalized in others into *de qua agitur.* In Sallust, *Iugurth.* 61, 4, the codices alternate between *de Massivae nece* and *Massivae de nece,* but the latter reading, despite the contrary opinion of recent editors, is *difficilior* and hence, in all probability, authentic. In general, on the tendency to banalize word-orders, see manuals on textual criticism, as well as e.g. George Thomson, 'Marxism and Textual Criticism', in *Wissenschaftliche Zeitschrift der Humboldt-Univ. zu Berlin,* Gesellschafts- und sprachwiss. Reihe, 12 (1963), I, pp. 43ff – even if I personally, as a Marxist or would-be Marxist, cannot quite understand why certain types of textual corruptions not having a 'social' cause should be seen as more likely to occur than others from the Marxist point of view.

have been a consequence of the first, viz. the forgetting of *aliquis*. Since this case concerns a young man who had been to school in Austria, it seems likely that he would have had a good recollection of elementary Latin prosody and metre, and would have kept up the habit of reading and reciting Latin hexameters according to the so-called *ictus* (rhythmic stresses) rather than the grammatical accents on individual words (had he gone to school in Italy, this would have been less probable). He would therefore have noticed, in a more or less conscious fashion, that the string of words *exoriare nostris ex ossibus ultor* could never be found in a hexameter, while this could well be the case for *exoriare ex nostris ossibus ultor*.[12]

---

[12] An analogous case can be found in the quotation from Terence, *Phorm.* 243, given by Cicero in *Tusc.* III 30. Cicero forgot *exsilia* (a word which was indispensable neither to the meaning nor to the grammar, following as it did the two synonyms *pericla damna*) and then turned the line around by inserting a *secum* (recalling the previous line): see W. Zillinger, *Cicero und die altrömischen Dichter*, Würzburg 1911, p. 74 (containing other examples) and Terence, *Phormio*, comment by Dziatzko-Hauler, Leipzig 1913, pp. 238ff. Another case – concerning a copyist's error this time, not a quotation – can be found in Dante, *Inferno* IV 83: the correct version *quattro grand' ombre* evolved into *quattr' ombre verso noi* in some manuscripts (all going back to a common model, or linked by mutual contamination): Dante, *La Commedia* edited by G. Petrocchi, I, Milan 1966, p. 137. This corruption originated as the omission of an epithet that was poetically advantageous but not 'necessary' in the sense defined above; subsequently it was followed by a metrical adjustment.

4

Dido, San Gennaro and the Spectre of an Unwanted Pregnancy

At this point I am satisfied – as perhaps any other specialist in textual criticism would be – that the double error of quotation perpetrated by Freud's interlocutor has been adequately explained. The explanation certainly has nothing brilliant about it, nor is it even particularly intelligent (and if I have expounded it in so much detail, it is because I want what I write to be clear even to Freudians who have never had any contact with philology whatever); but it is the simplest and most 'economical' explanation possible. Now in what sense and within what limits is it correct to regard it as an explanation at all? To assist us in replying to this question, let us examine the quite different explanation given by Freud.

With the young Austrian's consent, Freud subjects him to a miniature 'analysis'. Obviously it cannot be considered as a real psychoanalytic session – just as in general *The Psychopathology of Everyday Life* is not concerned with real neuroses, but with those 'microneurotic' mechanisms that reveal themselves even in basically healthy people. However, the technique employed to go back to the cause of the young man's memory disturbance is, even in this case, that of 'free association'. Freud says: 'I must only ask you to tell me *candidly* and *uncritically*, whatever comes into your mind if you direct your attention to the forgotten word without any definite aim.'[1] Thus it happens that the young Jew, starting with the thought of *a-liquis*, and opportunely guided by Freud's maieutic method (we shall return to this point), associates this word in succession with *Reliquien* – *Liquidation* – *Flüssigkeit* – Fluid. Then

[1] P. 15=9.

with St Simon of Trent, the child whose murder was calumniously attributed in the 15th century to the Jews, and whose relics in Trent have been visited not long before by the young Jew. Then – through a succession of saints – with San Gennaro (St Januarius) and the miracle of the clotted blood that liquefies, and the excitement that grips the more superstitious people of Naples if this liquefying process is retarded, an excitement expressed in picturesque invective and threats hurled at the saint. Finally, with the fact that he was himself obsessed with the thought of an 'absent flow of liquid', since he was afraid he had made pregnant an Italian woman with whom he had been – among other places – in Naples, and was expecting to receive confirmation of his worst fears any day. But there is more: one of the saints the young man thinks of after St Simon is St Augustine, and Augustine and Januarius are both associated with the calendar (August and January), i.e. with expiry dates that must have had a sinister ring for a young man afraid of becoming a father (it is unimportant that the two months were so far separated, and not even separated by the fatal nine months for that matter). Yet again: St Simon was a child saint, another unpleasant idea. He had been killed while still a baby: this connects with the temptation of infanticide – or abortion as equivalent to infanticide. 'I must leave it to your own judgment', Freud concludes with satisfaction, 'to decide whether you can explain all these connexions by the assumption that they are matters of chance. I can however tell you that every case like this that you care to analyse will lead you to "matters of chance" that are just as striking.'

Is the chain of associations linking the young Jew's forgetting of *aliquis* in that line from Virgil with his confession of the fear afflicting him at the time as cast-iron as it seemed to Freud – and, so far as I can make out, seems today to all, or at least a majority of Freudians?[2] I would answer no; indeed I am of the opinion that, beneath the brilliance of the intellectual fireworks, few procedures

---

[2] See Bleuler's enthusiastic judgment quoted by Freud himself in a note added in 1924 (p. 17 n 1 = 11 sq. n 1). The narrative that Freud devises in connexion with this is reproduced, as a particularly exemplary and convincing 'anthology piece', in Robert, pp. 183ff. and in Fornari, pp. 161ff. We shall shortly draw attention to a different explanation proposed by P. Wilson, but one which is still couched in the same doctrinal framework.

can be reckoned so anti-scientific as the one followed by Freud in this and so many other analogous cases.

The 'associations' that Freud, in accordance with his well-known method, allows his patient to generate spontaneously are of various kinds. There are phonic similarities between words having quite different meanings or even belonging to different languages (e.g. between *aliquis* and *Reliquien*). There are affinities between the meanings of phonically dissimilar words (and here again it is irrelevant whether they belong to the same language or not – e.g. the affinity between *Liquidation* and *Flüssigkeit*-Fluid). There are also all sorts of factual and conceptual connexions (Simon, Augustine and Januarius were all saints; St Januarius – San Gennaro – is connected with Naples, and the miracle of San Gennaro concerns the liquefying of blood, etc.). Now we are not concerned to deny, in the abstract, the possibility of all these forms of association (except in one case: the excessive ease with which translation from one's mother tongue into other languages is employed). Rather, our concern is to point out that by passing through so wide a range of transitions, one can reach a single point of arrival from any point of departure whatever.

If there really did exist a causal relationship between the young Austrian's forgetting of *aliquis* and his fear of the Neapolitan woman's pregnancy (and by this we mean a relationship of strict causality: in his last chapter, and for that matter in every exposition of his own concept of a neurotic symptom, Freud speaks of determinism, notwithstanding the unpleasantly '19th-century' ring this may have for Freudians today), then one would have to conclude that the young man had to disturb *that* word and no other – either by forgetting it, or remembering it in an altered form, or introducing it in a context where it was not needed. Stretching the point a little, one might go so far as to admit that a single unpleasant thought, if consciously repressed, might give rise to diverse symptoms – in this particular case, the forgetting of various words. But one certainly could not admit that the imperfect recall or outright forgetting of *any* word in the line from Virgil could equally well be counted as a symptom. In that case, with the one cause producing any number of effects, the concept of causal relationship would lose all significance. Se we should expect that if we take a series of counter-examples – i.e. if we suppose that some other word in that line from the *Aeneid* was forgotten – then the chain of associations will break down, or will be less convincing than in the 'authentic' case narrated by Freud.

Very well then, let us suppose that instead of forgetting *aliquis,* the young Austrian slipped up on *exoriare,* 'arise'. He would have had no difficulty in connecting the idea of 'arising' with that of 'birth' (*exoriare* can have both meanings): the birth, alas, of a child – so feared by him. Next let us suppose that he forgot *nostris*: the Latin adjective *noster* would have brought to mind the Catholic *Pater noster* (we have seen that even though Freud and his inter-locutor were both Jewish, much use was made in the 'authentic' episode of associations between ideas taken from the Catholic religion), and he could easily connect God the Father with the saints, and – passing from saint to saint – eventually with San Gen-naro and the feared failure of the woman to menstruate; or more directly, the thought of the Father in heaven would have aroused in the young man his fear of soon becoming a father on this earth. Now let us suppose he forgot *ossibus*: bones are typical relics of Catholic saints, and having once reached the thought of relics of various kinds, the way was again wide open to San Gennaro; or the well-educated young man's mind might have connected *os* 'bone' with *os* 'mouth' (pronounced with a long ō), and thence with the passionate kisses between himself and the woman, and with all the compromising events that followed the kisses (perhaps Freud would at this point have added one of those polyglot digres-sions he loved so much, on the euphemistic use of the verb *baiser* in French). Finally, what if he forgot *ultor*? In this case several itineraries were possible. *Ultor* does not sound too different from *Eltern* ('parents' in German), and this word would have led our young man back to the painful thought of himself and the woman as parents of the child that was perhaps already conceived. Or else the wish-threat (recalling the devotees of San Gennaro) that the woman's menstrual flow must begin shortly, otherwise . . . could have become embodied in the word *Ultimatum,* which is again phonetically not far from *ultor.* Or thirdly, the concept of 'vendetta', expressed by the word *ultor,* could have led the young man to think of the ill-fated St Simon, associated with all the plans for

revenge which the Catholics had calumniously attributec
Jews in order to have a pretext for their own vendetta ᵃᵍᵃⁱⁿˢᵗ
them – and hence with the infanticide-abortion temptation we
noted above.

Are these connexions that I have amused myself thinking up
(and which could be varied and expanded at will) grotesque ones?
Of course they are. But are the connexions via which Freud
explains, or rather makes his interlocutor explain, the forgetting
of *aliquis* any less grotesque or less 'random'? For that matter,
several orthodox Freudians and even Freud himself have furnished
counter-examples that weaken still further the latter's explanation.
Freud says that forgetting a word is only one form of memory
disturbance, and not even the most frequent one. Usually the
disturbance is manifested not as simple omission, but as substitution
of a mistaken word for the correct one, or even as the converse of
omission, when for instance a correct word – which happens to be
connected with a repressed thought – comes to mind 'with peculiar
clarity and obstinacy'.[3] The young Austrian, when questioned
further, confessed in the end that *exoriare* was the word from
Virgil's line which he had initially seen most vividly. 'Being
sceptical', Freud comments, the young man attributed this to the
fact that it was the first word of the verse. To my mind, the explanation shows not his scepticism, but his rationality. How often does
it happen that we remember only the beginning of a poem (though
usually more than just the first word), when we have learnt it by
heart or read it carefully some time before! Are we to believe
that, every time this happens, the first line or first few lines are
serving as a 'cover' for repressed thoughts, or that every time
there is an analogous psychopathological motivation for our forgetting the rest of the sonnet? So far as this verse of Virgil's is
concerned, I would only add that the position occupied by *exoriare*
(an exceptionally long word: hexameters beginning with a penta-
syllable were not common, especially in the poetry of the Augustan
era) at the beginning of the line gives it a particular emphasis, so
that the 'peculiar clarity and obstinacy' with which it comes to
mind, before it corresponds in any way to the young Austrian's

3 P. 18 n 1 = 12 n 2.

emotional state (yet to be demonstrated), corresponds to a carefully-planned stylistic effect on the part of Virgil. But the analyst, who so far as his own science is concerned suffers from many defects but certainly not that of 'scepticism', unerringly identifies the 'clarity and obstinacy' with which the word comes to mind as a tell-tale symptom.

The 'interpretative mechanism' of psychoanalysis, rightly observes Gilles Deleuze, 'can be summarized as follows: whatever you say, it means something else'.[4] In compliance with this norm, Freud asks the young man to 'attend all the same to the associations starting from *exoriare*', and he gives him the word *Exorzismus*. This reply, we may note, should scarcely come as any surprise, for if one consults a German dictionary, one finds that, apart from *Exordium* and *Exorbitanz*, both rare words, the only German word beginning with *exor-* is precisely *Exorzismus*. But Freud at once sees in the word *Exorzismus* a harking back to the names of the saints (insofar as they were endowed with the power to exorcize the devil), with once again the possibility of connecting with San Gennaro and everything that follows. Later, in an addendum to this same footnote written in 1924, Freud refers to the opinion expressed by P. Wilson, who attributed even more significance to the idea of exorcism, but interpreted it in yet another way, without passing via San Gennaro: 'Exorcism would be the best symbolic substitute for repressed thoughts about getting rid of the unwanted child by abortion.' Here is Freud's unruffled comment: 'I gratefully accept this correction which does not weaken the validity [literally: the rigorous, inexorable character, *Verbindlich-keit*] of the analysis.' Thus, provided one eventually succeeds in establishing a causal link between the unfortunate young man's

---

[4] *Psicanalisi e politica*, Milan 1973, p. 9. Cf. p. 8: 'The patient speaks in vain: the whole analytic mechanism seems designed to suppress the conditions for real enunciation. Whatever you say is put into a sort of mill, an interpretative machine. . . .' I believe these critical comments by Deleuze (and those of Felix Guattari, co-author with Deleuze of *Anti-Oedipe,* Paris 1972 – a book which has made a great impact) are correct, though I do not go on to accept their claim that psychoanalysis and Marxism have equally been superseded, or their invocation of the 'production of the unconscious', which has a suspect irrationalist flavour to it. See also the interview with Deleuze and Guattari in *L'Arc* 49 (1972), pp. 47ff., which contains many very perceptive individual observations.

quotation from Virgil and his fear of the woman's pregnancy, it is irrelevant whether one takes as the revealing symptom his forgetting of *aliquis* or his particularly intense recollection of *exoriare* (explained in turn, as we have seen, in two different ways)! The curious thing is that Freud sees this profusion of competing explanations as confirmation of his method's validity, without ever asking himself whether this superabundance, this unlimited supply of explanations might not be an indication of the weakness of his construction, or without asking himself whether this might not demonstrate the 'non-falsifiability', and hence absence of any probative value, of the method he employs.

I have used a term, 'falsifiability', which may legitimately give rise to interminable epistemological disputes – arguments between 'verificationists' and 'falsificationists'; arguments over the so-called *experimentum crucis,* to which strong objections have been made and whose validity is now generally denied; arguments over the distinction between 'verification' and 'confirmation' and over the priority of the latter.[5] However, I would maintain that the counter-examples given here and others developed later are pertinent at a much more modest and artisanal level, and for that very reason are valid irrespective of rarefied epistemological debates. Even if one acknowledges, as I believe one must, that there can be no such thing as a definitive *experimentum crucis,* it will nonetheless always be true that a theory, or a particular explanation that claims to be scientific, must not be such as to elude all forms of control. One must be able to conceive of an empirical fact that, if it were true, would disprove the theory or explanation in question. If this is not possible, if the explanation for one determinate fact could with equal facility explain any other fact, then one must conclude that this explanation has no scientific value. Such an objection is being

---

[5] For the discussion between falsificationists and verificationists one must go back to Popper, *Conjectures and Refutations,* London 1969 (3rd edition), pp. 228ff. On the collapse of illusions concerning the possibility of there being an *experimentum crucis* that definitively establishes the truth or falsehood of a theory, see L. Geymonat, *Filosofia e filosofia della scienza,* Milan 1960, p. 192. See also A. Meotti's chapter on 'Sviluppi dell'empirismo logico', pp. 242ff. (esp. pp. 257 and 285) in Geymonat's *Storia del pensiero filosofico e scientifico,* VI, Milan 1972. Also M. Galzigna in *Rivista critica di storia della filosofia,* 28 (1973), pp. 427–31.

more and more frequently levelled at psychoanalysis;[6] and to my knowledge it has not yet been answered. Cesare Musatti emphatically asserts that 'this presumed freedom of interpretation does not exist at all; the psychoanalytic technique is remarkably binding on the practitioner, and . . . the principal danger in psychoanalytical interpretation is not so much that of seeing too much as that of not seeing anything.'[7] I believe that this statement is not only quite obviously sincere, but also important in giving us an insight into the eminently experimental concept of science which has always inspired Musatti. But I have the impression that Musatti has never measured how far this ideal of his deviates from Freudian technique and from basic ideas of psychoanalysis, and that he has too easily believed it is enough for him to dissociate himself from the 'mythical' speculations of the later Freud.[8] The result of our examination of slips, omissions and losses of memory will be, I think, to convince us that the Freudian technique is in fact *not binding enough*.

[6] See especially E. Nagel in Hook, p. 38 sqq. ('a theory must not be formulated in such a manner that it can always be construed and manipulated so as to explain whatever the actual facts are', p. 40), and Hook himself, ibid. p. 212 sqq. The chapter entitled 'The Evidence for the System' in Rapaport, *Structure*, p. 111, sqq. does not seem adequate to me. In fact Rapaport's whole book, perhaps unduly praised, wavers between a somewhat exaggerated demand for epistemological rigour and a contrary claim that psychoanalysis is a *sui generis* doctrine, exempt from any criteria of 'scientificity' in the usual sense of the word. (See further here, p. 216 sqq.).

[7] C. L. Musatti, *Psicoanalisi e vita contemporanea*, Turin 1960, p. 365.

[8] The discussion between the Soviet psychologist F.V. Bassin (whose article was published in Italian in the *Rivista di Psicoanalisi*, 5, 1959, p. 93 sqq.) and Musatti (from whose reply the above quotation is taken) leaves the reader – especially fifteen years later – with a sense of dissatisfaction. The Soviet scholar displays a notable ignorance of the development of Freud's thought, an ostentatious Pavlovian orthodoxy that is no aid to an understanding of Pavlov's real greatness, and an unacceptable reduction of all bourgeois science (at least in psychology) to ideology. Musatti, for his part, reveals an undue confidence in the wholly scientific character of psychoanalysis, ignoring its extensive ideological elements.

5

The Not So Free Associations
and the Coerced Consent
of the Patient

There is still ample scope for a Freudian to retort to the argument developed so far, and we must now consider his probable reply. He might well say: your counter-examples, though they may be of general value as an admonition to caution in the use of the analytic technique, have no pertinence at all as an argument against the specific Freudian interpretation of the forgetting of *aliquis*. For the validity of the latter was acknowledged by the subject himself once his resistances – for the most part, highly predictable – to the course of the analysis were overcome. It is a fact that he had really had an amorous relationship with the Italian woman, and that he feared he had made her pregnant; it is a fact that Freud, starting from an apparently quite insignificant symptom such as the forgetting of *aliquis,* was able to gain access to the anguished thoughts afflicting his interlocutor. By contrast, what have you achieved with your so-called philological method (which is itself too none other than a psychological method, though belonging to a superficial pre-Freudian psychology)? Nothing but to dissolve that *particular* patient's specific case of neurosis into generic categories – tendency towards banalization, omission of words inessential to the context, and so forth. To be sure, you textual critics are for the most part concerned with the 'slips' made by authors and copyists of past ages; and you cannot resuscitate the dead in order to psychoanalyse them. In any case, the field of your study is the transmission of written and oral texts and the restoration of these to a form most nearly matching the original; thus the particular experience of the individual responsible for a 'slip' (for example, the sexual repression of a mediaeval scribe in his monastery), even if one could reconstruct it, is hardly within the scope of your interests. But we psychoanalysts work in much more favourable conditions: we have the patient alive before us, and we can submit him to analysis.[1] Nor is it the correction of 'slips' which is our concern but their study as micro-neurotic symptoms that aid an understanding of the genesis of real and actual neuroses.

I imagine Freud would have said something along these lines, and that a Freudian would argue similarly today. I shall wait until Chapter 7 to deal with the argument about the 'generic' character of my explanation as opposed to the 'individualizing' nature of Freud's, which will be one of the central themes of this debate. To the other objection, however, I would like to reply immediately. Is it a valid proof of the correctness of Freud's explanation that he who arrives at it is not Freud but the interested party himself 'aided' by Freud, and that the conclusion of the analysis (that is, the fear that the Italian woman had been made pregnant) undoubtedly corresponds to reality – that, in short, *habemus confitentem patientem* ['we have the patient's confession']? I do not think so.

In the first instance (although this is not, in my opinion, the essential point), we may note the 'suggestive' character of many of Freud's interventions in the dialogue. The method of 'free association' (*free* from external interferences and from critical inter-pellations by the subject himself, and precisely for that reason conforming to a strict causal concatenation), which the person under analysis is requested to respect, ought, as we know, to be matched by a corresponding method of 'suspended attention' on the part of the analyst: up till the moment of interpretation, the analyst, like his patient, should abstain from any critical filtering of the discourse that would prematurely privilege certain of its

---

[1] This last distinction between the method and feasibility of the work of the philologist, as opposed to that of the psychoanalyst, has only a very general validity, since, as is known, Freud frequently indulged in 'analysis from a distance': the most sensational case is possibly to be found in Freud's study of President Wilson, written in collaboration with W. C. Bullitt and not published until 1967: *Thomas Woodrow Wilson, eighth President of the United States: a psychoanalytical study* (Boston, 1967). See P. Roazen, *Freud: Pol. and Soc.* p. 300 sqq., which has sound observations to make on the general problem of analysis from a distance. But there are also examples even in *The Psychopathology of Everyday Life* (p. 91 sq. = 67 sq. and elsewhere).

elements at the expense of others. Adherence to this norm is difficult, if not impossible, and this is known to be one of the main reasons – there are others – why it remains an issue of contention among Freud's successors, many of whom have abandoned it. On the other hand, in very few accounts of cases of analysis does it appear to be so openly flaunted as in the episode currently engaging our attention. It might be said that the very patency of Freud's 'dishonesty' here testifies to an exemplary honesty. For example, when the young Austrian says that he recalls a companion he encountered on a journey the previous week, by the name of Benedict, Freud intervenes to say that this name, like those previously recollected, Simon and Augustine, is that of a saint, and thus puts the sequence of remembrance 'back on the track' from which it had threatened to go astray. Indeed, since this Benedict was described by the young man as *ein wahrer Original* ('a real original'), Freud adds, with apparent indifference, that 'There was, I think, a Church Father called Origen': the remark is not followed up directly then, but it represents a kind of 'card up the sleeve' whose value is by no means negligible, be this because Origen's principal claim to fame lies in his self-castration, or because the second element of the name, derived from the Greek root designating generation or birth, can summon forth various associations of a sexual nature, should there be a need of these. We have another suggestive intervention in the remark that both Augustine and Gennaro are connected with the names of months. In other words, so far from Freud's attention being 'suspended', we have a series of explicit interventions, thanks to which the analysis becomes not unlike the 'maieutic' Socratic or Platonic dialogue. It is, of course, well-known that the function of maieutics is to allow the pupil-patient to arrive 'by himself' at precisely the conclusion that the investigator of souls intends that he should: they induce the disciple to recollect from among the host of things which he sees in the world of Ideas or has buried in his own unconscious, exactly that which confirms an already established doctrine.

More significant, however, than Freud's particular interventions in the dialogue, is the generally suggestive atmosphere in which the young Jew found himself immersed from the beginning of the conversation. Though he had only once met Freud in person before, on an earlier holiday trip, he was acquainted with Freud's writings on psychology – as Freud himself tells us. Immediately after his misquotation of Virgil's line, he says in a nervous tone: 'Please don't look so scornful: you seem as if you were gloating over my embarrassment . . .'. When Freud reminds him of the complete line, he adds: 'How stupid to forget a word like that! By the way, you claim that one never forgets a thing without some reason. I should be very curious to learn how I came to forget the indefinite pronoun *aliquis* in this case'. Here we are presented with that compound of curiosity and fear which typifies the state of mind of someone entering analysis – and must have done so even more at the beginning of the analytic movement. I do not think it would be an exaggeration to say that the young man feels 'bewitched'. He knows he is face to face with the fearsome Doctor Freud, who, they say – and it seems true from what he has read himself – is able to extort confessions even of what is least confessable. He is intrigued as to whether Freud will succeed in this respect with him too, though he is already half convinced that he will; and he is further confirmed in this belief because Freud cheats a little: whereas in the past he has admitted that analyses have failed because the resistances were too strong, on this occasion he boasts a complete confidence, claiming that the analysis 'should not take us long'. Before the analysis has proceeded very far, the young man asks: 'Have you discovered anything yet?' It is the creation of this sort of fatalistic conviction – that 'one cannot oppose Freud'; that no matter how strong one's resistance, one's secret will certainly be extracted – which, more than any of the specific promptings we have noted, is the most powerful means of suggestion at Freud's disposal.

This is even more true of the present case, where the secret is not concealed in the depths of the unconscious: the young man's anxiety about the Italian woman's possible pregnancy was actual and present, and not a repressed thought. At most, we might wonder whether this worry had been temporarily forgotten at the start of the interrogation, or whether it was not already preoccupying him then. Freud's written account lends credence to the first alternative (it is only towards the end of the dialogue that the youth says: 'Well, something *has* come into my mind . . . but it's too intimate to pass on . . .'). Yet the anxiety the young man displays right from the initial stages of the conversation, his fear that Freud had even at that point already 'found him out', give some justification for supposing the second alternative to be the true state of affairs.

In any case, even if we accept the first alternative, it is precisely because the fear of becoming a father was the secret 'dominating' the young man's thoughts, that it was also the idea which he found the most unpleasant to disclose, and yet, whether consciously or not, most drawn to confess. If this was the situation, it matters little that what gave rise to the interrogation was the forgetting of *aliquis*. Some other 'slip', some other parapraxis, some more trivial manifestation of nervousness, could have functioned just as well as the starting point for an analysis which in each case would have led to the same conclusion. This is the value of the 'counter-examples' provided in the previous chapter: they demonstrate (we have seen that Freud himself does so too, by the ease with which he accepts two further, quite different explanations, based not on the forgetting of *aliquis,* but on the stress laid on the word *exoriare*) that the connexion established by Freud between the misquotation of Virgil's line and the anxiety afflicting the young man has not the slightest substance. There is no demonstrable causal relationship between the two facts, except, *possibly,* one of the most general kind – namely, that someone highly preoccupied with other concerns is more susceptible to forgetting things and making 'slips of the tongue'. But if we question at this point why it was precisely *aliquis* which was forgotten and not some other word, we shall have to have recourse to an explanation of the kind advanced in our third chapter.

Yet Freud still induced his interlocutor not only to confess his anxiety, but also (albeit while still retaining certain doubts) to grant the correctness of Freud's explanation of his 'slip'. We touch here on a problem which Freud dealt with explicitly in the third of his *Lectures* of 1915–16 (*GW* XI 43 sq. = *Introd. Lect. Psych., SE* XV 50 sq.), where he speculates on the possibility of a psychoanalytic explanation being rejected by the person who committed the 'slip'. Whom ought we to believe in such an event? According to Freud, the analyst. But, he goes on to say, his audience will object:

'So that's your technique (. . .) When a person who has made a "slip of the tongue" says something about it that suits you [i.e. admits to the repressed thought responsible for its production] you pronounce him to be the final decisive authority on the subject. (. . .) But when what he says doesn't suit your book, then all at once you say he's of no importance – there's no need to believe him'. Freud then replies: 'That is quite true. But I can put a similar case to you in which the same monstrous event occurs. When someone charged with an offence confesses his deed to the judge, the judge believes his confession. If it were otherwise, there would be no administration of justice, and in spite of occasional errors we must allow that the system works'. Thus to the question he then imagines put to him: 'Are you a judge then? And is a person who has made a "slip of the tongue" brought up before you on a charge? So making a "slip of the tongue" is an offence, is it?', he replies: 'Perhaps we need not reject the comparison', and proposes to his audience (my emphasis) 'a *provisional compromise*, on the basis of the analogy with the judge and the defendant. I suggest that you shall grant me that there can be no doubt of a parapraxis having sense if the subject himself admits it. *I* will admit in return that we cannot arrive at a direct proof of the suspected sense if the subject refuses us information, and equally, of course, if he is not at hand to give us information'. But this does not mean, concludes Freud, that we have to abandon explanations based on 'circumstantial evidence', which are always endowed with a significant degree of probability and can be confirmed by a study of the total 'psychical situation' in which the 'slip' occurs and of the character of the person who commits it.

An exhaustive commentary on this passage would involve no less than a critical examination, on the one hand, of the entire Freudian theory of interpretation (not only of the 'slip', but also of dreams, of the specific symptoms of actual neuroses, etc.);[2] on the other hand, it would also have to confront (as, in fact, many commentators have done already from a wide range of standpoints) the problem of the ideological limits which Freud's bourgeois

[2] For objections of a general kind to the acceptance of the interpretation on the part of the patient as proof of the interpretation itself, see E. Nagel in Hook, p. 48 sq.

formation imposed on his own scientific research. That is not possible here: although I shall continue to exercise the right I have hitherto reserved to digress from my central theme whenever circumstances demand it, it is also part of my contract not to lose sight of the specific subject of this work, which is the 'slip'. So I shall restrict myself to a few remarks. The comparison between the relationship of judge and defendant and that of analyst and patient reveals a generally authoritarian conception of psychiatry and medicine; moreover, even within the framework of such a conception, the psychological criteria to which it appeals are extraordinarily short-sighted. One is inclined to say that this investigator of the many complexities of 'depth psychology' was possessed of an oddly simplistic vision when it came to certain mechanisms of 'superficial psychology', with which even a bourgeois judge of not particularly retrograde tendency or a moderately enlightened teacher is familiar – and would have been in Freud's day also. The truthfulness of any confession is accepted by Freud without question, and the judge (and the psychologist and the teacher) is thereby exempted from any further need to verify it. The possibility that, even apart from any violent form of coercion, an accused (or patient, or pupil, or child) might be induced by the suggestions of an interrogation to 'confess' to things which he had not done – taking 'things' to include not only actions themselves, but as least as much thoughts, intentions, motivations of acts – is blithely ignored. Furthermore, when Freud speaks of 'the admission of the sense of a parapraxis' here he conflates two very different facts. We have already remarked on the difference between them in our treatment of the forgetting of *aliquis*: on the one hand there is the fact – this, to be sure, is undeniable – that the young Austrian feared news of the Italian woman's pregnancy; on the other hand, there is the presumed causal chain which is supposed to link this fact with the forgetting of *aliquis*. Now, confronted with a Freud already possessed of a theory of 'slips', who is in a position (by way of the acrobatics and 'unfalsifiable' links we have noted) to conjoin everything with everything, and who responds to a doubt expressed by the young Austrian as to the relationship between two thoughts with brusque authority: 'You can leave the connexion to me' (p. 16 = 11), the patient is in an obviously inferior situation because he has no alternative explanation at his disposal. He is therefore inevitably induced to believe that if Freud, who has taken his cue from a true fact (the forgetting of *aliquis*), has managed to make him 'blurt out' another true fact whose confession is unpleasant (the fear of the woman's pregnancy), then the procedure adopted must have been scientifically correct. However, the counter-examples given in the last chapter have showed us that things are not as straightforward as that.

Moreover, for Freud any denial of the charge by the defendant, or of the explanation of the 'slip' by the patient, though it is certainly regarded as a complicating factor in the work of the judge or the analyst, cannot be allowed as much weight as attaches to the conviction that the charge or the explanation is justified. Let us take heed of those words we have just stressed: 'provisional compromise'. Freud contents himself with this formula because he cannot hope in a single lecture to overcome the scepticism and, above all, the 'resistances' of his audience. But the word 'compromise' clearly indicates that, in his opinion, the real solution is something other than this: the patient is always, or nearly always, wrong when he makes a denial, because every negation on his part is in reality a manifestation of resistance, and thus an involuntary confession. Freud makes this very clear in his paper on 'Negation' (*Die Verneinung*, in *GW* XIV, pp. 11–15 = *SE* XIX, p. 235–40), on which Francesco Orlando* has written an acute commentary.[3] The principle enunciated by Freud in this brief essay is, so to speak,

---

* Francesco Orlando: professor of French literature at the Universities of Pisa, Naples and now Venice, and author of works on the relationship between psychoanalysis and literary criticism, particularly *Lettura freudiana della 'Phedre'* and *Per una teoria freudiana della letteratura*.

[3] See E. Fachinelli's translation, preceded by the German text, in 'Corpo' (1965) and in 'Nuova corrente' 61–62 (1973), pp. 123–7. See also F. Orlando, *Lettura freudiana della 'Phèdre'* (Turin, 1971) Chap. II. The issue of 'Nuova corrente' already mentioned contains a good 250 pages of comments on Freud's brief essay written by philosophers and psychoanalysts ranging from Hyppolite to Lacan, from Fachinelli to Rey and Perlini, and many others. But, except in rare instances, these are comments which 'overwhelm' the Freudian text, rather than interpret it: the 'Freudian negation' in the hands of these adroit conjurors is transformed into a Hegelian or Adornian negation; it is loaded with implications which are at times existentialist, at others pseudo-structuralist. How much more lucid and useful are Orlando's few pages!

a variant of the ancient maxim *excusatio non petita, accusatio mani-festa* ['an unsolicited excuse is a manifest (self-)accusation'], which could be formulated: *negatio non petita, affirmatio manifesta* ['an unsought denial is a manifest consent'].[4] Every time, says Freud, that one of our patients for example declares: 'You ask who this person in the dream can have been. It was not my mother', we can be sure that it is his mother. He concludes (p. 15 = 185): 'There is no stronger evidence that we have been successful in uncovering the unconscious that when a patient reacts with the words "I didn't think that" or "I never thought of that".' He thus goes so far as to formulate, quite directly, a heuristic rule. One asks the patient: 'What would you consider was the most unlikely thing in the world in your situation? What do you think was furthest from your mind at the time?' – 'If the patient falls into the trap (N.B.!) and names what he thinks most incredible, he almost invariably in doing so makes the correct admission'.

There is no doubt (and Orlando has some important observations on this point) that Freud isolated a particular mode of 'confessing what cannot be confessed by means of denying it', that is a feature of human behaviour – whether at the unconscious or conscious level – which will persist so long as there are things which 'cannot be confessed' to the persons themselves or to others – that is, as long as there is repression, or, in the wider sense, suppression.[5] On

---

[4] There also exists in Freudian methodology, although it does not have the same importance, an *affirmatio non petita* which has the value of a *negatio manifesta*. See Maeder, *Nouv. contributions* (cit. above Chap. I note 3), p. 298: 'Il est bien des *oui* prononcés d'une certaine manière qui veulent dire *non*, et les psychiâtres ne sont pas les seuls à le savoir' ['There is certainly a *yes*, which when pronounced in a certain manner means *no*, and the psychiatrists are not the only ones to know about it'].

[5] The extension of the Freudian concept of 'repression' to the much wider one of 'suppression' (which also includes suppression of what is consciously known to the subject, and extends beyond the field of sexuality or at any rate of individual psychology to every form of suppression, including that of a political and social nature) has allowed Orlando, in the book already cited, and in another which represents its logical development, *Per una teoria freudiana della letteratura* (Turin, 1973), to trace an aesthetic which has nothing in common, in the rigour of its method and its anti-biographical and anti-psychologistic orientation, with the rather barren products of some of the Freudians and of Freud himself in this field. Orlando shows himself to be fully conscious that he is not an 'orthodox' Freudian; but he is possibly even less of one than he maintains, at once because he makes the (conceptual and not purely terminological) extension

the other hand, while Orlando is right to extend the applicability of this Freudian interpretative criterion to include not only 'repression' but also 'suppression' (of every kind – not just sexual, but also, for example, political suppression), he nonetheless feels obliged to remark (op. cit. p. 15): 'It would certainly be wrong to think that the interpretation that Freud suggests of his patients' denials would be applicable on every occasion on which we make a verbal or written denial of something.' He is right, but this is perhaps an understatement. Even in the specific cases of those delicate issues, to which we 'cannot confess' for moral, political or other reasons, the criterion of *excusatio non petita* must be wielded with extreme caution. Not only is there the risk that a more or less conscious emotional charge will be detected in a perfectly 'calm' denial, free of *arrière-pensées,* such as even a neurotic might express (since it is not the case that every single affirmation or denial made by a neurotic, even in the course of analysis, is a specific neurotic manifestation); but there is also the possibility that we may fall prey to the mistaken belief that the truth is to be extracted from the pure and simple 'negation of the negation', where in fact a much more complicated and reflexive mental process could have occurred. Anyone who feels himself suspected of thinking something which he has not thought (and this is a condition experienced, at least at certain moments, by almost all those who undergo analysis – these being persons who already know, if only in a very approximate way, of what psychoanalysis consists, and where the analyst, from his starting point in the Oedipus complex, is bent on arriving), will be very likely to want

---

we have mentioned, and because of the respect he pays to linguistic content. He has developed the original idea that the elements for a Freudian theory of art are to be found not in Freud's writings on artists and works of art, but in his book on *Jokes and their Relation to the Unconscious* (*SE* VIII). I remain more dubious about the debt which Orlando declares he owes to Lacan. I must confess that I am incurably committed to the view that in Lacan's writings charlatanry and exhibitionism largely prevail over any ideas of a comprehensible, even if debatable, nature: behind the smoke-screen, it seems to me, there is nothing of substance; and it is difficult to think of a pioneer in the encounter between psychoanalysis and linguistics who has more frequently demonstrated such an erroneous and confused knowledge of the latter, whether structural or not.

to ward off the suspicion; but he will then find himself in a dilemma, because an *excusatio non petita,* however truthful, will be taken for an *accusatio manifesta.* Any judge or lawyer, or indeed any teacher too, who is possessed of a minimum of psychological penetration knows very well that it is just these very mechanisms (fear of confessing what is blameworthy or punishable) which exist, and always will exist, as long as there remains even a moderate degree of suppression, and which give rise to both the 'Freudian negation' and also to 'preventive defences' which it would be utterly wrong to consider always as unrepresentative of the truth. A teacher notices some breach of discipline, and asks: 'Who did that?'. A young pupil, either because he knows he is already 'under suspicion' for his misbehaviour on other occasions, or because he sees, or thinks he sees, the teacher's gaze fixed on him, hastens to answer: 'It wasn't me!'. If the teacher (though the same applies, with minor modifications, to the officer of the law, or the psychoanalyst) concludes: 'So it was him', he will err in a very high percentage of cases. Thus once again we register the way in which his zeal for his own theses rendered the master of depth psychology extraordinarily unaware of any of the subtleties of 'superficial psychology'.

It is intriguing to imagine Freud's reaction if one of his patients – a neurotic, but a politically lucid one – in reply to the question which according to Freud was the best means of 'ensnaring' the patient: 'What would you consider was the most unlikely thing in the world in that situation? What do you think was furthest from your mind at the time?' – had answered: 'I consider the most unlikely thing in the world would be to see a capitalist renounce his own privileges without any use of force on the part of the workers he exploits.' At this point, there would surely have been an exchange of roles: Freud would himself have succumbed to the behaviour typical of a 'patient', he would have lost his temper or changed the subject – in short have revealed 'resistances' so strong that he would not even have been aware of their existence.

But this hypothesis is deliberately provocative. What we should really keep in mind is the fact already mentioned: that the patient finds himself (whether he accepts Freud's interpretation or persists in denying it) in an inferior position because he is not able, save in exceptional circumstances, to advance an alternative explanation of his 'slip' that he can adequately defend. So he is usually constrained, if he is unwilling simply to accept Freud's explanation, to fall back on a line of defence which is much more easily attacked: 'My "slip" did not have any particular significance: it happened by chance.' We have seen (Chap. 4) that this was the defence attempted by the young Jew, and *The Psychopathology of Everyday Life* records other reactions of the same type. In his reply to it, both in *The Psychopathology* and in the *Lectures,* Freud insists on two points: 1) chains of connexions of the type which led from the forgetting of *aliquis* to the thought of the unwanted pregnancy cannot be due to chance – on the contrary 'every case like this that you care to analyse will lead you to "matters of chance" that are just as striking'. (But we have seen, and we shall further see, how fragile and arbitrary most of these chains are); 2) no event, however insignificant, is without a cause: 'If anyone makes a breach of this kind in the determinism of natural events at a single point, it means he has thrown overboard the whole *Weltanschauung* of science. Even the *Weltanschauung* of religion, we may remind him, behaves much more consistently, since it gives an explicit assurance that no sparrow falls from the roof without God's special will' (*GW* XI 21 = *Introd. Lect. Psych., SE* XV 28). We can accept this profession of 'determinism' (understood in the not strictly technical sense); it would be irrelevant, in my opinion, to appeal to Heisenberg's principle, which is so often mistakenly invoked in this connexion, and which, in any case, implies a reformulation and not a negation of the principle of causality. However, there is always *one* sense in which it is perfectly legitimate to resort to the notion of 'chance' – and this is a refusal to allow that a cause-effect nexus exists between two particular events, without at the same time for a moment doubting that each of the events has a cause. We have seen that the forgetting of *aliquis* by the young Jew was in no way due to chance: it has an excellent explanation as we have illustrated above. But the coincidence of the forgetting of *aliquis* and the fear of the Italian woman's pregnancy – that indeed is 'merely fortuitous', because the two events belong to two different causal series. It is merely fortuitous in the same way as the fact that Signor Tizio who has fallen ill with pneumonia happens to have red hair.[6] But we will revert to the Freudian concept of 'explanation' in Chapter 7. It is time now to take issue with the episode narrated in the first chapter of *The Psychopathology*.

[6] Musatti, *Trattato,* p. 401 sqq. makes some good remarks in principle on this question. But he is not convincing in his comments on Freud and 'slips': 'If scientific progress in a given field of phenomena consists in an increasing application of a causal interpretative schema to facts that were previously theorized as *chance* events, one can affirm that Freud constructed for the complex of these slight psychical disfunctions a new science.' If the causal interpretative schemas are unduly arbitrary and unverifiable, there is no new science; while a claim to establish a causal relationship (in the sense elucidated above) between two facts which are unconnected in this sense, is an anti-scientific operation.

6

Love and Death at Orvieto and in Bosnia-Herzegovina

Freud, journeying from Dalmatia to Herzegovina 'in the company of a stranger', asks the latter if he has ever seen the famous frescoes at Orvieto by . . . and fails to recall the name of Signorelli. The names of two other Renaissance painters come to his mind, Botticelli and Boltraffio (the latter being a minor painter of the Leonardo school); but he is aware that neither of the two names is the correct one.

Freud rightly dismisses the explanation that a traditional psychologist would provide – 'proper names succumb more easily to the process of being forgotten than any other kinds of memory-content' (p. 5 = 1) – as too vague, even if not without some foundation. He also forestalls the hypothesis of a banalization, which, on this occasion, he for once foresaw: 'The name I had forgotten was just as familiar to me as one of the substitute names – Botticelli – and much *more* familiar than the other substitute name – Boltraffio' (p. 7 = 2). So far as Boltraffio is concerned there is no doubt that Freud is right. In the case of Botticelli, we might legitimately query his assertion;[1] but let us not lose ourselves in uncertain

[1] In an article which one can regard as a first edition of this chapter of *The Psychopathology*, (*Zum psychischen Mechanismus der Vergesslichkeit*, in 'Monatsschrift für Psychiatrie und Neurologie' 4, 1898, reprinted in *GW* I 519 sqq.; see in particular p. 521 note 1 = *SE* III 287 sqq., p. 291 note 2), Freud says: 'der erste dieser Namen [i.e. Botticelli] mir sehr vertraut' ['the first of these names was very familiar to me'], without adding that Signorelli was equally familiar to him. I have the impression (though it would need to be checked) that to a cultivated German of the late 19th century works by Botticelli such as the Primavera and the Birth of Venus appeared more typically 'Renaissance' and for that reason were better known than Signorelli's frescoes, despite the fame of the latter. But the question has minimal importance so far as our problem is concerned, as we explain immediately in the text.

conjectures: let us assume, then, without more ado, that for Freud it was true that *Botticelli* did not constitute a banalization of *Signorelli*. But textual criticism teaches us that one of the most frequent category of errors is a confusion between words of an equal number of syllables which are also connected by a marked phonic similarity, or even better, by assonance or rhyme. The great majority of errors are not derived from misunderstandings of the signs used in the text to be copied: many of the letters that compose the respective words have a different form, and cannot be confused in any type of script.[2] Rather, they are cases of faulty memory, and usually not so much visual in nature as auditory. They are errors that occur in 'self-dictation', whose mechanism, as we illustrated in Chapter 2, is substantially the same both in the case of transcription of a text (where 'memory is short-lived'[3]) and in the case of genuine quotations from memory. Sometimes there is no affinity of meaning between the two words. On other occasions, there is, and in this event a further element common to both words has facilitated the error; but, I repeat, this is not a necessary condition.[4] In many cases, one of the two words is rarer

[2] It can also happen that an error, which is explicable in a given text as originating from a confusion between similar signs, is found in exactly the same form in another text that has been preserved in manuscripts antecedent to the appearance of the type of writing in which such a confusion could occur. This leads one to suspect that a certain number of errors, which, in the absence of evidence to the contrary, we take to be palaeographic, are in reality of psychological origin, or at least that their production is the result of a conjuncture of both causes. In this connexion see Dain, pp. 47–8.

[3] In Italian 'breve ha la memoria il corso' – an expression taken from Leopardi's poem 'Alla Luna'.

[4] For a good collection of examples taken from Latin texts, see Willis, p. 74 sq. ('Whole Words Similar in Appearance'). For Greek texts, see Bruhn (cit. above p. 21 note 3) and Pasquali, p. 114. One could easily multiply the examples: in Isaeus, *De heredit. Cleon* 46 a codex has αἰτίαν in mistake for οὐσίαν (see Leopardi, *Scritti filologici*, Florence, 1969, p. 128); in Diogenes Laertius III 24 two codices have ποιήματα for ποιότητα ; in the so-called Latin anthology *tenerum* has come down to us instead of *generum* (15, 37); *iura* instead of *iuga* (16, 25); *sedes* instead of *seges* (17, 256). In Piero Calamandrei's *Scritti e discorsi politici* II (Florence, 1966) p. 448 note 1, the expression 'lavori scientificamente molto pregevoli' ['works of great scientific value'] has been restored on the basis of a conjecture, but one that is certainly correct. The first impression from which this work was reproduced had, instead of 'pregevoli', 'presenti'; in this instance, the assonance of the word 'scientificamente' may also have contributed to the error. See also the interesting examples of errors of this type in

and more difficult than the other, and then the error comes to constitute a particular case included in the wider category of banalization. But in many other cases, we must admit that there is no genuine and original *lectio difficilior* ['harder reading']: the manuscript tradition of Homer's poems and, in general, of Greek poetry written in hexameters – perhaps also, to a lesser degree, of Latin and of Romance and Germanic Mediaeval poetry – presents a great number of these 'indifferent variants', which in certain cases (Homer, Mediaeval epics) will partially date back to an earlier phase of oral or semi-oral tradition. It is often impossible to choose between these variants without an appeal to external criteria (the greater authority of one codex or group of codices etc.).

Proper names – which are of particular interest to us here, given the *Signorelli–Botticelli* analogy – are very frequently found to be affected by errors of this kind. We have already seen (p. 22, note 4) how Cicero, when he wanted to name Ulysses' nurse called her *Anticlea* instead of *Euryclea*: here the equal number of syllables, the rhyme due to the identity of the second element of the two compounds, the affinity in role between the two characters – the one the mother, the other the nurse of the same Homeric hero – are more than sufficient to account for the 'slip'. In a passage from Macrobius' *Saturnalia* (V 18, 10: quoted in a fragment of the Greek historian, Ephorus, *FGrHist* 2 F 1 Jacoby) the codices have Ἀγησίλαος , instead of the correct Ἀκουσίλαος. One can speculate as to whether the error has its source in Macrobius himself or in the lost codex from which all the codices in our possession derive, but in both cases the confusion between the two proper names has been facilitated by their possession of the same number of syllables, by their rhyming, and by their nearly identical phonic content (only the second syllable is different). There is not, in this instance, an affinity between the two characters, but the Spartan general Agesilaus was much better known than the historian Acusilaus, and thus a process of banalization has intervened to render the error more likely. In the *Gerusalemme Liberata* (XI, st. 34, v. 5) the first editions all contain the name *Adrasto*, while it is

---

quotations from memory of Latin authors, collected by G. Friedrich in his commentary on Catullus (Leipzig-Berlin, 1908), p. 291.

clear from the context that one should read *Alcasto*.[5] Adrasto too is a character in the *Liberata*, but he appears much later in the poem, and he plays a quite different role. Do we have a case here of a 'slip' by the copyist or printer, which was thereafter passively repeated by others, or is it a case, not indeed improbable, of distraction on the part of the author himself? In either event, whichever of the two hypotheses one opts for, the mechanism of the error is again almost identical: the principal cause lies in the phonic similarity of the two names; to which we can add the fact that Adrastus is a well-known name in Greek mythology, a hero of the Theban cycle with which Tasso and his contemporaries were very familiar – primarily through Statius' *Thebais* – while Alcastus is a name of Greek *formation* but practically unknown; and again, Adrasto's role in Tasso's poem, from canto XVII onwards, is by no means insignificant, while Alcasto (who in the *Conquistata* will appear again under the name of Ermanno) is only mentioned, apart from the disputed passage, on one other occasion. Alcasto is, then, a 'doubly *difficilior*' reading.

I shall now give some modern examples, where there is no doubt that it is the author, and not the copyist or printer, who is responsible for the error. In Heine's *Die romantische Schule*[6] a list of feminine characters from Goethe is cited – 'a Filina, a Käthchen, a Klärchen and such like charming creatures' – who lend themselves to the criticisms of the moralists despite the fact that they are stupendous artistic figures. It has been correctly remarked that Heine must have made a 'slip of the pen' when he wrote *Käthchen* instead of *Gretchen*, the heroine of Faust whose 'morals are open to criticism'.[7] Here, too, the pair of names that have been exchanged are phonically very similar. They are two of the most prevalent

[5] See *Tutte le poesie di T. Tasso* edited by L. Caretti (Milan, 1957), I, p. 685 note 21.

[6] Book I (Ital. trans. by P. Chiarini in Heine, *La Germania*, Bari, 1972, p. 47).

[7] See Chiarini's note loc. cit. In many of the German editions the 'slip' is not pointed out; but Cesare Cases referred me to H. Jess' edition, Heine, *Gesammelte Werke* (Leipzig n.d.), III, p. 894, which comments as follows: 'Käthchen, gemeint ist Gretchen; in der französischen Ausgabe steht richtig Marguerite' ['By Käthchen he really meant Gretchen; in the French edition' – written by Heine himself and revised by others – 'he wrote Marguerite']. I have not had access to other critical editions in process of publication, to which my colleague Cases also drew my attention.

feminine diminutives (which is not to say that one can speak of a 'banalization' in the substitution of one for the other), and they are both names found in Goethe, and even belong to persons in his *life,* since there was both a Gretchen and a Käthchen (Anna Katharina Schönkopf) among the loves of his youth: in short, we have more than is needed to account for the 'slip'.

In the first edition of *Virgilio nel medio evo,*[8] Domenico Comparetti quotes Dante's lines, evidently from memory, (*Par.* XXIII 25 sq.), in the following way: '*Come* ne' plenilunii sereni/*Cinzia* ride fra le ninfe eterne' ['*How* when the moon is full, the night serene/*Cynthia* smiles mid nymphs eternal']. The first mistake (*come* for *quale*) is one of the usual banalizations on which there is no point in dwelling. The second, *Cinzia* for *Trivia,* is more interesting. Here we have the same number of syllables; the same stressed *i*; the same ending with -*ïa*, which in both words is to be read as di-syllabic; finally, more than an affinity, there is a semantic identity between the two names since Cinzia and Trivia are both appellations of Diana, who is identified with the Moon. Can one speak of banalization? *Possibly* – for throughout the whole corpus of Latin and of Italian poetry in the classical style, it is probable that *Cynthia (Cinzia)* is more frequently found than *Trivia*; on the other hand, Virgil – the Latin author with whom Comparetti was most familiar, especially during the period when he was writing his study of him – uses *Trivia* many times but never uses *Cynthia,* and even in the *Divina Commedia,* which Comparetti must certainly have re-read and thought about again before writing the last three chapters of his first volume, which are expressly devoted to the presentation of Virgil in Dante, *Cinzia* is never to be found. All in all, then, we seem to have a simple case of an exchange of synonyms which sound alike, though we cannot be certain that we are right to regard the incorrect as more banalized than the correct one.[9]

[8] Livorno, 1872, vol. I, p. 266. In the second edition 'revised by the author' (Florence, 1896), I, p. 268, the oversight is corrected; so too, of course, in Pasquali's new edition (Florence, 1943), I, p. 247.

[9] Another possible conjecture is that *Trivia* had been unconsciously 'repressed' by Comparetti because of its connexion with the notion of 'vulgarity' ('trivial', 'trite language' and so on). This would be a Freudian, or quasi-Freudian explanation nearer to the truth, if I am not mistaken, then the majority of these worked out by Freud for other 'slips'. But even here one would be reluctant

Let us descend from the heights of Comparetti to the literary mediocrity of Barna Occhini: in the Florentine journal 'La Rinascita' (the organ of the Istituto di studi sul Rinascimento then edited by Giovanni Papini, 1942, p. 423), he wrote an article *A proposito del Wölfflin,* in which he attacked – from the right! – Benedetto Croce, exposing him as 'anti-nationalist' i.e. as anti-fascist, and saying that his prose resembled the sorceress Armida, exquisite in appearance, in reality putrid. Croce ('La Critica' ·1943, p. 51) did not fail to note – it provided him with the occasion for a barbed remark – that *Armida* was a 'slip of the pen' for *Alcina.* In this instance, too, there was a fairly marked phonic similarity (three syllables of which only the first ends in a consonant, the identical vowel sequence *A-i-a,* and the same stress on the *i*); on the other hand, there is an affinity between the two characters, in that both are sorceresses who make their appearance respectively in *Gerusalemme Liberata* and *Orlando Furioso* – that is, in two 'rival' poems which have proved the object of innumerable comparisons. It is not, I think, either demonstrable or probable that Armida was more familiar than Alcina to Barna Occhini, so that we cannot speak of banalization here either.

In his last, grotesque speech before the Anglo-American landing in Sicily, Benito Mussolini said: 'The Greek philosopher *Anaxagoras* (forgive my erudition) said that man is the measure of all things'. I am quoting from memory, and perhaps inexactly in some insignificant respect, but as to Anaxagoras and the clumsily ironic parenthesis I have no doubts. Moreover, very many of my contemporaries or those somewhat older or younger than me will certainly remember the speech. In this error (*Anaxagoras* instead of *Protagoras*) we are confronted with a new problem, to which we shall have occasion to return later (Chap. X). The previous errors considered, those made by Heine, by Comparetti and even by Barna Occhini, were effectively cases of 'slips', that is, of momentary disturbances of memory, which would have been easily acknowledged as such by the parties concerned themselves. In the case of Mussolini, we should probably speak not of a 'slip',

---

to posit it as anything more than a very uncertain hypothesis, which is, in any case, far from essential to an explanation of Comparetti's lapse in memory.

but of ignorance and lack of culture. It is true, of course, if we are to believe Emil Ludwig, that Mussolini, when he was not as yet the criminal which he soon became, had read with interest a master-piece on the history of Greek thought, *Griechische Denker* by Theodor Gomperz, and had even conceived the notion of writing a history of philosophy on that model.[10] But a lot of water had passed under the bridge since that time, and a lot of presumptuous inanity had accumulated in that brain. The newspapers, which in their first editions had faithfully printed *Anaxagoras,* published the correct name *Protagoras* in their subsequent reports: in all prob-ability, it was not Mussolini himself who insisted on this 'papering-over', but some intellectual in the notorious Ministry of Popular Culture.[11] But despite the distance between a 'slip' (to which even a highly educated person is subject) and an error due to ignorance, there was nevertheless a reason for Mussolini's 'erudite' attribution of the saying to Anaxagoras, and not, for example, to Democritus or Plato; and this was the phonic similarity between *Anaxagoras* and *Protagoras* – though this does not allow us, even on this occasion, to assert that Anaxagoras was a banalization. We shall see how at other times it is not so easy to draw a sufficiently sure distinction between a 'slip' and an 'error'.

The examples I have cited – and I could add to these if I were not reluctant to weary the reader – are all analogous to the *Signorelli-Botticelli* 'slip'. Once again we find an equal number of syllables, a

[10] See E. Ludwig, *Colloqui con Mussolini* (1932), new ed., (Milan, 1970), p. 203. It is not easy to know what is more contemptible in this book: Mussolini's capacity for histrionics or the gullible admiration (despite occasional and marginal reservations) of the Central European Ludwig for the 'strong man' who had preserved Italy from communism, and would do the same for the whole of Europe. Among other things, Ludwig passes – like so many of his illustrious German contemporaries – a derogatory judgement on a man of genius like Gomperz; while he is quick to justify Mussolini's crimes as far as possible, he politely reproaches him for wasting so much time reading Gomperz!

[11] To avoid misunderstandings, I should make it clear that for me, as for every Marxist, it was not its lack of culture as such which was the most basic and infamous characteristic of fascism, but the viciously anti-proletarian function which it performed. It was because of this that its enemies finally came to include the most enlightened sectors of the Italian bourgeoisie, who wanted to fight or neutralize communism by less violent means. If a militant of the working class were to confuse Protagoras with Anaxagoras, it would clearly be stupid to adopt an attitude of erudite condescension towards him.

similarity (even if it occurs in reverse order), in the vowel sequences of the first two syllables (*i–o/o–i*), and a rhyming of the two names. We have already seen that banalization is not a necessary condition here. It is true that the inverse process to that of banalization – the substitution of a *lectio facilior* ['easier reading'] by a *difficilior* – is exceptional and would be difficult to explain; but exchanges between words which are, as it were, 'on equal terms' with each other, are quite normal. That a relationship should exist between the true or fictional characters answering to the names is not absolutely necessary, but it is commonly found to be so (the only exception to this among the examples to which we have appealed is the *Agesilaus–Acusilaus* substitution, but here the tendency towards banalization exercized a particular force): as for *Signorelli–Botticelli*, this fully satisfies our condition, since we are dealing here with two Italian Renaissance painters who were directly contemporary.

I have no right as yet to claim, on the basis of what I have said so far, that any Freudian would consider the *Botticelli* 'slip' to have been *explained*. He could object that a collection of analogous cases does not constitute an explanation. That is true; and I am forced to ask him to bear with me patiently until the next chapter. I would like now, however, to draw attention to the 'quantitative' character of the errors belonging to this type. Even in medicine, of course, the same symptom can be caused by different illnesses: not even a layman is so naive as to believe that there exists a one-to-one correspondence between symptoms and diseases. But is it likely that symptoms which are all of one distinct type are produced, not by two or three or ten different causes, but each one by a different cause, each one as the outcome of a strictly individual history? I am content, for the moment, merely to pose the question, and will now proceed to examine the case narrated by Freud.

How did it happen that, after Botticelli, the name of the obscure Boltraffio also entered Freud's mind? Must we here acknowledge a breach of the principle we have only just now insisted upon, according to which the substitution of a rare name for one much better known is extremely unlikely?

The answer lies in the fact that *Boltraffio* does not constitute a 'slip of the tongue', nor a case of what in textual criticism we call a primary corruption, but rather an unsuccessful attempt at correction, a 'disimprovement' (in German *Schlimmbesserung*). Once the *Botticelli* 'slip' has occurred, Freud takes his cue from it in an attempt to recover the correct name; and in the course of this attempted emendation he recalls the name of another Renaissance artist beginning with *Bo-* like *Botticelli* – namely, *Boltraffio*. In other words, he fails to isolate the element of the original word in which he effected an alteration, and thus, instead of correcting the first part of it (*Bottic* to *Signor*), he takes the initial element (*Bo-*) to be right, and tries to correct the rest of it accordingly: nothing better than *Boltraffio* comes to mind (and maybe, given the nature of the mistaken first syllable, there were no other solutions available), but he realizes at once that this is not the right name.

Here too textual criticism can furnish perfect analogies. The history of the misfortunes suffered by a text in the course of its transmission from one copy to another is not the outcome merely of primary errors, but of bad correction of errors, or, frequently, of poor emendations due to a failure to understand the correct reading. To use Louis Havet's felicitous terminology, in addition to *fautes serviles,* there are *fautes critiques,* i.e. 'disimprovements';[12] and very often, exactly as happens in the *Botticelli–Boltraffio* case, the correction goes astray because of an incapacity to *localize* the fault[13] – so that the authentic word in a given phrase is emended instead of the corrupt one, or, within the body of the word itself, the authentic part instead of the corrupt part.

I shall not pause here to go into examples which one can find in any manual of textual criticism, but restrict myself to a few, which have to do with proper names. In Cicero's *Tusculanae,* I 89, the name of a locality of Cisalpine Gaul, *Litana,* appears in all our codices in the corrupt form *Latina.* This is a primary corruption:

[12] Havet, p. 301 sqq. But see the article by the same author in 'Mélanges Ch. Graux' (Paris, 1884), p. 803 sq.

[13] 'His first problem [for the person, that is, who has realized that a passage has been transmitted in an incorrect form] is to discover as precisely as possible where the corruption lies. (. . .) Finding the exact location of the corruption will sometimes lead him at once to recognize its nature, and perhaps to see the solution' (West, p. 57). Havet, p. 101, deals at length with the question of the *localisation de la faute,* on the methodology of which he makes some acute remarks, even if here, as frequently elsewhere in the work, he is too precipitate in his diagnosis and treatment of many of the particular examples.

it is a combined case of an anagram[14] and a gross banalization, since a rare place-name has been substituted by the commonest of ethnic adjectives, although wholly unsuitable to the context. But an emendator of the codex Vaticano lat. 3246, who had access to a lost manuscript which is full of excellent readings that cannot be the result of conjecture, but also full of good and not so good conjectures, has cancelled *Latina* and written *Hirpini*. Here we have a typical 'disimprovement': the person who thought it out realized that *Latina* was inadmissible, but did not succeed in restoring, either through conjecture or consultation of another codex, the difficult *Litana*; and since he saw that the *Lucani* are named a little further on, it occurred to him to introduce the name of another Latin people, the *Hirpini* – of vague assonance with *Latina* – in order to correct the sense in the least damaging way.

In another of Cicero's works, the *De divinatione* (I 48), the original reading – restored as the result of a conjecture by a philologist of the Humanist period: and here the conjecture is indisputably

[14] Anagrammatic errors are among the most frequent in the manuscript tradition (for Greek see J. Jackson, *Marginalia scaenica* edited by E. Fraenkel, Oxford, 1955, p. 208 and note 1; for Latin, Housman's edition of Manilius, I, p. LIV sqq., with its very rich choice of examples, and now Willis, p. 81 sqq.), and in typing and printing (Willis, ibid.). It should be noted that often such errors do not originate from mistaken reading or writing, but from faulty memory – so much so that even the spoken word is subject to exchanges of sounds (the extreme case is provided by the errors to which we are liable when we recite a so-called tongue-twister – we shall have reason to come back to these). The term 'anagram' is therefore often a misnomer because it is based on a confusion between sounds and alphabetical letters (a confusion which, as we have seen, persisted for a long time even in modern linguistic theory, at least up to and including Jacob Grimm). W. Schulze, *Kleine Schriften* (Gottingen, 1966²) pp. 307 sq. and 711, provides the best, although brief, assessment of these errors. Nor is the phenomenon restricted to mistakes made by any one individual, but becomes an instance at times of collective linguistic innovation, of 'metathesis' (early Italian *drento, formento, strupo* [instead of *dentro, frumento, stupro*] and so on). On other occasions, although it does not permeate the language, it is nonetheless widespread: one thinks of how often one happens to read or hear the word *fisolofia* instead of *filosofia*. Finally, there are anagrammatic errors in which the tendency to banalization has exerted an influence probably greater than that of a simple disturbance of reading or pronunciation: such is the case, for example, with the error *Veronesi Pesciolini* instead of *Venerosi Pesciolini* (the Fascist podestà [i.e. administrative head] of Florence), which one finds repeated pp. 19 and 40 of Orazio Barbieri's work, *Ponti sull'Arno* (Rome, 1964²). Veronesi is much more widespread as a surname, and as a typical instance of a name derived from the designation given to the inhabitants of a particular city.

correct – is *in fano Iunonis Laciniae* ['in the temple of Juno Lacinia'] (the reference is to the Lacinian promontory near Croton). As a result of a mechanical double corruption, due to an exchange between the so-called open *a* (which is common in pre-Carolingian lower-case script and in the first phase of Carolingian) and the *u*, and a *saut du même au même* within the self-same word (see above, p. 36), *Laciniae* was curtailed to *Luci(a)e* in the Mediaeval codices; and here too a tendency towards banalization operating alongside the mechanical processes just described cannot be ruled out. Lucia, the name of the Syracusan martyr, was well known in the Middle Ages. An emendator of the codex Vossiano 86, who found himself confronted with either this *Luci(a)e*, or perhaps with another manuscript which contained the only half corrupted *Luciniae*, and understood that neither *Lucia* nor *Lucinia* could be epithets of Juno, wrote *Lucin(a)e*[15]: a disimproved emendation which reveals a certain intelligence and degree of culture, since *Lucina* (protectress of those in child-birth) was indeed an appellation of Juno, though scarcely apposite in this context.[16]

A further example is to be found in the codices of Macrobius' *Saturnalia*. An allusion is made to Xenophon's *Symposium* (Macrob. *Sat.* VII 1, 13): one of the guests is mentioned in the accusative case as a certain *Charmadam*. This must certainly be corrected to *Charmidam*. Is this a 'slip of the pen' by Macrobius (as Ludwig von Jan in his ancient commentary chooses to suppose, and as recent editors, who leave the variant in the text, would appear to believe), or is it, as I would be inclined to think, an error of the manuscript

---

[15] For the reader who is not a philologist it should be explained that the dipthong *æ* is nearly always written as *e* in mediaeval codices.

[16] For reasons of space I shall not deal with other interesting cases in the Ciceronian manuscript tradition: see, for example, the oration *cum senatui gratias egit*, 9 (where *Cinnano* first undergoes the corruption *Germano* and is then disimproved to *Cesonino* by an ill-educated copyist, and is finally later, but still erroneously, altered to *Cesonini*); *Lucullus*, 14 (*Xenophanem* reduced simply to *Xeno* either because of a *saut du même au même* with the next word *Platonem*, or because the manuscript had been damaged and a poor disimprovement had been made by the corrector, who wrote *Xenophontem*, a better known name). Again, see Lucius Septimius (p. 40, 14 Eisenhut): *Iolchorum* corrupted to *Colc(h)orum* in some codices as a result of the preceding *Colchis*, and subsequently disimproved by other copyists who wrote *Graecorum*, which gives an acceptable sense, but is much more banal than the original reading.

tradition? The issue cannot be resolved for certain, and in any case, it matters little for our purposes. What is interesting is that, at the instigation of this erroneous variant, a codex of the Humanist era (referred to as *T* in Willis' critical apparatus) bears the disimproved correction *Carneadam*. Minimally less ignorant than Don Abbondio,[17] this copyist of the 15th century knew Carneades at least by name; but not well enough to realize that the founder of the New Academy was not in a position for reasons of chronology, to figure in one of Xenophon's Socratic dialogues.

On other occasions, these two distinct stages of a primary error followed by an disimproved correction have not reached us in a recorded form in two different manuscripts, but can be distinguished and reconstructed only on the basis of a hypothesis – one, however, of which we can in many cases be fairly certain. In Athenaios XI 506 D the manuscript tradition has τὸν ἀδελφὸν δὲ τοῦ Ἀλκιβίαδου καὶ Νικίαν, while is is clear that, as Valck realized, followed by recent editors, καὶ Νικίαν must be corrected to Κλεινίαν. We have two errors here belonging to an earlier phase (the one due to the pronunciation of ει as ι in the Byzantine era, the other to the confusion, which is very frequently found in upper-case writing, between the signs Λ and Α). At a later stage we have a disimprovement: the incomprehensible καινιαν has been 'emended' to καὶ Νικίαν [18]. Alcibiades' name served to remind the copyist-conjecturer of that of his rival Nicias, who is mentioned so many times in connexion with the former; and it is probable that he was also influenced by the fact that a few lines above (vol. III, p. 119 line 13 in Kaibel's edition) a Nicias is named. The man referred to, it is true, is not Alcibiades' famous rival, but the copyist either did not know this or else was unconsciously

---

[17] A character in Alessandro Manzoni's *Promessi Sposi* (Chap. VIII: 'Carneades! Who on earth was he? – pondered Don Abbondio to himself') [Carneades was a Cyrenian philosopher, a pupil of the Stoic Diogenes, and founder of the New Academy in Athens. Don Abbondio's ignorance has since become an Italian proverb – to the point where a completely unknown person is referred to as a 'Carneade'. Trans.]

[18] It goes without saying that regular spacing between words, accents, the use of capitals for the first letters of proper names in texts written wholly in lower-case, are all devices used in writing which were unknown (or had only a sporadic use) in Antiquity and the Middle Ages.

affected by his reading and transcription of the same name a little earlier.

That we distinguish between the two separate stages represented by the mechanical error and the disimproved correction does not necessarily mean that we must attribute them to different copyists. It is often the case, as in the examples from Cicero and Macrobius, that there is evidence for the existence of two distinct sources responsible for the primary error and the attempted correction respectively. In other instances, as in the example from Athenaios just cited, this is not the case. This is not to suggest that the issue depends on whether or not the manuscripts which would have contained only the primary error have been lost to us. One and the same copyist is capable, after an initial misreading, of more or less unconsciously disimproving, a correction of his first error in the process of 'self-dictation' and writing. A *faute critique* can moreover also be an instance of accurate intuition; it is not always a wholly conscious conjecture, but can be the result of a virtually automatic attempt at correction, analogous to the motorist who swerves to avoid a skid or a collision without a full rationalization of his responses beforehand. So there is nothing to prevent the hypothesis (I would even be prepared to regard it as certain) that Freud himself, in his effort to recall the right name, Signorelli, first committed an involuntary banalization (*Botticelli*), and than an equally uncon-scious or semi-conscious disimproved correction (*Boltraffio*).[19]

But, and otherwise than in the case of primary corruptions, such disimprovements do not always consist of banalizations, but very often of 'learned' (in inverted commas!) reminiscences that come to mind at some inappropriate moment. Instances of these from among the examples quoted are *Hirpini* for *Latina*, καὶ Νικίαν for Κλεινίαν. *Boltraffio* for *Botticelli* is another. It is precisely because of the 'secondary' rather than 'immediate' nature of such disim-provements that they do not always consist in banalizations. It is

---

[19] In the first version of this chapter (see above, note 1) Freud makes it very clear that the disimprovement has a 'secondary' character relative to the first error (p. 521 = *SE* III 291: 'Botticelli und *in zweiter Linie* Boltraffio' ['*Botticelli* and, in the second place, Boltraffio']). He is less precise in the definitive edition (p. 6 = 2): 'the names of two other painters – *Botticelli* and *Boltraffio* – thrust themselves upon me'.

obvious – even when such mistakes are made automatically rather than in full awareness – that the more numerous the uncommon words in someone's vocabulary, the more likely it will be that in the disimproved correction of a previous *faute servile* one of these rarities will spring to mind. The fact that Freud recalled, even if in error, the name of the obscure Boltraffio confirms, if there were any need of it, his excellent knowledge of Italian Renaissance art. But the reason in the first instance for the production of an disimproved correction (rather than the accurate name, *Signorelli*) lies in what, we repeat, is a very common failure to locate an original error.

In this case too, however, as in that of the forgetting of *aliquis*, Freud's line of approach is very different. Before the Orvieto frescoes became the topic of conversation, he had told his travelling companion a story he had heard from a doctor whose practice was in Bosnia-Herzegovina, about the exceptional resignation of the Turkish peasants in that area before incurable disease. They would say to their doctor, simply: '*Herr* (Sir), what is there to be said? If he could be saved, I know you would have saved him' (p. 7 = 3). But Freud, because of his reticence in conversation with a stranger, withheld the other piece of information the doctor had given him – that the resignation of these peasants in face of death was matched by the profundity of their despair in the event of a loss of sexual potency: '*Herr*, you must know that if *that* comes to an end then life is of no value'. Moreover, this privileged theme of 'death and sexuality' had surfaced in a painful way only a few weeks previously when Freud had happened to be at Trafoi in the Alto Adige: he had there learnt that one of his patients 'Had put an end to his life on account of an incurable sexual disorder'.

At this point everything is clear to Freud, and he presents it in an even more graphic fashion by means of a diagram (p. 9 = 5). Why did he forget the first part of the name of *Signorelli*? Because *Signor* = *Herr,* and the vocative *Herr* had figured both in the anecdote which he had narrated a little earlier to his travelling companion, and in that which he had kept to himself for reasons of discretion; and, in addition, because *Her-* constitutes the beginning of *Herzegovina*, which, with Bosnia, made up the geographical region to which the account referred. But taken as separate elements, Bosnia and Herzegovina were submitted to an advantageous 'division of labour': while the latter, with the reinforcement lent by the vocative *Herr*, served to repress the first part of *Signorelli*, the former served to furnish by substitution the first two letters of *Botticelli*. What of *Boltraffio*? That was the result of a somewhat approximate fusion between the *Bo-* taken from *Botticelli* and *Bosnien* on the one hand, and *Trafoi*, the name of the hamlet in the Alto Adige on the other.

Once again, we must question whether there is anything which could *not* be explained, given such a measure of freedom in associations, suppressions, substitutions and translations from one language to another. Have you forgotten something? Then you have repressed it from consciousness because it was connected with a memory which was unpleasant or impossible to confess (even if the connexion is based not even on so much as an entire syllable, but wholly on the conjuncture of two single phonemes: *Bo-*!). Do you remember something in a particularly insistent way? In that case you are obsessed with that same unpleasant memory to such an extent that you have not succeeded in repressing it.[20] The *lucus a non lucendo* and the *lucus a lucendo*[21] are equally valid in psychoanalysis. The ancient grammarians managed to resolve any etymological problem on the basis of an unconditional admission of either of these types of connexions between word and concept, or by recourse to a practically unlimited manipulation of the words that could be put into an etymological relation, thanks to the four operations of 'addition' (whether of letters or of sounds – for them the distinction did not exist as yet), of 'subtraction', of 'alteration' and of 'transposition'.[22] Even in the 18th century critics spoke ironically, and rightly so, of this omnipotence (and thus immunity to proof or disproof) of etymology – the

---

[20] Again in the first edition (p. 526 note 1 = *SE* III 296 note 1) Freud hypothesized another reason for his forgetting of *Signor(elli)*, based not on the breaking up into *Her-zegovina*, but into *Herz-egovina*, and thus on the fear of *heart (Herz)* disease which could have produced the repression. Later he rejected this hypothesis, because he was forced, for once, to acknowledge that it constituted an unnecessary complication.

[21] A well-known example of a false ancient etymology: 'a wood (*lucus*) is so called because it gives no light (*lux*)'. Trans.

[22] See, e.g., Quintilian, I, 5, 6; Charisius, p. 350, 6 sqq. Barwick.

science for which 'the difference between the vowels counts for nothing, and that between the consonants counts for very little'. The establishment of etymology as a true science dates from its imposition of specific limits on such freedom, whereupon its explanatory force became that much greater *precisely because it was no longer in a position to explain everything with absolute ease*. Now, it would certainly be mistaken to pretend that the associations made by psychoanalysis should obey rules of the kind appropriate to historical comparative etymology (more legitimate, instead, would be to compare it with so-called 'folk etymologies'); but that the freedom of associations 'permitted' should be such as not to render any attempt at verification futile – this, by contrast, is an indispensable condition of validity.

I shall spare the reader the tedium of a mass of 'counter-examples' such as I presented in the case of *aliquis*. Here I wish only to call attention to the problem of those associations which depend on *translation* from one language into another. Freud never seems to have asked himself how it is, that in his own unconscious or in that of his interlocutors, associations dependant on translation could occur with such ease: from *liquidus* to *flüssig* (or derivations of the respective words) in the episode of the young Jew (above, Chap. 4); from *Signore* to *Herr* in the *Signorelli–Botticelli* one; from *homo* in such wholly innocent phrases as *ecce homo* and *homo sum* to the neuter *Mensch* with the sense of 'a prostitute',[23] and numerous other cases. This would presuppose, if I am right, that translation

[23] See, e.g., pp. 33 = 26, where the 'repressed' name of Jung is supposed to have made its reappearance in an account by a young woman in the form of the adjective which in Hungarian corresponds to *jung* ('young'), and, be it noted, without her account appearing to be in itself in anyway confused; 37 sq. = 30 (on which see below p. 133); 92 note = 82 note (below, p. 135); 134 = 122 (*Achol*: see below p. 141); and in many other cases. See furthermore the article written in 1936, *Die Feinheit einer Fehlhandlung*, in *GW* XVI 37–9 = *The Subtleties of a Faulty Action*, *SE* XXII 233–5, in which the transition is made from the German *bis* ('until') to the Latin *bis*. Groddeck allows himself to indulge in equally, if not more bizarre, polyglot associations both in *The Book of the Id* (London, 1950), and in his letters to Freud. One patient told Groddeck that he had read a book in which mention was made of the sea. Groddeck's comment is: 'The patient has an unresolved Oedipus Complex, and he is a fool not to have realized [!] in fact that by means of the association *Meer = la mère* he was speaking of himself' (*Carteggio Freud-Groddeck*, Milan, 1943, p. 69). One should note that the patient was German; his unconscious, nonetheless, made its confession in French!

from one language to another was a constant habit and that the subjects in question were possessed of an equal mastery of both languages: in short that they were in every sense bilingual – so that the translation of certain associations between words and sounds as much as between ideas and images occurred to them at a virtually instinctual level. Now, there is no doubt that Freud had a very good knowledge of Italian, but he was certainly not bilingual in German and Italian;[24] while the young man who failed to recall *aliquis,* despite his dalliance in the company of an Italian lady and his past as a worthy student of the Latin language, was unlikely to have been as bi-lingual as Freud in Italian and it is even more improbable that he would have spoken Latin with the casual ease of the humanist man of letters of the old school. In fact, in the two accounts that Freud gives, as in others which we shall examine subsequently, the translation happens to involve an even more complex and mediated process. *Liquidation* in German is a term of economics and commerce, as is *liquidazione* in Italian; the same is true of the adjective *liquid,* which means either 'ready' (said of money), or 'solvent' (said of a person), or 'payable, liquidable'. The passage from *Liquidation* to *Flüssigkeit* (Fluid) is not made via the simple association between synonymous words nor even via a simple transposition of a 'Latinism' into the purely Germanic word, but depends on a prior reference to the Latin *liquidus* in order to pass back to the German *flüssig* and thence to the abstract *Flüssigkeit.* Likewise, the immediate equivalence *Signore= Herr* is one thing, the extraction of *signor* from Signorelli and of *Her(r)* from *Herzegovina* is another.

It is precisely in reference to foreign words that Freud remarks, at the beginning of chapter II of *The Psychopathology,* that these are forgotten more readily than those of one's own language, so that 'an early stage in functional disturbance is revealed by the fluctuations in the control we have over our stock of foreign words',

[24] Hans Sachs, whose book on Freud is marked by an intense admiration which constitutes both its merit and its limitation, attributes to Freud 'full command of English and French', but adds 'he could read Italian and Spanish fluently' (*Freud, Master and Friend,* London, 1945, p. 102). However, Freud did not speak Italian fluently enough to be considered a German–Italian bi-lingual. It should be emphasized the one thing of which Sachs cannot be suspected is underestimation of any intellectual quality of Freud.

while the current vocabulary of our own language 'seems to be protected against being forgotten'. We have no quarrel with Freud's observation, but the use which he makes of it in both the *Signorelli* and the *aliquis* case is aberrant. It is exactly the 'associations dependant on translation' which presuppose, as we have said, a mastery of a foreign lexicon (of its semantic content and not merely of its superficial phonic similarities) on a par with that of one's mother tongue. I find myself much more able to accept that unconscious processes could issue in false equivalences of the type *caldo-kalt, alto-alt, stufa-Stufe, ruota-route*[25] and so on, rather than in exact translations such as those to which Freud appeals. One of my relatives once asked an astonished shopkeeper in Berlin for 'Ein Paar alte Schuhe' (i.e. for a pair of *old* instead of *high-heeled* shoes); these are the kind of tricks that a moment of distraction or haste play on us even when our overall knowledge of the foreign language is quite adequate, although not perfect.

I am well aware of the expedient to which a Freudian might have recourse in order to defend the conception of a 'polyglot unconscious'. He would perhaps say that mental processes that are accomplished only with difficulty at the level of full consciousness (e.g. complicated arithmetical calculations) are performed with surprising facility at the unconscious level. This is an assertion which, I would venture to suggest, still stands in need of more experimental confirmation, and a more precise definition of the limits of its applicability. For the present, I am reluctant to treat it as anything more than an insufficiently proved assumption. Moreover, I do not consider that an arithmetical calculation can be assimilated to a much less 'mechanical' process such as translation: after all, computers which are much 'cleverer' than any human being have existed for some time, whereas nothing similar in the way of translating machines has hitherto proved possible to construct.

We shall have something more to say on this much debated problem in the last chapter. All the same, neither in *The Psychopathology of Everyday Life* nor even in the *Lectures* do we in fact

[25] The Italian-German pairs mean: 'hot-cold'; 'high-old'; 'stove-step'; the Italian-French one 'wheel-route'. Trans.

find a defence of the 'polyglot unconscious' along the lines we have just suggested. One might expect to find something in one of Freud's later works. But except for a very brief note written in 1936[26] and a passing remark in *An Outline of Psychoanalysis*, published after his death,[27] Freud in his last years did not concern himself with 'slips', and above all did not ever feel the need to reformulate *The Psychopathology* in order to bring it into line with the two theories of the Unconscious which he subsequently developed (that presented in the essays on 'Metapsychology', which makes the distinction between the Preconscious and the Unconscious, and that of the system Id/Ego/Super-ego).[28]

In the first edition of the chapter on *Signorelli–Botticelli*,[29] Freud tried to justify in a much simpler way the ease with which associations dependant on translation were made: 'The whole process [of association] was clearly made easier by the fact that during the last few days at Ragusa I had been speaking Italian continually – that is, that I had become accustomed to translating German into Italian in my head'. This justification was not included later in the definitive edition, though nothing was put in its place. It is legitimate to suppose that Freud became aware either of its intrinsic weakness (the regular use of a foreign language for a short period does not render one bi-lingual!) or of the fact that a similar explanation did not apply in the case of the forgetting of *aliquis*, nor to the incident which depends on an equivalence between *homo* and a particular meaning of *Mensch*, nor to many other unconscious translations postulated in *The Psychopathology*.

[26] Cit. above note 23.

[27] *GW* XVII 63 sqq. = *SE* XXIII 141 sqq.

[28] From a remark in the second series of *Lectures* (*GW* XV 77 sq. = *New Introd. Lect. Psych.*, *SE* XXII 70 sq.) it appears that Freud assigned 'slips' whose cause the subject immediately acknowledged to the realm of the pre-conscious, and reserved for the unconscious proper those whose interpretation by the analyst was 'repudiated as something foreign' by the subject. In both cases it went without saying that the author of the 'slip' was right when he admitted to it, wrong when he denied it. The problem of the 'polyglot unconscious' is not, however, dealt with by Freud on this occasion.

[29] Cit. above (note 1), p. 523.

7

'Abstract' Science and 'Concrete' Magic

At the beginning of Chapter 5 we mentioned the accusation of excessive generality levelled by Freud and the Freudians against attempts to explain 'slips' and parapraxes by methods other than their own. We must now examine this charge in more detail.

Freud found himself confronted by two types of explanation. One was strictly neurophysiological: 'slips' and instances of forgetting were to be attributed to tiredness, or to arteriosclerosis, or to general functional disturbances of the cerebrum (p. 27 = 21); there was, for example, the frequency with which instances of forgetting had been found to accompany attacks of migraine. The other was a psycholinguistic explanation: 'slips' were due to a mistaken transposition of sounds belonging to the same word or to contiguous words (as in those cases on which we commented above p. 72 note 14), or to the transposition of entire words (as in 'the Milo of Venus' instead of 'the Venus of Milo'), or to substitutions based on phonic or conceptual similarities. Given a certain relaxation of attention – and here neurophysiological factors came into play again– there might occur 'an uninhibited stream of lexical and phonetic associations'.[1]

Freud allows that such considerations have a certain validity. He impresses on us many times that there is no contradiction between them and psychoanalysis. But what the psychologists and psycho-linguists among his contemporaries regarded as *causes* of instances of forgetting or 'slips', Freud counts only as *Begünstigungen*,

[1] See in particular the beginning of Chap. V of *The Psychopathology*, and p. 68 = 61. This last phrase is Wundt's, reported by Freud himself. See also *GW* XI 25 sq., 39 sq. = *Introd. Lect. Psych.*, *SE* XV 32 sq., 46 sq.

that is, as circumstances *favouring* the production of such disturbances of memory, but in no way constituting either necessary
conditions (since 'slips' and instances of forgetting can occur even
'at a time of perfect health and unimpaired efficiency') or sufficient
conditions (because still too generic). Freud wittily remarks that
it is as if the victim of a robbery were to report to the police that
'I was in such and such a street, and there *loneliness* and *darkness*
took away my watch and purse', instead of saying that '*favoured*
by the loneliness of the place and under the *shield* of darkness
unknown malefactors robbed me of my valuables'.[2] So we are left
with the problem of identifying the 'unknown psychic forces'
which, favoured by arteriosclerosis or fatigue on the one hand,
by phonic and conceptual similarities on the other – or even in
the absence of such favouring circumstances – produced the psychic
disturbance.

I think it could rightly be claimed that, in comparison with the
explanations criticized by Freud, those advanced here are much
more specific. Possibly this is because, compared with the psycho-
linguist or physiologist, the textual critic, as we have already noted,
necessarily has a greater awareness of the multiplicity and complexity of the causes which conjoin to produce a 'slip'[3] and is thus
much more alive to the fact that his task cannot be restricted to
grouping 'slips' within wholesale categories, but demands an
effort to understand how various general tendencies contribute
on any given occasion to the production of a single and particular
error. All the same, a Freudian might be inclined to accuse even

[2] p. 27 sq. = 21; *GW* XI 39 = *Introd. Lect. Psych.*, *SE* XV 46 sq.

[3] We have already seen the extent to which the explanation of errors of
transcription also nearly always refers us to a conjuncture of several causes
(palaeographic, psychologico-cultural, and so on); and we shall also see in what
follows the extent to which virtually all errors are multi-determined. The
concept of 'overdetermination' (*Überdeterminierung*) is a term used in textual
criticism too, although not with quite the same meaning and without the
more specific sense which Freud on occasions, though not always, assigns to it
(see J. Laplanche and J.-B. Pontalis, *The Language of Psychoanalysis*, London,
1973, p. 292). Our own difficulty in accepting the majority of the Freudian
explanations of 'slips' does not lie, however, in any reluctance to admit to the
concomitance, with the more general causes considered by us, of causes more
closely connected to the psychic history of the individual. It lies entirely in the
relative lack (and sometimes complete absence) of any means whereby to check
the explanations themselves.

our explanations – those we have already given, and those we shall give in what follows – of generality and superficiality. There is no doubt, he might say, that there exists a tendency towards banalization; we might even admit that in the famous line from the *Aeneid* the word *aliquis* was the most likely one to be forgotten; but that has not prevented, nor will it prevent, innumerable other persons, equipped with a knowledge of Classics more or less equivalent to that of Freud's young interlocutor, from remembering the entire line perfectly; and probably the young Austrian himself had quoted it on other occasions from memory without forgetting any of it. How then, was it, that precisely that individual, in that situation, forgot the word that he did? Likewise a Freudian might well say that the exposition of the disimprovement mechanism at work in *Botticelli–Boltraffio*, while in itself acceptable, does not allow us to understand why it was just that mistake which Freud made on this occasion, when on a hundred others he had remembered the name *Signorelli* perfectly, nor why, from among the possible emendations he could have made to the erroneous *Botticelli*, he happened to settle for *Boltraffio*.[4]

By way of reply, then, let us first point out that so-called 'generality' is an ineliminable feature, or, if you prefer, necessary price of any scientific explanation. In comparison to any scientific explanation a 'magical' one, by contrast, nearly always has a more 'individualizing' quality. The distinction has been particularly clearly stated by Ernst Cassirer;[5] and it retains its validity even for one who, like myself, rejects Cassirer's Kantianism or neo-Kantianism, and his conceptualization of scientific law and of causality. For reasons of space I shall not cite the whole passage,

[4] In this specific case, however, there is a very restricted range of possible errors that Freud could have made. For it would be difficult, I believe, to point to another Renaissance painter whose name presented so much phonic similarity with that of Signorelli as does the name of Botticelli; nor do I believe (once the false path of disimprovement had been taken) that there exist other Renaissance painters with names beginning with *Bo-* other than Boltraffio and Botticelli (none are recorded in Thieme and Becker's dictionary).

[5] E. Cassirer, *Determinism and Indeterminism in Modern Physics* (New Haven, 1956), p. 99. (The work was first produced in German in 1937.) Cassirer himself points out in a note that Lucien Lévy-Bruhl had made a similar observation: see *Primitive Mentality* (Boston, 1966), p. 442, and the other passages cited in the content index under 'causality'.

but limit myself to a few sentences: 'For myths there can be no accidental event in the course of human existence . . . Everything has to be strictly determined; but it is determined not by general principles underlying events, as expressed in the sciences by 'natural laws', but by individual purposes and forces servile to them. . . . This magical causality therefore penetrates much further into detail than the causality of theoretical science . . . it demands a definite cause for every case of illness or death, to be found in some individual act of will, in some antagonistic sorcery worked upon the person. Here we find, in a certain sense, instead of an absence of all causal explanation, a hypertrophy . . . and only the character of the causes differentiates between mythical and theoretical thinking, in that mythical causality is based on intentions and acts of will as contrasted with rules and laws'.

Thus Freud's analogy with the victim of theft who accuses not his assailants but the darkness and loneliness of the night, can legitimately be countered by another analogy – one not so witty, but perhaps more appropriate to clarify the divergence involved in the concept of causal explanation. If I have a sore throat and I consult the doctor, who diagnoses pharyngitis, I can complain that in its recourse to a general category this diagnosis obliterates my own specific and highly personal affliction. If the doctor, in order to better satisfy me, specifies that my pharyngitis was caused by streptococci which found a favourable environment in my pharynx and in my organism as a whole as a result of the cold and of the generally debilitated state that I happened to be in at the time, I might still reply that all this is still too general. Why, after all, did the streptococci attack me in particular rather than my friend X, who had been exposed to the cold just as much as I, whose general condition of health was worse than mine, who worked in a less wholesome environment and was subject to greater exploitation? Indeed how was it that I myself did not contract pharyngitis a month ago, when the illness had much more epidemic proportions and when my physical condition was no better? Since there is no science without generalization, one can always accuse science of excessive generality.

This charge may appear all the more justified when levelled at sciences such as medicine and philology. Despite their thousandfold differences in other respects, these disciplines have two features in common. On the one hand, they are both obliged – in response to practical as well as theoretical dictates – to retain the specificity of the individual case. The dictum of the Belgian philologist, Joseph Bidez, *tous les cas sont spéciaux* ['every case is special'] was regarded by Dain and Pasquali[6] as the golden rule of textual criticism. 'There is no disease, there is only the patient' is the rather more famous medical aphorism. The painstaking exactitude and extreme scruple of Augusto Murri's study of the problem of medical causation is well-known – a study which equally never succumbed (any more than the work of Dain and Pasquali in philology) to the opposite temptation to reduce a science to an 'art' entrusted to an intuition of 'case by case', without regulative laws and general principles. Secondly, philology and medicine are both diachronic sciences, whose phenomena – by contrast with those studied by mathematics and physics – are not reproducible under identical conditions, and are therefore for the most part not susceptible to direct experimental verification.[7]

Now let us suppose that I had consulted a magician instead of a doctor about my sore throat. In that event my demand for an individualizing explanation would apparently find much greater satisfaction. The magician will not, in fact, talk to me about an abstract 'pharyngitis', but will first elicit an account of myself and my woes. If he then discovers, let us say, that on the day before I fell ill I had quarrelled with my neighbour, he will proceed to explain that it was the latter who cast an evil eye on me. True enough, I can then return home satisfied that I have obtained a strictly individual explanation! If, moreover, the magician is sufficiently astute and up-to-date (a far from unlikely supposition in these days when the vogue for 'call-up consultants' in superstition among the upper-classes is on a scale reminiscent of the success of Babylonian astrology during the Roman Empire), he will in

6 See Dain, p. 181; Pasquali, p. 480. The principle was formulated even earlier by A. L. von Schlözer. See E. J. Kenney, *The Classical Text* (Berkeley-London, 1974) p. 98.
7 One might want to recall the traditional distinction between 'experimental sciences' and 'sciences of observation'. Giuseppe Prestipino has examined the problem in terms of a revised methodology, *Natura e società* (Rome, 1973), Chaps. XI–XII and passim.

no way claim that what the doctor had told me was mere humbug. Indeed, he will concede the part played by pathogenic bacteria, the cold and my general state of debilitation, provided these are regarded only as circumstances favouring the development of my pharyngitis. Whereas the real cause, which explains my pharyngitis and mine alone, is the evil eye.

It might be thought that with this paradoxical example I am trying to insinuate that psychoanalysis is nothing more than a contemporary form of witchcraft. But it would be utterly ridiculous, though not unprecedented, to condemn it in this way. I am well aware that among those who have pronounced such a sentence must be numbered the most diehard reactionaries (not only in matters of science but in their general vision of reality), and the outright slanderers and persecutors of Freudianism. On the other hand, I certainly believe that Freud often arrived at wholly arbitrary constructions in his quest for certain typically 19th century forms of deterministic explanation. I also believe that his explicit attempt to achieve the most individualizing explanation possible was a significant factor in these aberrations. Not that such an attempt is in itself wrong, provided that the advantage gained by a greater degree of individualization is not purchased at the unacceptable price of an explanation that is immune to any real verification.[8] This is the sense in which I believe that the explanations of the forgetting of *aliquis* and of the *Signorelli–Botticelli–Boltraffio* 'slip' which I propose can be said to be of the 'pharyngitis type', while Freud's explanations are those of the 'evil-eye type'. To say this is not to overlook – the warning should be superfluous – the immensity of the gulf which separates a thinker who for better or worse was unquestionably one of the intellectual giants of our century

[8] I have elsewhere argued against the prejudice that every attempt to relate natural and social factors to the individual subject is necessarily contaminated with irrationalism and 'historicism': see *On Materialism*, London, 1976, p. 188 sqq. It is curious that the major advocates of the view that the only valid form of scientific knowledge is abstract, the prime antagonists of any concrete study of the individual (especially in the human sciences) should be, at the same time, extensively influenced by Freudianism. One has only to think of Lévi-Strauss or Althusser. The paradox is no more than apparent, and we shall comment on it shortly. But it would need a separate treatment to do it justice, which we cannot provide here.

and who pioneered new horizons *even for science,* from an obscure practitioner of textual criticism, who may be right in one or two or even many individual cases, and formulate objections to psychoanalysis with some foundation, but who nevertheless will always remain the average intellect that he happens to be.

Of course, once we have chosen the Freudian path, we can soon find that Freud himself is too much a 'man of science', i.e. too general and abstract in his approach. In this connexion, it is worth recalling Georges Politzer's *Critique des fondements de la psychologie,* since it is the work of an acute intellect and a highly developed political and moral consciousness.[9] Here we find Freud criticized from what one might call an ultra-Freudian standpoint. Politzer's objection is that Freud does not remain consistent to his own pioneering conception of psychology as 'individual drama' and that in his recourse to abstract categories he falls back into the older tradition of a generalizing and de-humanizing psychology. Of course, there is much more than this to Politzer's critique of Freud. In its demand for a 'concrete' psychology, for a psychology of the 'first person' which would not be treated with the naturalistic niethods of the 'third person', Politzer's youthful work opened the way to a study of man as a being who is simultaneously natural and social; whose multitude of unsatisfied needs and complex sufferings can by no means be explained simply by reference to the traumatic experiences of his infantile sexuality, but must be related to the whole set of frustrations and oppressions to which he is subject in a profoundly anti-egalitarian society. Here we can already discern the path that was to lead Politzer to Marxism, and which, after his death during the Resistance, Lucien Sève was to pursue in *Marxisme et théorie de la personnalité.*[10] But even if we acknowledge all this, we must still grant that the *Critique des*

---

[9] Written in 1928, this monograph was published in Italian in the volume: G. Politzer, *Freud e Bergson* (Florence, 1970), with an introduction by Pierre Naville which gives a very good account of Politzer's personal itinerary from psychologist to militant Marxist. See, in particular, the defence of Freud which Politzer develops in Chaps. I–II and the criticisms he makes of him in the following chapters. See also L. Sève, cit. in the following note. By and large, Politzer's essay has been unjustifiably neglected in works dealing with the psychoanalytic movement and its 'heretics'.

[10] An English translation is now in preparation.

fondements de la psychologie contained the risk of widening the gap between psychology and neurophysiology (which was already responsible for anti-scientific elements in Freud's work). More generally, in the urgency of its pursuit of the 'concrete' it tended to overlook the actual nature of scientific knowledge.[11]

Let me repeat that this does not mean that one should not seek the most 'individualizing' explanations possible that are consistent with the scope of any given science. We have earlier commented on the way in which a shared necessity for such explanations links the so-called humanities (of which philology is one) to medicine, and thus also to psychology and psychiatry, sciences which in a certain sense belong to both camps. But individualized explanations, if they are really to improve on generalized explanations, must satisfy conditions which Freudianism usually fails to do. Every relationship they posit, every link they add to the causal chain uniting a symptom to its presumptive original cause must be, if not amenable to absolute confirmation, at least demonstrably more probable than other alternative explanations. Considering the question of medical diagnoses, Augusto Murri wrote: 'The more numerous the intermediate links in the chain, the greater the danger of an unjustified connexion being made'.[12] This is even more true in the case of Freudian analyses in which we are very often dealing with symbolic interpretations which leave a very wide margin for invention.

Nor is it enough, in order to substantiate an avowed determinism, to assert that every 'slip' has a cause and thereupon present extravagant causal connexions as certain. Even the magician whom it occurred to me to consult about my sore throat – this is the last time that I shall appeal to my earlier provocative analogy – could

[11] Here Sève (op. cit. pp. 337–44) seems to me too impassioned in his unconditioned defence of Politzer's 'concrete psychology' against Althusser's criticisms. Certainly as a polemical riposte to the cloud of presumptuous Platonism foisted upon him by Althusser, Sève's reply has its merits. But the potential dangers of a 'concrete psychology' (at any rate in the formulation – which we should remember was provisional – that Politzer made of it) cannot be denied. In this respect, Naville's introduction, though much briefer, reveals a greater awareness of the difficulties (which were not exclusively due to the priority he gave to political action, or to his heroic and premature death) that prevented Politzer from advancing his project of a concrete psychology.

[12] A Murri, *Il Medico pratico* (Bologna, 1914), p. 73.

rightfully claim to be a 'determinist' in this sense of the term. 'No sore throat develops by chance', I might be told, 'there is an evil eye responsible in every instance'.

Furthermore, *non-scientific individualizing* explanation, precisely because of the weakness of its experimental basis or indeed its outright arbitrariness, nearly always ultimately resolves itself into its opposite. After registering all its painstaking individualization, we cannot but become aware of the extremely impoverished set of causes that Freudian theory advances in explanation of neurotic disorders. We know, in fact, that there is basically only one cause. We shall shortly see that it is actually the Freudian theory of 'slips' that partially evades this criticism, not so much in its general formulation as in its particular applications; but we shall also see that the extent to which it does so constitutes an objection to Freudian theory itself.

Freud himself was acutely aware of the contrast between the description of a certain type of neurosis (together with its related diagnosis, which is always an instance of the reduction of a particular case to a general category, of a substitution of the 'patient' by the 'disease') and that which is strictly specific to each case of individual neurosis. He expresses his awareness of the distinction in a page of the *Lectures* which has possibly not received all the attention it deserves. Towards the end of Lecture XVII of the first series (*GW* XI 278–280= *Introd. Lect. Psych.*, *SE* XVI 270 sq.) he introduces an antithetical distinction between the 'typical' symptom and the 'historical' symptom which seems to anticipate the objection raised later by Politzer (see above, p. 89), and which has an undoubted affinity with similar problems that were an issue of debate for other human sciences during the same period – for example, for Saussurian linguistics (*langue* and synchrony on the one hand and *parole* and diachrony on the other). These were problems which all arose from the schism between science and history which became manifest in European culture towards the end of the 19th and the outset of the 20th century.[13] The solution which Freud merely mentions in that Lecture, and which he later developed in other works, was to be contained in the notion of

[13] See *On Materialism* cit., p. 149.

the collective unconscious. It was, as we know, a solution that posed more problems than it resolved. But it would nonetheless have been interesting, even if to my mind unconvincing, had an attempt been made to apply it to the theory of 'slips', whereas neither Freud nor the Freudians have ever done so.

The Freudian, for his part, can in turn ask in what sense, and within what limits, the explanations we have given of the *aliquis* and *Signorelli* cases (and others similar to these which we expound later) are causal analyses rather than simple descriptions of phenomena.

The phenomenon of banalization (which we have already examined, Chap. 3) provides a starting-point from which to develop our reply. Every time that anyone learns a new or at least unfamiliar linguistic expression (and it matters little, in this instance, whether the 'novelty' is restricted to the mode of expression or also relates to the content of the expression) he finds himself called upon to insert it into a cultural-linguistic patrimony long since acquired, and for that reason already much more familiar to him. There is always the danger, therefore, that what is new or rare will cede place to the more usual, that what is familiar will be substituted for that which, precisely on account of its novelty and rarity, is less easily assimilated and fixed in memory. This danger is present not only at the moment of the *initial* contact with the unusual expression: unless the expression subsequently becomes absorbed through a context of work or study, the danger is constantly present and can reveal itself even after some lapse in time (as in the examples we have given and shall give of quotations from memory).

What is involved here is essentially a process of 'mental economy'[14] – an unconscious tendency towards the exertion of the least effort. The same holds true of the tendency to 'eliminate the superfluous' (see above, p. 36 sqq.). This latter, in fact, is a primary cause not only of many individual omissions and simplifications

[14] I am, of course, speaking of 'economy' here in the sense of an (unconscious) tendency towards least effort: in a more general and traditional sense, that is, than Freud's when he speaks of 'the economic point of view' (see Laplanche and Pontalis, cit. above note 3, pp. 127–31) or Reich's later usage, when he speaks of *Sexual-Ökonomie*.

of phrases, but also of those 'generalized' errors which constitute linguistic innovations. We have only to point to the elimination of the dual form which is already clearly evident as a tendency in Homeric Greek, and to which, of the Indo-European languages alive today, only Slovenian has offered any resistance; or else to the process of simplification which the verb system of the various Indo-European languages has undergone (for example, the reduction in the number of preterite tenses, the gradual disappearance of the subjunctive, the elimination or drastic reduction of verbal inflexions); or indeed, to any of the innumerable examples cited in all the handbooks of linguistics. While it is certainly not my intention to present the tendency towards least effort as the cause of every morphological or syntatical alteration – it would be extremely wrong to do so – the enormous influence which it has exercised, and continues to exercise, remains nonetheless undeniable.[15] The same holds true, furthermore, for the substitution of sounds or groups of sounds which are hard to pronounce by others which are easier: here, in contrast to the two categories of errors we have already noted, the 'ease' and the 'difficulty' have to do with habits acquired by our vocal organs in speaking our own language, and are not related to the 'mental habits' developed as a result of the regular correspondence of certain words with certain concepts. But even in these cases a tendency towards 'economy' in our sense of the term occurs, and its influence is not restricted to cases of phonetic changes alone, but permeates the entire system. The seminal work on this aspect of linguistics is still André Martinet's *Economie des changements phonétiques* (1955), even though at times it yields unduly to the teleologism of the Prague School of linguistics.

Is it appropriate in all these cases to speak of 'psychopathological' factors, or even of that form of psychopathology that Freud quite rightly maintains is revealed even in subjects who are basically free of neurosis? I would say not. Likewise, I would also want to

---

[15] Stylistic-syntactic features such as elision are also to a large extent to be explained in these terms. See in the *Handbuch der erklärender Syntax* by W. Havers (Heidelberg, 1931), p. 162 sqq., the chapter entitled '*Das Streben nach Kräftersparnis*'; and also the essay on 'Le besoin de brèveté' in H. Frei, *La grammaire des fautes* (Paris, 1929), Chap. III, p. 109 sqq.

claim that even forgetting is more 'physiological' than 'pathological' when, as in the case of *aliquis*, it too conforms with the principle of simplification. The *Signorelli–Botticelli* type of 'slip' is perhaps more obviously pathological, at any rate in those cases where it is not accompanied by a banalization, but consists simply in a substitution of words which are linked by some conceptual and especially phonic affinity. But even here, there is no need to invoke an 'individual drama' or depth psychology in order to provide an explanation. If, as Saussure claims, a linguistic sign is the association of a concept with an acoustic image, one can assume that the human mind has a capacity to 'associate' (and thus easily confuse) not only similar concepts but also similar acoustic images; and also that the danger of confusion will be obviously that much greater whenever a *coincidence* of both conceptual and acoustic association is possible. Of course, one must be able to posit an instigating cause of such a confusion. Freud places great weight in his argument on the fact that 'slips' are produced not only at times when little attention is being paid to what one is saying, but also at times when we are especially concerned to express ourselves exactly.[16] This is true, but it represents a particular instance of a whole set of 'counterproductive' features to which our emotional states give rise. It is precisely my fear of bungling things on an occasion when I both wish and need to make a good impression – for example, when addressing a select public or a large crowd – that makes me do so, whereas this does not happen when I have no such fear. Similarly, there is a whole set of nervous symptoms (tremors or missed heartbeats) which are excited at just those times when we least need them, and when we are most anxious to preserve our composure.[17] At the same time, the *other* cause – the lapse in our attention due to preoccupation with other thoughts, or to boredom or fatigue[18]

[16] See *GW* XI 23 = *Introd. Lect. Psych., SE* XV 30.

[17] 'Slips' provoked by means of suggestion (or auto-suggestion) come into this category. Such, for example, are the 'slips' made by amateur actors whose friends amuse themselves in attempts to induce them to stammer their lines: see *GW* XI 32 = *Introd. Lect. Psych., SE* XV 43; A. Maeder in 'Archives de Psychol.' (1908), p. 290 (the 'pièce du répertoire classique allemand' which Maeder was no longer able to identify, was, of course, Schiller's *Don Carlos*).

[18] It is true, as Freud notes, (p. 145 = 132, see *GW* XI 22 sq. = *Introd. Lect. Psych., SE* XV 29 sq.) that it often happens that we read or recite a text 'automatically',

when we are speaking or writing or copying – should be given more weight than it is by Freud.

There is no doubt that the explanation we have outlined in terms of banalization, elimination of the superfluous, and transposition of phonically similar words, needs further development. But this development should be the object of a study of the physiological mechanisms of the process of memory, forgetfulness and concentration, and of the emotional disturbances to which they are subject. This is a rapidly developing field of work, though much remains to be clarified.[19] However, from this point of view, Freud's explanations are no more 'developed' than ours: those we have hitherto considered in Freud's writings, and many we have yet to investigate – we shall see that none of these are less improbable – are, if anything, more arbitrary.

Moreover, it is always useful to keep in mind the distinction between two ways in which a causal account can be developed. There is one that is genuinely scientific, and there is another which dismisses the explanations of science as merely 'empirical', and insists on the existence of something more arcane beneath the level of empirical reality. This anti-empirical bias may be said to attain its apotheosis in the work of Jung and, nearer our own time, in that of more lightweight figures such as Lévi-Strauss. Yet

---

while thinking about something else, and yet make no mistakes. It is also true that someone who walks on the edge of a precipice without looking into it is *in one respect* better protected from falling than a person who is looking or has been advised by others to pay attention, and is thus nervous. But *in another respect*, a situation of this kind has its disadvantages, because one can make a false step not only as a result of nervousness, but straightforwardly as a result of inattention. Equally, we may say with regard to 'slips' that an instinctive reflex on the one hand, and conscious attention (accompanied nearly always by anxiety) on the other, are two different mechanisms of defence, each of which has its pros and cons.

[19] See, e.g., in *La fisica della mente* by K. S. Lashley and others, edited by V. Somenzi (Turin, 1969), the papers by Lashley *Alla ricerca dell'engramma,* p. 80 sqq. [*In Search of the Engram* in 'Symp. Soc. exp. Biol.' 4 (Cambridge, 1950)] and H. Hyden, *Aspetti biochimici dell'apprendimento e della memoria,* p. 301 sqq.; see also Somenzi's introduction and bibliographical notes. These references are not intended to do more than indicate a field of study to those who (like myself) have no specific knowledge of it. But it is clear that it was Pavlov, and not Freud, who initiated research in this direction – though it has scarcely proved unitary in character, as Somenzi makes very clear.

Freud, despite the materialist character of his initial intellectual formation (which we shall discuss in the final chapter), was among its initiators. It has Platonic credentials: in a famous passage from the *Phaedo* (98 sq.), alongside a correct acknowledgment of the distinction between efficient and final causes, there is an illegitimate promotion of final causes to the rank of 'uncaused causes'. Freud was sincere, and to a large extent justified, in his conviction that he had dealt a mortal blow to 'free will'. Nevertheless, his own theory of the unconscious – and to this too we shall return – gradually became the locus not of a psychic mechanism but of a more profoundly mysterious (and frequently unverifiable) finalism. However, anyone who is in a hurry to dismiss efficient causes as mere *Begünstigungen* of other profounder causes, would do well to recall Spinoza's famous passage (*Eth.* I, prop. 36, appendix). In reference to those who attribute to God an anthropomorphic finalism, Spinoza says: 'For example, if a stone falls from a roof on the head of a passer-by and kills him, they will show by their method of argument that the stone was sent to fall and kill the man; for if it had not fallen on him by God's will, how could so many circumstances (for often very many circumstances concur at the same time) occur together by chance? You will reply, perhaps: "That the wind was blowing, and that the man had to pass that way, and hence it happened". But they will retort: "Why was the wind blowing at that time? and why was the man going that way at the time?" If again you reply: "That the wind had then arisen because of the agitation of the sea the day before, after the previous weather had been calm, and that the man was going that way at the invitation of a friend", they will again retort, for there is no end to their questioning, "Why was the sea agitated, and why was the man invited at that time?" Thus they will pursue you from cause to cause until you are glad to take refuge in the will of God, that is, the asylum of ignorance'. It must not be forgotten, of course, that Freud never himself took refuge in the notion of a divine will, and never induced anyone else to do so. But the procedure whereby causes are introduced one after the other only to be rejected as at once too superficial and at the same time too general, to the point where we are left with an unverifiable 'unconscious will', is highly analogous to that described and satirized by Spinoza.

There is, moreover, a quite different set of 'slips' which are due to the influence of the context in which they occur – that is, unlike banalizations, they are not the result of a process of assimilation into the subject's cultural-linguistic patrimony, but of assimilations to preceding or subsequent words belonging to the same phrase. Or else, as in the case, for example, of copyists who already know the text they are copying quite well, or of those who are sufficiently educated to be familiar with the author they are quoting from memory, they are cases of assimilations made 'from a distance' – cases of recollection of similar expressions found in other, not necessarily juxtaposed, passages of the same work, or in some other work of the author.[20] I remember many years ago, during a performance, given in the Roman amphitheatre at Fiesole, of a mediocre jingoistic drama on the foundation of Rome, having heard the actor who played Romulus declaim in full voice at the climax of his account of the fratricide: 'Reso rise' ['Rhesus laughed'] instead of 'Remo rise' ['Remus laughed'], by an unfortunate anticipation of the *s* of the following word in the word before it; so that it was not only Remus but also the audience who laughed (though it did not suffer so direly in consequence), at precisely that point when it should have been most gripped by the tragedy of the situation. The actor, while pronouncing the first of the two words (which, of course, shared a distinct phonic similarity) was already thinking of the second. It is no accident, in fact, that the majority of errors of assimilation found in Greek and Latin codices and in modern manuscripts and typescripts are 'regressive' in this way, rather than 'progressive' (the same phenomenon occurs linguistically when consonants belonging to different syllables are assimilated). It is true that sometimes what has already been uttered or written then impinges on what follows, but more usually the speaker or writer is preoccupied with what he is about to say or write, and it is this preoccupation which gives rise to the mistaken anticipation. [21]

[20] On recollections and assimilations 'from a distance' see, e.g. A. E. Housman, *Classical Papers*, edited by Diggle and Goodyear, p. 436 sqq.; Willis, p. 99 sq.; Fränkel, p. 77 sq.
[21] See also below pp. 136–40.

In all these cases, and in various others which we shall later examine, what authorizes anyone to consider what we count as 'causes' as actually only 'favouring circumstances'? Is it the fact, perhaps, that the same kind of 'slips' and instances of forgetting do not always occur? By no means. The tendencies which operate to alter an expression are obviously countered by an opposite tendency (which in the majority of cases will prevail) towards an accurate registration of the concepts and their acoustic images, their preservation in memory and their pronunciation and transcription at the correct time and place. It is precisely because of this that banalization, confusions between similar sounds, and so on, are *tendencies* and not laws. Even the most slovenly and ignorant copyist, or the most distracted or emotional speaker, always writes or pronounces infinitely more 'correct words' than 'slips' (except, that is, in cases of genuine and severe psychosis). We find the most difficult, recondite and archaic of expressions preserved intact in Greek and Latin manuscripts which post-date the originals by thousands of years and have passed through the hands of innumerable copyists during that time.[22] Likewise, we can point to the way in which relatively uneducated persons preserve over decades the memory of passages of poetry and difficult proper names. Thus, it is quite impossible to predict that, for example, a given text will be corrupted by a given error at a given point in a given copy. But the situation is very different at the statistical level. While I can in no way commit myself to the prediction that the word *cultuale* will be banalized to *culturale* by a particular typist or printer, I am able to predict that in all probability if the passage is given to a hundred typists or printers to reproduce, the majority of them will fall into the error. The same can be said of the banalization of *teleologico* ['teleological'] to *teologico* ['theological']. Here the *saut de même au même* operates as an additional cause in conjunction with the tendency towards banalization, while the latter is further assisted by the fact that the two adjectives, though their meanings are significantly different, are often appropriate enough to the same context: belief in a finalism of nature is obviously related to

[22] See the well-deserved 'eulogy' of copyists (who are all too often reviled by the philologists for their errors) in Dain, p. 17 sq.

a conception which can loosely be termed religious or 'theological'. We must also take, as another example from among innumerable possible instances, the high chance that a little used adjective such as *rabidus* will be substituted by the commoner *rapidus*. In the case of Latin texts which have been transmitted through many codices one can be practically certain that there will be at least one in which that banalization has been effected.[23] Certain proper names suffer the same fate. Two distinguished Hellenists, Vigilio Inama and Emidio Martini, who lived at the end of the 19th century, were forced to resign themselves to the frequent banalization of their names to Virgilio and Emilio, and it is not unknown even today to see their names in this form (the fault is not always the printer's; sometimes it is that of scholars who refer to them).

It is also clear that there are banalizations which are less apt to recur than those we have cited; there are some which are extremely unlikely, but which nonetheless have occurred at least once. Take the mistake whereby Amatore Sciesa, the heroic Milanese worker who was shot in 1851, was named in the sentence delivered by the Austrian tribunal as Antonio Sciesa (as a result, the incorrect name then became widely recorded, and one might well still find it in some textbook today). This is undoubtedly a case of banalization. A very rare name has been replaced by one of the commonest, also beginning with an *A* and with the accent on the same penultimate syllable – *to-*. Yet the difference in the two names is nonetheless considerable, and the chances that Amatore has been banalized to Antonio in another instance, independent of this one, or that it will happen again in the future, are slight. Of one point, however, we can be sure: *if* a mistake occurs in the remembering of a word or phrase, in the vast majority of cases it is due either to banalization or to the attraction exerted by its context or to one of those equally frequent exchanges between words which share

[23] The corruption is so frequently found that modern philologists, through an excess of zeal, have 'restored' *rabidus* where *rapidus* (in its original sense of 'rapacious' or 'over-powering') fitted the context very well! See F. Calonghi in 'Rivista indo-greco-italica' 19 (1935), p. 47 sqq., who is generally convincing, even if he in turn, occasionally overdoes his defence of *rapidus*. In the same way, *nomen* is a frequently found corruption of *numen*, but it has at times been wrongly altered to *numen* (see 'Studi in onore di G. Perrotta', Bologna, 1964, p. 384 sq.).

phonic, and also often semantic, similarities of the kind that we find in the *Botticelli–Signorelli* case. What is very much more uncommon, as every philologist and proof-reader knows, is to find an easier reading replaced by one which is harder or more archaic.

Very much less common, but not impossible. Here too, we must not disregard the existence of counter-forces which at times may prevail over the tendency to banalization. We have already encountered an instance of these in our treatment of 'disimprovements', which often, it is true, consist of banalizations, but by no means always do so (for example, not in the substitution of *Botticelli* by *Boltraffio*, see above, p. 75 sq.). In the same way, the attraction exerted by the context – or by another text not directly before us, but in some way connected by its similarity to the one with which we are concerned – cannot be reduced in every instance to a case of banalization or to 'an exchange of equals'. One often happens to hear the line from Dante's *Purgatory* XVI 97 cited by way of a proverb in the following form: 'le leggi son, ma chi pon mano ad *elle*?' ['the laws are there, but what hand makes them good?']²⁴ instead of 'ad *esse*', the latter being the correct and easier reading (it is confirmed, amongst other things, by its rhyming with lines 95 and 99). The memory of another famous line by Dante: 'Voci alte e fioche e suon di man con *elle*' (*Inferno* III 27) ['fierce yells and hideous blether and clapping of hands thereto']²⁵ evoked by its vague similarities to the former (in both lines the word *mano* or *man* occurs in the same metrical foot, and possibly the purely phonic similarity between *son* and *s(u)on* has played a part), here produces a mistaken *lectio difficilior*.

Finally, apart from other possibilities which interest us less, we must not forget that 'easy and difficult are not absolute terms, and what is difficult, i.e. unfamiliar, to us, may have been easy to those alive at an earlier period'.²⁶ This holds not only as a warning against the transference of our own linguistic and cultural sensibilities and of our own criteria of judgement to epochs and social contexts that are not our own; it also holds for our own time, and our own

²⁴ *The Divine Comedy* (Harmondsworth, 1955) II, p. 190.
²⁵ Ibid. I, p. 86.
²⁶ Pasquali, p. 123.

society. The name of a sports celebrity or pop singer can be a household word for a brief period, and thus give rise to banalizations which when they crop up later will appear at first sight inexplicable. Even the fame of a political or literary figure, while usually somewhat less ephemeral than that of the stars of sport or popular music, is often at its acme only briefly, and thereafter goes into decline, so that the names of such personages are less readily amenable thereafter to 'slips'. In the proofs of a work of mine on the history of philology printed in 1963, I found, instead of 'codici Gottorpiani', 'codici Gattopardiani'. The 'slip' was a testimony to the extent of the fame acquired by *Il Gattopardo* [*The Leopard*] in the years following its publication (1958), and which Luchino Visconti's film of the same name – appearing in the same year as my book – had the effect of diffusing on a mass scale. Tomasi di Lampedusa's renown is far from exhausted today (the recently published book by G. P. Samonà will help to keep it alive, and encourage assessment at a more serious level); all the same, the chances that a printer today would commit a 'slip' like this are very much less now than in 1963, because *The Leopard* is no longer the subject of quite such vociferous publicity as it was at that time; and even if the mistake were, oddly enough, to be repeated, one would be inclined to wager that the 'culprit' would prove to be a printer who was no longer all that young, and on whom the cult of *The Leopard* had impinged with particular force. In the proofs of a volume by Zeller-Mondolfo (*La filosofia dei Greci nel suo sviluppo storico,* part I, vol. V) I once found *Empedocle e gli autonomisti* instead of the heading *Empedocle e gli atomisti*. This was in 1961 or 1962 (the book was published by *La Nuova Italia* some years later after further revisions had been made to it). At that time, the struggle within the Italian Socialist Party (PSI) between the so-called 'autonomists' under the leadership of Pietro Nenni, and the left wing of the Party was at its height – with the result that *autonomisti* was a term of current parlance in all the debates on the Italian left and in all the newspapers. Today it has virtually disappeared and Leucippus and Democritus no longer risk being numbered among the followers of Pietro Nenni.

But it is not only to certain epochs and social contexts that 'ease' and 'difficulty' may be relative; they can be relative even to a single individual (or to a restricted group of individuals whose cultural-linguistic patrimony is, in certain respects, different from the average – as in the case of jargon or specialized professional vocabularies). Giorgio Pasquali once mistakenly corrected, in the proofs of one of his articles, the word 'traduzione' to 'tradizione', although the first and commoner word fitted very well in the context and had in fact originally been written by Pasquali himself. It was he who later explained the reason for his blunder: 'I had written a book on the *tradition* ['tradizione'] of classical languages, whereas I have only perpetrated a single *translation* ['traduzione'] from these, and that a mere trifle; so that in this case I must be judged to have been the victim of a *lectio difficilior*.'[27]

With this last example, we have ourselves arrived at an 'individualized' explanation, although very different in kind from those we find expounded and 'explained' in Freud's book. But, as we have already seen and shall continue to see, the great majority of 'slips' are explicable in terms of 'general' causes. We shall come back to this point in Chapter 9 rather than pursue it immediately, because it seems politic to continue to alternate discussions of matters of principle with analyses and critiques of particular Freudian explanations.

[27] Pasquali, p. 485. Pasquali, of course, uses the word 'tradition' in the specialized sense of the manuscript tradition, the transmission of texts. The particular translation which he speaks of having 'perpetrated' (his tone is one of genuine dissatisfaction with this piece of juvenilia, but it hints ironically at the innumerable and frequently careless and D'Annunzio-esque verse translations of Romagnoli and Bignone) is of *The Characters* of Theophrastus.

8

The Slips of the Good
Citizens of Vienna

If we now move from the interpretations of 'slips' contained in the first two chapters of Freud's book to the very many others which he expounds much more briefly in the subsequent chapters, we will note certain differences which may allow us a better understanding of the privileged position which Freud reserved for the first two cases.

These cases – provided, of course, one accepts Freud's explanations of them, which for us lack verisimilitude – present a very clear analogy with a genuine and specific neurotic symptom. They are expressions of a thought which the unconscious ego has repressed, and which nonetheless succeeds in making itself felt in a disturbance of 'normal' speech – not, however, in a complete usurpation of this, but by means of a compromise between the disturbed conscious intention and the unconscious disturbing intention. The words *aliquis* and *Signorelli* (replaced by *Botticelli–Boltraffio*) are not only forgotten against the conscious wishes of the subject, but in addition, the subject himself, once he has acknowledged the error, is not immediately aware of the motive for it. He comes to understand this only through a miniature analysis (a self-analysis in the case of *Signorelli*) based on the method of free association; and this proceeds only by breaking down a whole series of resistances imposed by the subject, and by the interpretation of a series of symbols (especially in the *aliquis* case) which serve to disguise the true origin of the 'slip'.

By contrast, in the majority of the cases given later, the cause of the 'slip' is presented as immediately obvious to the speaker or listener (who is sometimes right about it, but sometimes wrong –

we shall come back to this point). Or if an analysis is needed, it is only a very brief and elementary one, in which the number of 'steps' and possible symbolic interpretations is reduced to the minimum. A member of the German parliament, concerned to persuade his colleagues to demonstrate their 'unreserved' (*rückhaltlos*) loyalty to the Kaiser, comes out with *rückgratlos* ('spineless') and thereupon immediately exposes the hypocritical servility which he was at such pains to keep hidden (p. 105 sq. = 95 sq.). A Jewish convert to Christianity, who found himself the guest of an anti-semitic family with which he nonetheless wanted to keep on good terms, and who feared that his children would reveal the unpalatable truth of their Jewish origin to his hostess who was ignorant of it, meant to say to them: 'Go into the garden, children', but instead of *Jungen* ('youngsters') says *Juden* ('Jews') – the very word that he least of all wanted to utter (p. 103 = 93). The only truly convincing examples given in *The Psychopathology* and in the *Lectures* are of this type, which we can call verbal *gaffes* (an expression I adopt in the absence of anything better). A *gaffe*, in fact, can also occur when a speaker is unaware of how tactless it would be to mention certain matters or to use particular expressions in a given situation, whereas in our case the speaker is all too cognizant of the inopportuneness of what he actually happens to say.[1] Freud himself does not fail to emphasize the fact that errors of this type had for a long time been known to occur and that there are examples of them in celebrated literary works which are not due to the inadvertance of the author, but to his subtle perception of this psychological mechanism.[2] Moreover, common expressions such as 'he gave himself away' or 'he didn't mean to say' etc. testify to

[1] For the two types of *gaffe* mentioned here, and the similarity and difference between 'slip' and *gaffe*, see Musatti, *Trattato*, p. 423 sqq.

[2] See, for example, the passages from famous authors (Shakespeare, Schiller, Meredith, Theodor Fontane) cit. pp. 107 = 96; 108 = 97; 111 note 1 = 100 note 1; 170 note 1 = 154 note 1; 196 = 176-7; and this list is anything but complete. See also *GW* XI 29 = *Introd. Lect. Psych.*, *SE* XV 36, where Freud's declaration is a rather significant indication of his attitude to 'official' psychology: 'nor would it be surprising if we had more to learn about "slips of the tongue" from creative writers than from philologists and psychiatrists'. (By 'philologist' (*Philolog*) Freud in reality means 'glottologist' (*Sprachforscher*): the 'philologist' and the 'psychiatrist' are, as usual, Meringer and Mayer, with whom, as we have seen, Freud had had especial reason to quarrel.

the fact that we have always recognized that it is difficult to maintain perfect control over what we say, and to avoid half-revelations of what we would rather keep from others, and in many cases from ourselves too.

This is not to deny that Freud has given us a clearer understanding of the psychological process which gives rise to the *gaffe*. All we wish to point to is the way in which Freud's explanations increasingly lose verisimilitude the further we move away from the *gaffe* type of 'slip' towards the 'slips' that can be said to be more typically 'Freudian' – that is, towards the *aliquis* or *Signorelli* type. To gain the reader's assent to his account of the latter type of 'slip' – which was obviously the project most important to him – Freud adopts two contrasting approaches in *The Psychopathology* and in the *Lectures*. In the former, as we noted, the reader is taken by storm: if the explanations given in the first two chapters appear convincing to him, he will thereafter be quite prepared to accept the others which generally refer to simpler cases. In the *Lectures*, which were published many years after the first edition of *The Psychopathology*, concern at the prejudicial hostility or incredulity which psychoanalysis still had to overcome is more evident. So that here Freud initially selects elementary and (at least to his mind) obvious examples, and once he has convinced his audience of these, he then proceeds to persuade it that more complex cases are no different in kind and so may command a similar consent. Yet each of these procedures depends more on Freud's ability as an advocate than on any intrinsically persuasive force. One is left with the impression, it seems to me, that wherever the explanation is certain or highly probable, there is no need for a Freud (except, as I say, to improve our understanding of a psychic phenomenon with which we are already substantially acquainted), whereas where we do need a Freud, the explanation is forced. It relies too often on the postulation of arbitrary or undemonstrable intermediate links between the 'slip' and its presumed cause. We shall see, for that matter, that even in the examples of the more elementary kind there is no lack of capricious explanations.

Another surprise for anyone who comes to *The Psychopathology* after a reading of Freud's principal works (especially those written before the crisis and reorientation of his thought provoked by the dramatic and unexpected experience of the First World War), is the relative dearth of 'slips' with a sexual reference. Even in this respect, the first two chapters, both of which are devoted to explanations of 'slips' of sexual origin (I am obviously referring to Freud's explanations and not those which I would hold to be correct), stand out from the others. Real or allegedly sexual 'slips' are certainly not absent from the later examples, but there are at least as many, if not more, which have to do with politics, with racial prejudice, with pursuit of money,[3] and, in a quite particular way, with frustrations over issues of career, scientific prestige and professional rivalry.[4] Freud and his circle, as we know, swiftly came to experience frustrations of this sort to an obsessive, even pathological, degree. Isolated as they felt themselves to be from the academic world, spurned by a society which abhorred the desecrations of psychoanalysis, they nevertheless yearned for acknowledgment by that very world and that same society. Thus it was that Freud, despite his hostility to universities, displayed side by side with an undoubtedly heroic independence and non-conformism, many of the defects of the university professor in their most heightened form; and between the master and his pupils, and among the pupils themselves, everything worst about academic life – the authoritarianism, the bitter competition, the love–hate relationships – was reproduced on a magnified scale.[5]

[3] Here too I give only a selection of examples. Politics: pp. 67 sq. = 59 (we will have more to say on this case on p. 147 sqq.); 80 sqq. = 71 sqq. (where the 'slips' concern not so much politics in the strict sense as the discontents and moral conflicts of wartime); 125 = 114 sq. (idem); 133 sq. = 121, and also the case already cited, 105sq. = 95 sq. Racial prejudice: *Juden/Jungen*, already cit. Miserliness (mostly in connexion with the medical profession): pp. 100 sq. = 91 (which has an ulterior sexual explanation. J. Stärcke is responsible for the report and explanation of the case); 252 sq. = 232 sq.; 246 = 226 sq., etc. (again, in a late writing devoted to the analysis of a parapraxis, *Die Feinheit einer Fehlhandlung, GW* XVI 37–9 = *The Subtleties of a Faulty Action, SE* XXII 233–5, the cause is traced back to Freud's reluctance to make a gift of something).

[4] Here there are countless examples. I shall cite only: pp. 29 = 22 sq., no. 2; 32 = 26 no. 7; 78 = 68 sq.; 78 = 69, no. 19; 88 = 78, no. 36; 129 sq. = 118 sq.; 130 sq. = 120 sq.; 159 sq. = 143 sq., no. 11.

[5] We shall return to this later. Particularly striking testimonies to the predominance of such an atmosphere in Freud's circle are to be found in E. Fromm, *Sigmund Freud's Mission* (London, 1959) (especially in Chaps. 6, 8 and 10) and in Roazen: *Broth. Anim.*

The Psychopathology of Everyday Life is, in large part, a reflection of the day-to-day life of Freud and his pupils. In another aspect, it provides a portrait (to which Freud brings all his great gifts as a writer – qualities which never deserted him even in his scientifically weakest works) of the highly complex and 'respectable' society of Vienna at the turn of this century.

To say this is not to reiterate in any way the moralistic judgement – which, as we have already seen, Freud rightly rejected – that psychoanalysis could 'only have originated in a town like Vienna – in an atmosphere of sensuality and immorality foreign to other cities', and that it therefore constituted 'a reflection, a projection into theory, as it were, of these peculiar Viennese conditions'.[6] Such comments are mere stupidity, and have already been refuted by the facts themselves – by the extent of the diffusion and success of psychoanalysis throughout the Western world. But it is perhaps not so stupid (even though it would be wrong to reduce the entire significance of Freud's work to this) to suggest that psychoanalysis reveals the imprint of that 'singular synthesis of implacable critical spirit and implacable bourgeois correctness' which Claudio Magris argues[7] was characteristic of Central European civilization – though less so of Germany than of Austro-Hungary. The Habsburg State represented a particularly notable focus of contrasts. On the one hand, it contained an exceptionally archaic social and political structure, one that in many respects was still pre-bourgeois: a

[6] *GW* X 80 sq. = *On the History of the Psychoanalytic Movement, SE* XIV 39–41. Freud's reply is remarkable, all the same, and reveals the ambivalence of his feelings towards the city in which he passed nearly his entire life. He first of all argues that in Vienna there is somewhat greater freedom of sexual behaviour, and somewhat less prudishness than in other European towns 'which are so proud of their chastity', so that the city is less likely than any other to generate neuroses. He then, *without any pause*, proceeds to state that 'Vienna has done everything possible, however, to deny her share in the origin of psychoanalysis' and that psychoanalysis feels itself surrounded at Vienna more than elsewhere by the hostility and neglect of 'the learned and educated section of the population'. Both arguments militate against the idea that psychoanalysis was intrinsically 'Viennese'; but they are to some extent contradictory.

[7] C. Magris, *Lontano da dove* (Turin, 1971), p. 151 and passim. See also Magris, *Il mito absburgico nella letteratura austriaca moderna* (Turin, 1963). Rapaport, *Structure*, p. 15 cites the article by E. H. Erikson in 'Internat. Journal of Psycho-Anal.' 36 (1955), p. 1 sqq., with reference to the influence of 'Victorian Vienna' on Freud; but the citation is not pertinent.

multi-national State that was an anachronism among the national States of the rest of Europe; a monarchy which outdid every other dynasty in Central and Western Europe for antiquity and 'venerability'; a generally low level of industrial development; severe restrictions on the rights of national minorities and Jews; a marked clericalism, an old-style militarism and a rigid moralism. On the other hand, the bourgeoisie of the big cities, and of Vienna in particular, sensed a crisis of traditional values, and a climate of sophisticated decadence and psychologism was more noticeable there than elsewhere. I am aware that this is a very summary characterization – I have no wish to pretend that I am any specialist in Central European culture and society, and it is certainly not enough to refer to an authority like Magris to compensate for my own very superficial acquaintance with it. I also realize that the contrasting elements I have indicated are essentially common to every bourgeois civilization once it has reached a certain stage of development and crisis; but for the reasons that I have had to touch on all too briefly, these contrasts were exceptionally prevalent in Austro-Hungarian society, which was simultaneously both behind and in advance of its time.

A member of that society had to be on guard against referring to a host of what were considered disconcerting topics; against touching on a multitude of burning issues, from sex to politics, from money matters to concerns of social and professional prestige, from the Jewish question to myriad other ethnic conflicts and their often unspecified social basis. On the other hand, he or she would have been aware to a greater or lesser extent that what all these 'forbidden topics' reflected was not a genuine respect for a set of values – objectively false and reactionary, yet firmly believed by the ruling class and its intellectuals – but rather a climate of utter crisis of all these pseudo-values within the bourgeoisie and aristocracy itself. Hence the continual temptation to infringe the rules, to say (and do) what was forbidden: 'their fear is changed into desire'.[8]

Within such a climate, even the sexual 'slip' does not emerge as substantially different from the other kinds of 'slips' we have

---

[8] Dante, *Inferno* III 126 [Eng. trans., *The Divine Comedy* cit. I, p. 88].

mentioned. The explanations of 'slips' and instances of forgetting which presume a sexual origin never – or hardly ever[9] – refer us back, in fact, to the very first stage of infancy which Freud would have us believe constitutes the primal source (a-historic, independent of all social conditioning, save for the very general fact of being alive in society at all) of the majority of the neuroses. Even the *aliquis* and *Signorelli* cases hinge not on the Oedipus complex but on recent adult experiences – whose confession is only so painful because of prudish embarrassment. This is even more obvious in the case of 'taboo words' which we happen to utter at the wrong moment, or only in a 'hybrid' and thus incomprehensible form, that reflects their half-suppressed status. We have only to think of how many words can be voiced today which even as little as thirty years ago were strictly forbidden; and of the disappearance, which is more or less a *fait accompli* among the younger generation, of the hypocritical distinction between a vocabulary intended 'for men only' (itself an expression of sexual frustration) and one appropriate to 'women and children'. There will be sexual suppression, of course, as long as an inegalitarian society exists (taking the term to include bourgeois society, and Stalinist and post-Stalinist society with its revival of an out-dated bourgeois puritanism as a 'healthy' proletarian ethic). It was this which Reich understood, and which he rightly refused to accept as the necessary price of any form of civilization, seeing it instead as a mark of a false and retrograde civilization. For egalitarian societies – as Reich saw too – will be those in which not only the State but the family has also disappeared. There is nothing more paradoxical than to acknowledge (as Freud rightly did, even if some of his interpretations are arbitrary, and even if he wrongly neglected other institutions and relations which may equally give rise to neurosis) that the family is far from an idyllic environment, that it is in fact a centre of tensions, of misunderstandings, of morbid loves and frequently hatreds too – and then to proceed to eternalize the institution, and to limit oneself to curing (if, indeed

[9] The only exception of any relevance is Chap. IV on 'Childhood and Screen Memories', on which we shall again have occasion to comment in connexion with instances of forgetting, in the penultimate chapter of this book. But our remark holds true for the content of *The Psychopathology* as a whole.

that is ever really possible!) the damage it does, rather than seeking to prevent that damage by the suppression of the institution itself.[10] Yet this does not alter the fact that the nature of sexual suppression is changing in society today. In many respects, it is already transformed. It no longer appears as direct suppression, but as a transmutation of sex into a 'luxury commodity'. (This should be distinguished from the squalid commercialism of prostitution, which lingers on but whose days are numbered). It may also often take the form of a premature abandonment of sexual activity due to over-work – in many cases necessary simply to survival, in others to maintain a pointlessly high standard of living whose effect is to divert gratification towards the 'unnatural and unnecessary' pleasures of household display, automobile activity, and the ever more exhausting 'rest' of the weekend. In the atmosphere created by this new form of sexual suppression, disguised as sexual freedom, it is no longer the use of 'taboo words' which scandalizes. We can predict, therefore, and perhaps already confirm, the rapid disappearance of the sexual *gaffe* – unless the present, by no means short-lived, economic crisis results once more in the extension of 'austerity' from consumption to morality.

Does the attention we have drawn to the 'social' rather than sexual character of very many of the 'slips' (even where these have a sexual theme) that are cited and explained in *The Psychopathology* refute the charge of pansexualism often levelled at psychoanalysis (especially in its first phase, before its actual or presumed discovery of the 'Death Instinct')? I would say not. In the first place, it is a fact that in their explanation of genuine and specific cases of neurotic symptoms (with the exception of the 'actual neuroses' which they regarded as relatively unimportant), Freud and the Freudians consistently appealed to the sexual traumas of early infancy. The recent – and to my mind largely successful – attempts to interpret what real and demonstrable content there is in the Oedipus complex as the product of historical and social determinations, would have been deemed heretical by Freud. Even in a work such as *The*

---

[10] For some of the vigorous demands for reform of infantile sexual education which Freud advocated towards the end of the first decade of this century, and in a more qualified way in his later writings, see below, pp. 182–3 and note 11.

Interpretation of Dreams – which in common with *The Psycho-pathology of Everyday Life* is concerned not only with the victims of genuine neurosis, but with the neurotic element present in everybody – explanations whose character is sexual and refers back to the sexuality of early infancy are much the most prevalent. Within the Freudian 'system', therefore, (and the *Lectures* reveal this particularly clearly) *The Psychopathology,* together with the work on *Jokes and their relation to the Unconscious,* escapes the so-called pansexualism of psychoanalysis only to the extent to which it retains the role of an expository text. In other words, it is not as if, with this work, we have yet properly crossed the threshold of Freud's 'depth psychology'. This is the only way in which we can account for Freud's flat assertion, in one of his mature works: 'I used always to warn my pupils: "Our opponents have told us that we shall come upon cases in which the factor of sex plays no part. Let us be careful not to introduce it into our analyses and so spoil our chance of finding such a case." *But so far none of us has had that good fortune.*'[11] We too have our own reasons to regard the charge of pansexualism as inappropriate. We shall come to these in the last chapter.

Moreover, *The Psychopathology* itself, despite its unusually wide variety of explanations, has two important lacunae even if one accepts (as we do not) that all or nearly all 'slips' have their origin in repression. In regard to the first of these: we drew attention to diverse explanations of 'slips' which concerned either the economic sphere (e.g. unconfessed greed for money, or a secret miserliness) or relations of authority and prestige (especially in the medical-academic field) or politics (servility towards those in power, perfidious inter-state alliances, discontent over the privations of war). But one would search in vain among all these 'social' slips for one that referred to class relations, to the antagonism between the bourgeoisie and the proletariat. It might be objected that since Freud and his immediate followers found their patients among the wealthy bourgeoisie (Freud's opinions on psychoanalysis for the

[11] *GW* XIV 235, in the famous paper on *Die Frage der Laienanalyse* (1926) = *The Question of Lay Analysis, SE* XX 207. It would be easy to cite many other equally trenchant passages.

poor are well-known),[12] or else from among aspirant psychoanalysts who submitted to a teaching analysis, it is naive to expect
to find the class struggle reflected in their unconscious. Such an
objection is wholly invalid. Bourgeois society certainly imposes
a much greater toll, even psychically, on the proletariat than on
the bourgeoisie. But despite its position of power, the latter never
ceases to live in fear of the former. This is true of periods of
progressive reform of working-class conditions, as was the case
in Austria at the start of the century, since the fear is always present
for the bourgeoisie that social gains by the working class may,
albeit if only in the long run, surpass the 'safety-limits' of the system
and thereby threaten its stability, even when there is no majority
among the proletariat and its leaders for such an aim; or else there

---

[12] See especially *GW* VIII 466 = *On beginning the treatment*, *SE* XII 132 sq.
One should note that Freud's position is quite distinct not only from that of the
ideal of a communist doctor, with whom it would be unfair and anti-historical
to compare him, but also from that of the 'humanitarian' type of doctor seeking
to benefit the proletariat within the limits of reformism. There were many
instances of such practitioners towards the end of the 19th century. For Freud,
however, the 'poor' (a) were excluded from psychoanalysis at least for the
time being because they could not afford the fees incurred by the extended
treatment which this form of therapy demands; (b) were much less exposed
to neurosis since this was intimately connected to civilization, to a 'superior
moral and intellectual development' and was thus the misfortune, but also the
privilege, of the upper classes (particularly interesting is the apology for the
different fates experienced by the young daughter of the landlord and the
child of the concierge in *GW* XI 365–7 = *Introd. Lect. Psych.*, *SE* XVI 352–4;
(c) a neurosis, in short, was beneficial to a poor man because it allowed him to
claim 'the pity which the world has refused to his material distress'. Here we
appear to have a glimpse of some astringent vision, of a condemnation of the
bourgeois society which subjects a healthy proletariat to a life of such exhaustion
and alienation that, by comparison, the state of illness is a blessing. But it is clear
if one reads the whole passage that this is not what Freud has in mind, or at least,
it is immediately overlaid by a distinctively reactionary notion: the poor man
'can now absolve himself from the obligation of combating his poverty by
working'; in other words, the poor man is essentially either a good-for-nothing
or content to become one, so that he has only himself to blame for the social
condition in which he finds himself. Freud magnanimously concedes that among
the poor 'one does occasionally come across deserving people who are helpless
from no fault of their own': it is only for this tiny band of honest workers that
the problem of free psychoanalytic treatment arises. Freud's social blindness is
also revealed in his constant reference to the 'poor', a category which he fails
to define in any economic and social terms. Does he mean workers? or peasants?
or a *lumpenproletariat?* In actual fact, he tends, from the psychological point of
view, to assimilate the proletariat to the *lumpenproletariat.*

is the fear that revolutionaries within the working-class movement will gain ascendancy over reformists. It holds for historical situations of revolutionary or pre-revolutionary crisis such as were experienced in Germany and Hungary after the First World War; and also for periods of brutal anti-proletarian reaction, when there is the danger that even the slightest infringement of a violently re-established 'order' may expose the fragility of a regime based on a maximum of force and a minimum of consent. *The Psycho-pathology of Everyday Life* first appeared in 1904, but new examples were constantly added to it up to the time of the tenth and final edition of 1924. However, neither in the first nor the last edition do we find a single example of a 'slip' or instance of forgetting whose origin Freud ascribes to the fear of revolution. This is true even though the 1924 edition appeared during a period in which Austria had only just escaped from a revolution itself, had been encircled by explosive revolutionary forces abroad (the Spartacists in Berlin, the short-lived attempt at a Soviet republic in Bavaria, the government of Béla Kun in Hungary, radical ferments in Italy), and now found itself directly confronted by Italian Fascism and Horthy's equally ruthless dictatorship in Hungary. Granted that we accept Freud's theory of 'slips', is it really credible that in not a single one of his bourgeois patients did a repressed thought of this unpleasant kind ever surface precisely in the form of a 'slip'? What is more, in addition to the fear that the bourgeoisie will suffer a *general* defeat, which is shared by all its members who have not gone over to the side of the proletariat (and thus also by those of its members – for example, many intellectuals – whose employment is not directly concerned with economic production or with the maintenance of the State's repressive apparatus), there may also exist a more personal and day-to-day fear or discomfiture in the lives of industrialists, businessmen, officials of the State repressive apparatus, over some particular potential or actual strike, over this or that act of 'insubordination' and so on. It is typical that even when they emerge victorious from disputes of this sort, such persons are often never really satisfied. They would prefer to see the proletariat more submissive, more content with its lot, or more drastically punished for its rebelliousness. Then there is the whole stratum of petty bourgeois (this already existed in Freud's day, though its members were fewer) who are entirely in an employee condition, and are thus in a purely economic sense already proletarianized, but psychologically experience a conflict between their hatred of the proletariat, assimilation to which they refuse, and their frustrations at the 'ingratitude' of their employers, with whom they feel allied but who ill repay them for their solidarity. Now many of the patients of Freud and other analysts who supply the examples found in the successive editions of *The Psychopathology* were certainly industrialists, men of commerce, higher or middle ranking functionaries in State or industry. Some were even petty bourgeois. However, one searches in vain for cases of psycho-pathological manifestations whose source is those innumerable individual conflicts with superiors or subordinates which we have distinguished from the concern for the overall destiny of one's class. This is clearly a case of a 'censorship' imposed, whether consciously or not, by Freud and his disciples on the whole vast field of psychological conflicts deriving from class antagonisms, or economic and social enmities within any one class. This is equally true of *The Interpretation of Dreams* and of all the works in which Freud interprets neurotic or para-neurotic symptoms. *Not only does the proletariat not feature in these, but its absence results in a seriously deficient account of the neuroses of the bourgeoisie.*

The second lacuna of *The Psychopathology* relates to those unpleasant thoughts (to which the bourgeois no less than the proletarian is subject, even if for him they sometimes take a different form) that stem from the consciousness of our own biological frailty. This is the fear, which is sometimes general and sometimes related to a particular and imminent danger, of illness, senility, or death – of ourselves, our friends or our relatives. It would need a separate study to develop this theme. Here we shall limit ourselves to noting that despite the importance in Freud's personal history, firstly of his more or less unfounded – but for all that, profoundly disturbing – fear of a premature death, and then of his fifteen year struggle, waged with heroic fortitude and lucidity, against an inexorable disease, Freudian psychopathology has never provided an adequately systematic account of this source of anxiety. Neither in the original concept of narcissism nor in the later 'Death Instinct' are we provided with a principle capable of explaining the unhappiness inflicted on man by his own 'physical ailments' and those of his kind. It is true that *The Future of an Illusion* contains a passage on man's oppression by Nature[13] which is among the finest in Freud's writings, and displays surprising, though certainly quite incidental, affinities to Leopardi. But Freud is interested in that oppression only as a justification of the origin of civilization and of the set of sacrifices that its development imposes on our hedonism.[14] When he treats of the unconscious and the neuroses, by contrast, Freud's awareness of man's biological fragility is strangely distorted and defective. It would appear that thoughts about our own death no more preoccupy our unconscious than they allegedly do the mind of primitive man. The death of strangers? We contemplate it quite calmly – so much so, in fact, that in times of war we cheerfully kill them, and in peacetime harbour many more murderous thoughts than we care to admit (Freud's bourgeois asperity is antithetical to every form of philanthropy or love for mankind in general – a sentiment he considers impossible, and, in the last analysis, undesirable: no more than a subject of hypocritical rhetoric). The death of those dearest to us? The fear, and the actual experience, of this are real enough, and they disturb us profoundly, yet our feelings are *always* ambivalent, a compound of fear and longing, of pain and pleasure.[15] If we ask how this is proved, Freud will answer: psychoanalysis.[16] In reality, the proof is obtained only by means of quite arbitrary manipulations. Perhaps most capricious and scientifically dishonest of all is Freud's 'proof' that all dreams, even anxiety dreams, are the expression of a repressed wish.[17] Here we indeed appear to be confronted with a psychiatrist

[13] *GW* XIV 336 sq. = *The Future of an Illusion, SE* XXI 15 sq.

[14] Ibid: 'But how ungrateful, how short-sighted after all to strive for the abolition of civilization! What would then remain, would be a state of nature, and that would be far harder to bear.' The argument, as is known, was more fully developed by Freud two years later (1929) in *Civilisation and its Discontents*, (*SE* XXI 57 sqq.).

[15] See *Zeitgemässes über Krieg und Tod* (1915), *GW* X 341 sqq. = *Thoughts for the times on War and Death, SE* XIV 290 sqq.

[16] Ibid. p. 350 = 297.

[17] See especially Chaps. III–V and VII of *The Interpretation of Dreams*, and the corresponding section (II) of the *Lectures* of 1915–16. Freud reaches the heights of 'dishonesty' in the eleventh Lecture (and already in an article of 1910, in *GW* VIII 214 sqq. = *The Antithetical Meaning of Primal Words, SE* XI 155 sqq.),

suffering from a captious psychologism, who was determined to present his own malady and that of his followers – whom he effectively held in the grip of a love–hate relationship (accountable not to their residual affinities with primitive man, but to their particular situation as members of a closed and authoritarian group) – as psychologically normal. In *Totem and Taboo* (which concentrates virtually all the elements of Freud's late writings) it is not so much the general model of an old-style bourgeois paternalistic authority which is projected back into pre-history, as the specific situation of the Society of Psychoanalysts, governed by a Father and Master who is the only analyst neither analyzed nor analyzable by others, and who maintains a relationship with his 'children' which is *doubly* unequal in that the latter are simultaneously both his pupils and his patients (or patients of his pupil-patients – whence the fearful rivalries and maniacal jealousies between them which Freud refused to analyse directly!).[18] Not, of course, that Freud was claiming 'all the women for himself' in any directly sexual sense. He was, indeed, the most abstinent of men in this respect. His methods of subjugation took a more subtly sublimated form;[19] while his acquaintance with the dire fate that lay in wait for the father at the hands of the sons in the primitive horde, led him to a preventive 'killing', i.e. eradication and banishment, of his potential 'murderers'. Here too his sentence was

---

where he appeals to what, from the linguistic standpoint, is a highly debatable work by K. Abel on the so-called *voces mediae* [i.e. primal words expressing opposites, for example Latin *altus* = 'high' or 'deep'. Trans.] and their frequency in the oldest languages (*Über den Gegensinn der Urworte*, Leipzig, 1884) for confirmation of the fact that any dream element can stand in for its opposite: given this, of course, there is nothing to prevent the interpretation of all anxiety dreams as dreams of wish-fulfilment! The partial exceptions, to which, as we know, Freud himself later admitted (see towards the end of Lecture XXIX of the second series of 1932), are far too few and marginal.

[18] Roazen, *Broth. Anim.* makes striking reading in this respect also. All the same, it is mistaken to attribute the rupture between Freud and Reich to 'the refusal of Freud to take Reich for personal analysis' as Roazen does (p. 152) on the basis of an assertion made by Reich's second wife. The quarrel between Freud and Reich was due to a radical divergence of ideas and political positions which it is too glib to relate to a mere psychological frustration on Reich's part.

[19] Again see Roazen, *Broth. Anim.*, passim, for Freud's relations with Lou Andreas-Salomé and Helene Deutsch, and for Tausk's role in these.

always pronounced in the name of science, even if it was based on a diagnosis of neurosis against which there was no appeal. In such a crazed environment, Freud's sentiments on the death of any of of his pupil-rivals were inevitably a mixture of grief and relief, and, if truth be told, the relief usually appears to have predominated.[20]

Thus it is that even in *The Psychopathology of Everyday Life,* Freud's explanations of 'slips' refer us to discomforting thoughts which have been repressed for diverse reasons, but never out of fear of illness or death or commiseration at the death of others. The particular case of *Boltraffio/Trafoi* is not an exception, because the discomfort of the memory relates not simply to the suicide of one of Freud's patients but to its sexual motivation – the distressing thought of death is admissible only in so far as the erotic compo-nent, as it were, guarantees its safe-conduct. If I am right, there is only one genuine exception which we shall examine in the next chapter (p. 142 sq.); that it was Jung who provided Freud with this example is perhaps no accident, but rather a certain reflection of Jung's tendency, even before his rupture with Freud, to minimize the sexual origin of neurotic symptoms. There is no need to emphasize that, so far as we are concerned, Jung's mystical fantasies greatly aggravate the evil they are supposed to remedy (and for that matter, the interpretation he gives of the 'slip' – which Freud accepts – is, as we shall see, itself mistaken or forced). All the same, it remains a fact that Jung's polemic against Freud's 'pansexuality' (we use the term for brevity's sake only) initially contained certain not wholly mistaken motives, even if its subsequent development was completely distorted.

On the other hand, even if we suppose that the unconscious as the 'archaic' locus of the human psyche does not have a subjective

---

[20] We have only to recall the notes in his correspondence on the deaths of Tausk and Adler. After Tausk's suicide (for which Freud must have known he had a certain responsibility), Freud wrote to Lou Andreas-Salomé: 'So he fought out his day of life with the father ghost. I confess I do not really miss him; I had long taken him to be useless, indeed a threat to the future . . . and would long since have dropped him had *you* not so boosted him in my esteem' (the complete text of the letter, originally published in a censored version, is given by Roazen, *Broth. Anim.,* pp. 139–40). Even harsher – if more understandable, given the genuine and complete nature of the rupture in this case, as distinct from that of Tausk – is the letter to Arnold Zweig on the subject of Adler's death (cit. by Jones, *Life,* III, p. 222–3).

fear of death, and experiences grief over the death of those we love only in an ambivalent form, we still have to ask ourselves what becomes of those 'present' thoughts that reflect the psyche of civilized man, when they become repressed. Does some process of transformation assimilate them all to the categories of a psychology of 'archaic' residues? Does repression involve no enrichment or modernization of that primitive basis? If such an enrichment does occur, it is not clear why there is no resurgence in the unconscious, even in the form of 'slips', of 'contemporary' thoughts and feelings such as those which relate to our own and others' biological frailty. If it does not occur, the Freudian explanation of innumerable other 'slips' remains incomprehensible – of those whose concern is career or financial matters as well as the *aliquis* example itself (primitive man, no doubt, was little obsessed with the menstrual delays of a woman with whom he had had sexual relations!). These difficulties derive, in my opinion, from that strange 'interpretation of prehistoric man in an autobiographical register' which is one of the weakest aspects of Freud's theory.

In conformity with Freud's views on death, we find quite a number of explanations of 'slips' in *The Psychopathology of Everyday Life* that refer us to secret desires for the death of some beloved person.[21] The Oedipal situation tends to assume the dimensions of a paradigm for any and every human relationship – at the price, on occasion, of curious contortions. A doctor prescribes, fortunately without serious consequences, an excessive dose of belladonna for his own mother; he later makes a similar mistake with regard to an elderly aunt (p. 136 sq. = 122 sq.). He had felt for some time that by sharing the same household as his mother he was 'inhibiting his erotic freedom': his unconscious desire, therefore, was to kill her. But while Freud would have been quite content with an analogous conclusion if the case had been that of a son who wanted to kill his father, or even of a daughter who wanted to kill her mother, or if the wish that emerged had been for fratricide or uxoricide, the case of a son wanting to kill his mother created some difficulty for him despite the presence of a desire for greater

---

[21] E.g., pp. 134 = 121 sq. no. 7; 209–11 = 197 sq. We shall deal with a further example directly in the text.

erotic freedom. Let us see with what sleight of hand he puts things to rights: 'We have, of course, learnt from psychoanalytic experience that such reasons are readily misused as an excuse for an internal (incestuous) attachment'. So: fathers are killed (or one wants them to die) because of rivalry; mothers because of an excess of affection, that is to say, in a desperate attempt to free oneself from temptations of incest; elderly aunts because they are 'mother-figures'. Once again we find ourselves confronted with a method of explanation that defies any imaginable refutation.

9

Freudian Slip and Forced Freudianization

The last example considered in the preceding chapter is a reminder of the constant need to respect the different levels, and the connexions and distinctions between them, on which any polemic against Freudianism should surely be conducted. If we were to assume that a denunciation of the class limitations of psychoanalysis sufficed as a critique of Freud, it might be enough to revise and expand *The Psychopathology of Everyday Life* to include, alongside the examples of 'slips' of a 'respectable-bourgeois' character, an equal or greater number related to the class division of society and the psychological malaise or genuine neuroses to which it gives rise. The result would be an enlargement of the conception of repression, which would then include every form of suppression, including that caused by the dominance of one class over another, or of one particular elite over the other members of a community.[1] If we were Marxists of Leopardian sympathies, as is the present author, we might go on to search for further 'slips' indicative of other repressed thoughts whose preoccupation was with man's biological frailty – with disease and old age (whose pain, *pace* Freud's Bosnian peasants, is not caused solely by a weakening and loss of sexual potency, but by a general decline of our physical, mental and affective powers), or with death itself (which certainly releases us from life's troubles, but at the same time severs our emotional, social and cultural bonds, and is thus the object of an

[1] Francesco Orlando has suggested such an enlargement in the two books already cit., p. 57 note 5, where I remarked on the importance I attribute to this extension of 'repression' to include all 'suppressed' unconscious and conscious material.

'instinctive fear', which creates its own unhappiness that the various *consolationes philosophiae* cannot easily exorcize).

All these areas can, and should be, investigated. But if we were to use the Freudian technique, with its pseudo-proofs and its symbols *bons à tout faire*, in order to arrive at 'Marxist' or 'Leopard-ian' explanations of 'slips' and neuroses, this would neither benefit Marxism nor assist its potential deepening and development in the direction of a hedonist-pessimist materialism of the kind anticipated by Leopardi (to which we have alluded elsewhere).[2]

We must ask ourselves, then: in what cases should we not be content with 'philological' explanations of the type already illustrated in chapters 3–6, and which will be further exemplified later? When should we look to the Freudian explanatory model for additional material?

To improve our formulation of the problem, it should be emphasized that the contrast between the two types of explanation is not to be made simply in terms of their more 'generalizing' or more 'individualizing' nature. (We remarked very briefly on this in Chapter 7.) The truly Freudian 'slip' or instance of forgetting presupposes the existence of psychic material which my conscious ego has repressed because it proved *displeasing* – or, given it was desirable from a hedonistic point of view, because my moral inhibitions prevented my confession of it even to myself, let alone to others. A 'slip' such as that committed by Giorgio Pasquali when he mistakenly corrected 'translation' to 'tradition' (see above, p. 102) is, in its own way, 'individual' – for Pasquali was exceptional in his greater familiarity with the word that for the vast majority of people is the lesser known of the two, especially in its sense of 'manuscript tradition'. But for Freud, a satisfactory explanation of it would have necessitated a further analysis which demonstrated that in Pasquali's psyche the manuscript tradition was linked to some unpleasant memory that had been repressed at an earlier date into his unconscious and now had surfaced again

---

[2] I have attempted a development of this sort (while well aware that it is no more than an attempt) in my earlier works, *Classicismo e illuminismo nell'Ottocento italiano* (Pisa, 1969[2]: see especially the essay 'Alcune osservazioni sul pensiero del Leopardi', p. 133 sqq.), and *Sul materialismo* (Pisa, 1970) – English edition *On Materialism*, NLB, London 1976.

in a disturbance of his discourse. Could some demonstration of this kind be made, or could it have been when Pasquali was still alive, without a descent into pure and simple absurdity? Pasquali was indeed, as everyone knows, a neurotic. Yet his mistake was not a symptom, even a minor one, of his neurosis. Here is another, even more interesting case: in a brief article which we found reason to cite at the beginning of this work (p. 28 note 13), Lanfranco Caretti examined a 'slip' contained in an article from *Gazetta dello Sport* of 23 August 1949. The footballer, De Gregori, whose name was reported correctly in the first instance, became De Gasperi, the Christian Democratic leader, a few lines below![3] Caretti rightly remarks that there are 'two competing reasons' for the error: 'one is the objective reason that the two names have an identical beginning (*De G* . . .);[4] the other is the psychological, and therefore subjective reason, that certain names which are dinned into us by the radio, constantly blazoned by newspapers and posters (especially so in the electoral climate of 1948!), interminably repeated in the weekly press, and crop up all the time in our daily conversations with friends, acquire an extraordinary persistence for us. In other words, *De Gasperi* was a *lectio facilior* then, even if it would probably no longer be today. Certainly, relative to the speed with which the name of the worthy footballer fell into oblivion, that of De Gasperi continues and will always continue to be remembered by many, even if only for his nefarious (or others might say 'providential') role in restoring capitalism and securing the 'continuity of the State' in Italy. All the same, his name could only be introduced as a 'slip' today by a student of post-fascist history or by someone who had personal reasons to remain intimately engrossed with that epoch – and not by an ordinary printer or journalist, even if he were a Christian Democrat.

[3] Alcide De Gasperi (1881–1954), leader of the Christian Democrats (the Italian clerical and conservative party), was Prime Minister from 1945 to 1953. He was responsible for the restoration of capitalism and the pre-fascist State, and integrated Italy into NATO.

[4] The similarity is reinforced by the fact that the two names end in -*ri*, and are of the same length. The difference lies in where the accent falls, which inclines one to think that the error is more likely to be visual, due to a 'synthetic reading' (see above, p. 21), rather than the result of the mnemonics of the spoken words.

But Caretti proceeds to find an explanation even more closely related to the person who committed the error: 'The unconscious, however, is moved by latent forces of attraction and repulsion; and in this case we cannot be sure whether the hidden motive for the irresistible resurgence of the name was one of sympathy or antipathy to the statesman. I believe . . . that if the (probably middle-class) reporter was responsible for the mistake it should in all likelihood be interpreted as a testimony, even if unpremeditated, of his loyalty to the government; if, on the other hand, the printer was the culprit, then it was probably incited by opposite sentiments, and witnesses to a quite different attitude.' That Caretti was influenced by his reading of Freud is clear enough; but one should note that his is not an orthodox Freudian explanation (and precisely to that extent is, I think, convincing), because it leaves open the possibility that the 'slip' was either 'sympathetic' or 'antipathetic', where Freud would have made a definite and unjustifiable option for the latter, the only hypothesis which presumes a repression. Naturally, we must not delude ourselves that the Freudian is ignorant of devices whereby a 'sympathetic' explanation can be rendered consistent with Freudian orthodoxy. If, as we saw at the end of the last chapter, even the desire to kill one's mother can be interpreted as a manifestation of love, it would be comparatively easy to reduce the 'sympathy' felt for De Gasperi by a loyal Christian Democrat to the ambivalence of the latter towards the Father who is at once tyrannical rival and at the same time protector. But the only result of this sophistry would be to obliterate the distinction, upon which Caretti is right to insist, between those who, in 1949 and the years that followed, were – for highly concrete political reasons – committed to De Gasperi, and those who opposed him.

The truth is that the sympathy we feel for a person, even when avowed and unsuppressed, can be the occasion for a 'slip', no less than antipathy. So too can dispassion, provided its object is someone widely known in one's particular circle, whose name is often mentioned, and thus 'sticks in the mind'. In the case of the *De Gasperi* 'slip', if we think back to the explosive climate of 1948–9, a neutral attitude is improbable. But the printer who in a relatively lukewarm political atmosphere set 'autonomisti' instead of 'atomisti' (see above, p. 101) could have been a socialist adherent of Pietro Nenni, or a supporter of the left of the Italian Socialist Party (PSI) or of the Italian Communist Party (PCI) which were hostile to Nenni, or else a relatively a-political worker who had nevertheless overheard the repeated debates between the 'autonomists' among his fellow-printers and others, and their opponents. The misprint 'Gattopardiani' for 'Gottorpiani' was the responsibility either of an 'indifferent' printer who had very often heard references to *The Leopard* (even if he had never read it), or more probably, of an admirer of the book. It seems much less likely to me that on this occasion the 'slip' was due to hostility, because I find it difficult to imagine that any potential animosity towards *The Leopard* (either the novel or the film) would, in the case of a printer, so far exceed boredom and detachment and become so emotional and tormented as to need burial in the unconscious.

If we are to have good grounds for accepting the 'Freudian' origin of a 'slip', the latter must satisfy at least two conditions: 1) that psychological processes of a relatively 'superficial' character, which themselves regularly give rise to 'slips' and instances of forgetting, are not sufficient to explain it; 2) that the 'Freudian' explanation does not rely on associations or symbolic connexions that are so forced as to make it wholly arbitrary and unverifiable. Among the mass of examples cited by Freud and by the Freudians, there are some which actually fulfil these two conditions. Let us take, for example, the case already cited (at the start of Chapter 8) of the German delegate who said *rückgratlos* ('spineless') instead of *rückhaltlos* ('unconditional'). The two adjectives are phonically similar, but instead of a process of banalization or an exchange of words uttered with a virtually equal frequency, we have the reverse mechanism: a very much rarer word has been substituted for the extremely common *rückhaltlos*. Furthermore, it is neither possible to attribute the *lectio difficilior* to the influence of its context, nor is it reasonable to suppose that, contrary to the case for the majority of Germans, the 'difficult' adjective was in fact more familiar to the delegate (as 'tradition' was for Pasquali relative to 'translation'). The first condition is therefore satisfied. So too is the second – the 'troubled conscience' which induced the hypocritical politician to give voice to the unfortunate adjective is all too obvious. We need have recourse neither to the existence of unproved connexions, not to translations into foreign languages, nor to symbolisms that adapt to all eventualities, in order to expose it. Here, then, the 'slip' is indeed an involuntary expression of the 'suppressed' even if not necessarily 'repressed' material.

The same applies in the case of another 'slip' cited above, that of *Juden* in place of *Jungen*. Here even the particular circumstances in which the 'slip' happens to occur (the visit to an anti-semitic family from whom the interested party is especially keen to conceal his Jewish origin) definitely orients us in the direction of the explanation given by Tausk and approved by Freud. Or again, take the case of the girl who lacked the courage to express to her mother the aversion she felt for the young man she was supposed to marry, and said of him that he was 'sehr liebenswidrig' when she meant to say 'sehr liebenswürdig' (p. 101=92). This is a 'slip' which in all probability is effectively 'Freudian'. Here too – and even more so than in the case of 'rückgratlos' – the word substituted is not only a *lectio difficilior*, but a neologism all too appropriate to the expression of the girl's true sentiments; but it is grammatically quite bizarre. Instead of 'worthy of love' ('lovable'), what is said is a literally untranslatable compound meaning something like 'repellent to love', in which the second part (-*widrig*), indicative of hostility or disgust, contradicts and annuls the first.

In these cases, and in certain others to be found in Freud's book,[5] it is indeed legitimate to consider the phonic similarity between the two words as a merely subsidiary cause, precisely because this similarity is not *in itself* enough to explain the 'slip'. But we must repeat what we have already said on p. 104 sq.: all the really

---

[5] Rather than a complete inventory, I shall cite what seem to me the most persuasive, or at least highly probable examples: pp. 78 sq.=69 sq.; nos. 19, 22 and 24; 81=71 sq., no. 28; 88=78, no. 36. In general, the examples which call for a lengthy exposition (and thus, in the great majority of cases, contain many passages which lack proof or verisimilitude) are the least convincing; those for which Freud has to provide only a brief exposition are the more persuasive. Is the fact that the 'simple' cases often invite our acceptance a good reason for us to feel the same in regard to the 'complex' cases? No, since the complication involves a forced and arbitrary interpretation. For that matter, we shall see that even many of the 'simple' cases can be explained quite differently.

persuasive examples belong to that type which we have called
a *gaffe*. 'Slips' of this kind certainly presuppose that something has
been suppressed, but the speaker is fully conscious of, and currently
preoccupied with, whatever it is that he wants to conceal from those
to whom he is speaking. It is not something which has genuinely
been 'repressed' (forgotten) and re-emerges from the depths of
his unconscious.

Even more persuasive would appear those 'slips' which, as
Freud himself pointed out, show marked resemblances to jokes.
A distinction is claimed for these on the basis of their unconscious
character.[6] Yet in several cases one can be highly dubious as to
whether they possess this. 'A father who was without any patriotic
feelings, and who wished to educate his children so that they too
should be free from what he regarded as a superfluous sentiment,
was criticizing his sons for taking part in a nationalist demonstration. When they protested that their uncle had also participated in
it, he replied: "He is the one person you should not imitate: he is
an idiot (*Idiot*)". On seeing his childrens' look of astonishment, he
then added apologetically: "I meant to say patriot (*Patriot*), of
course". (p. 100 = 90). Here, to my mind, one is given the distinct
impression that the 'slip' is 'feigned'.[7] In all likelihood, a father who
had such definite ideas about patriotism at a time when a zealous
love of one's country was the norm, was a socialist (a true socialist,
not a social patriot!) or, at least, a non-conformist radical. From such
a man, who evidently had in no way repressed his anti-chauvinism,
but professed it with full conviction, one would be inclined to
expect an intentional sarcasm rather than an involuntary 'slip'.
Moreover, although Freud's book on jokes is in many respects a

---

[6] See pp. 87 = 77 sq.; 92 = 81 sq. One should keep in mind that although the
first edition of *The Psychopathology* pre-dates the work on jokes (*Der Witz und
seine Beziehung zum Unbewussten*, 1905 = *Jokes and their Relation to the Unconscious*)
by four years, many of the additions to the successive editions presuppose the
existence of the later work.

[7] One finds a malicious example of a 'feigned slip' in Cicero, *Pro Caelio*, 32:
'I would respond even more vehemently, were it not for my enmity towards
the woman's husband – brother, I *mean*; I keep making mistakes!'. In the same
moment in which he declares himself to feel obliged to moderate his language
lest his personal hostility towards Clodius be thought to be the cause of his
invective, Cicero alludes with his 'feigned slip' to the rumoured incestuous
relationship between Clodius and his sister.

masterpiece that has played a part in the development of important trends in the theory of literature (I am thinking of Orlando's work again), the relationship that it asserts between jokes and the unconscious remains rather tenuous. Their resemblance appears greater than it is in reality, precisely because (under Brentano's influence) Freud ascribes to the category of the unconscious those aspects of intentionality possessed by conscious manifestations of our psyche, and relieves it as much as possible of those automatic and instinctual aspects which would differentiate it rather more from conscious psychic processes. Freud never consented, as Groddeck would have liked him to do, to a straightforward reduction of the Ego to the Id, but he did tend to make the Id the 'truer' aspect of human reality. We shall say something more of that in our last chapter.

Sometimes we are directly confronted not with a 'slip' nor even with a joke, but with a wholly conscious lie or falsification. Can we really believe that in the laws of 1867 concerned with the financial obligations of Austria and Hungary, the omission of a word in the Hungarian text is to be ascribed to 'the *unconscious* desire of the Hungarian parliamentary draftsmen to grant Austria the least possible advantages'? (p. 141 sq. = 128); such was B. Dattner's hypothesis, approved by Freud. These draftsmen will have been perfectly 'conscious', as is always the case in 'amicable' agreements of this type in which each party is trying to cheat the other. In the Uccialli treaty of 1889 between Italy and Ethiopia, for example, the Italian text spoke explicitly of Italy's protectorate over Abyssinia, while there was no mention of this in the Amharic text. This was certainly not a case of a 'slip' on the part of the Negus Menelik, nor of one of his scribes, but a ruse that was perfectly justified from his point of view.

Incidents of this kind, which by no means rule out the existence of Freudian 'slips', but impose strict limits to their frequency and their significance, would certainly have appeared to Freud – and could not appear otherwise to an orthodox Freudian – to be too exiguous to be of much use to psychoanalytic doctrine as a whole. Did Freud admit the existence of non-Freudian slips? His opinions always wavered. His statement at the end of the first chapter of

The Psychopathology remains very circumspect: 'We shall, I think, have stated the facts of the case with sufficient caution if we affirm: *By the side of simple cases where proper names are forgotten there is a type of forgetting which is motivated by repression.*' But immediately in the next chapter, commenting on the case of *aliquis* with which we have already dwelt at some length, Freud asserts that 'all' instances of forgetting have their origin in repression. Then in Chap. V (p. 69=61) he says: 'Among the "slips of the tongue" that I have collected myself, I can find hardly one in which I should be obliged to trace the disturbance of speech simply and solely to what Wundt calls the "contact effect of sounds". I almost invariably discover a disturbing influence in addition which comes from something *outside* the intended utterance; and the disturbing element is either a single thought that has remained unconscious, which manifests itself in the "slip of the tongue" and which can often be brought to consciousness only by means of searching analysis, or is a more general psychical motive force which is directed against the entire utterance.' The false choice with which we are presented here (we find it formulated by Freud and the Freudians on other occasions) helps to force the interpretation of 'slips' in a psychoanalytic direction. It consists in a restriction of the opposition *simply* to that between 'slips' that derive from repression and 'slips' due to the displacement of contiguous sounds (of the type *toppro* for *troppo, battecca* for *bacchetta*). The odd thing is that Freud has only that moment quoted a passage from Wundt in which there is an explicit mention of the existence, in addition to the merely phonic 'slip', of the 'slip' due to substitution of 'quite different' words which 'stand in an associative relation' with the words that the subject meant to utter; and his comment on this is (p. 69=61): 'I consider these observations of Wundt's fully justified and very instructive.' At that point he adds only a minor specification, but later, in the passage we quoted just now, he tacitly identifies Wundt's 'associative relation', which was the more or less traditional 'association of ideas', with his *own* associative relation between the disturbed elements in the discourse and the disturbing element which stems from the repressed thought. Thus, all non-Freudian 'slips', and not just merely phonic ones (but those due to banalization, to the exchange of synonyms, to the influence of context and so on), are implicitly discounted.

Again, on p. 90 sq. = 81, Freud reasserts his agreement with Wundt – of whom, as we have noted, he gives a Freudian interpretation – but then concedes: 'there is nothing, on the other hand, to prevent me at the same time from allowing that, in situations where speaking is hurried and attention is to some extent diverted, the conditions governing 'slips of the tongue' may easily be confined within the limits defined by Meringer and Mayer. For some of the examples collected by these authors a more complicated explanation nevertheless seems more plausible.' A little later, however, (p. 93 = 83) he says: 'But if I still secretly cling to my expectation that even apparently simple "slips of the tongue" could be traced to interference by a half-suppressed idea that lies *outside* the intended context, I am tempted to do so by an observation of Meringer's which is highly deserving of attention.' Then once again, a little further on, from a remark added in 1907 (p. 111 = 100) the hope appears to have become a conviction: 'The view of "slips of the tongue" which is advocated here can meet the test in the most trivial examples. I have repeatedly been able to show that the most insignificant and obvious errors in speaking have their meaning and can be explained in the same way as the more striking instances.'

Freud returns to the problem, though with no less ambivalence, in the Lectures of 1915 (*GW* XI 38 = *Introd. Lect. Psych., SE* XV 44 sq.), where he declares himself to be 'very much inclined' to believe that 'slips' have their origin in repressed thoughts because 'every time one investigates an instance of a "slip of the tongue" an explanation of this kind is forthcoming' (we have seen, and will see, at the price of what sophistry). He goes on: 'But it is also true that there is no way of proving that a "slip of the tongue" cannot occur without this mechanism. It may be so; but theoretically it is a matter of indifference to us since the conclusions we want to draw for our introduction to psychoanalysis remain, even though – and this is certainly not the case – our view holds good of only a minority of cases of "slips of the tongue".' Once again, any debate between Freud and his potential or actual opponents is vitiated by a characterization of the latter as incapable of doing more than express a general scepticism (or argument based on merely 'phonetic' explanations) and hence unable to oppose sufficiently well-reasoned and documented alternatives to Freud's theory.

That Freud, however, was not so 'indifferent' to the possibility that a greater or lesser number of 'slips' were not subject to his type of explanation may be seen in a passage from the following Lecture (*GW* XI 63 sq. = *Introd. Lect. Psych.*, *SE* XV 68 sq.). Here he actually posits a 'Freudian' explanation even of those 'slips' which are too slight and irrelevant for the explanation to appear to be demonstrable even to him. 'It is to be assumed that a purpose of disturbing the intention of the speech is present in these cases but that it can only announce its presence and not what it itself has in view. The disturbance it produces then proceeds in accordance with certain phonetic influences or associative attractions. (. . .) But neither this disturbance of the attention nor the inclinations to associate which have become operative touch on the essence of the process. This remains, in spite of everything, the indication of the existence of an intention which is disturbing to the intention of the speech, though the *nature* of this disturbing intention cannot be guessed from its consequences, as is possible in all the better defined cases of "slips of the tongue".' One might note that in the addition of 1907 to *The Psychopathology* quoted above, the explanation of the 'most trivial examples' was regarded as no less proved than that of the 'more striking' instances; whereas here it is admitted that the trivial cases are not as capable of interpretation as Freud would like. All the same, he by no means renounces the claim to *general* validity of his theory of the 'slip', which alone accounts for its 'essence', even if this – at any rate temporarily – remains to be specified.[8]

[8] See also, in a paragraph of *The Psychopathology* added in 1907 (p. 247 = 221 sq.): 'Every time we make a "slip" in talking or writing we may infer that there has been a disturbance due to mental processes lying outside our intention; but it must be admitted that "slips" of the tongue and of the pen often obey the laws of resemblance, of indolence or of the tendency to haste without the disturbing element succeeding in imposing any part of its own character on the resulting mistake in speech or writing. It is the compliance [*das Entgegenkommen*] of the linguistic material which alone makes the determining of the mistakes possible.' The 'slip' is helped on its way, then, thanks to the famous *Begünstigungen* (see above, Chap. VII), while on the other hand, the *Begünstigungen* obscure its 'true' cause. But what if they were, quite simply, themselves the 'true' cause?

What is chronologically perhaps the last evidence of Freud's views on the subject (it dates from September 1938, when he was already exiled in London, and not long before his death) is given by Smiley Blanton, *My Analysis with Freud* (cit. above, p. 16 note 6). There Freud admits that parapraxes, such as breaking a teacup, or even possibly typing errors, can occur purely by chance (i.e. in the absence of any unconscious intervention), 'but not the "slip"'. The distinction is hard to sustain. Is there really a difference between a typing error and a garbled pronunciation or confusion in writing, such as *partrerre* or *Schwest* on which we comment below (pp. 135–42)? How can one admit to the 'chance' nature (i.e. the 'mechanical' causation) of the former while asserting the unconscious determination of the latter?

Whoever embarks on a study of the 'slip' with such a strong and unfounded *a priori* conviction of its 'essence', or is so anxious to verify it at all costs that he takes as axiomatic what is only a working hypothesis, will force any interpretation to attain his ends. We have already seen this occur in the case of *aliquis* and *Signorelli,* and we can find confirmation of it in many other instances. The pages of *The Psychopathology* progressively reveal to us a relationship of antagonism, yet at the same time of collaboration and complementarity between Freud and his 'guinea-pigs'. We will not pause here to dwell again (see above, Chaps. 5 and 8) on the techniques of suggestion that Freud used on the 'bad conscience' of the respectable bourgeois about his repressed sexual desires, and the consequent ease with which the latter was induced to admit to the most far-fetched interpretations of his own 'slips'. We shall simply add that, alongside the 'old-fashioned' and 'crisis-stricken' bourgeois still reluctant to lose respectability either in his own or in Freud's eyes, another and more up-to-date type appears in *The Psychopathology* (especially in its later editions). This is the type who is quite prepared, in exchange for the release from anxiety promised him by Freud, to submit to psychoanalysis, and to start with the decipherment of his own 'slips'. (No such release is any longer afforded either by religion or by a combative secularism once prevalent in an epoch when the principal enemy was still to the right of the bourgeoisie and the latter felt itself, however mistakenly, to be the bearer of 'universal values'.) The neo-bourgeois of this sort, in contrast to his predecessor, has understood that just as Christ did not come into the world in order to abolish the ancient Laws but to accomplish them, so psychoanalysis does not demystify bourgeois values in order to destroy them, but to reinstate and consolidate them. Thus as psychoanalysis gradually ceased to be a moral scandal and became a vogue (prior to its submergence by a new and more serious wave of vicious intolerance with the Nazi reaction), so too explanation of 'slips' became a 'polite pastime'. The neo-bourgeois who had learnt to play this game would himself collaborate in the explanations, and – in part against his will, in part with a touch of conscious snobbery – furnish Freud with the 'free' associations needed for the smooth course of every analysis.

Freud described the phenomenon of these 'over-zealous' patients with relation to the interpretation of dreams: 'It looks as though the patient has been amiable enough to bring us in dream-form exactly what we had been "suggesting" to him immediately before.'[9] But he hastened to dismiss the problem with the remark that the expert analyst will not attribute these dreams to the patient's 'amiability', but to the influence of the psychoanalytic treatment. Such dreams were secondary effects, always outnumbered by dreams which 'forge ahead of the analysis'. The dismissal is too convenient. In reality, these dreams show that the psychoanalyst himself moulds the patient's neurosis to a significant degree, adapting it to his theory, and then seeing in the dreams produced – we could add in the 'slips' too – further confirmations of the theory. This is even more true of the numerous cases of self-analysis or analysis by one analyst of another, which are recorded in *The Psychopathology*. 'Two men, an older and a younger one' (p. 37 sq. = 31 sq.) discuss towns visited in the course of a trip to Sicily. Neither the elder nor the younger succeed in recalling the name of Castel-vetrano; the younger thinks of Calatafimi, the elder of Caltanis-setta. When the elder one says that Castrogiovanni was called Enna in antiquity, the younger one finally remembers Castel-vetrano. It is the older man who explains why he had forgotten the name: 'Obviously (. . . .) because the second half, "vetrano",

9 *GW* VI!I 356 sq. = *The Handling of Dream-Interpretation, SE* XII 96 sq.

sounds like "veteran". I know I don't much like to think about *growing old . . .*'. Why then did he remember instead Caltanissetta and Castrogiovanni? Because Caltanissetta sounded to him 'like a pet name for a young woman' and Castrogiovanni 'sounds like *giovane* (young)'. The story would scarcely be a good one even if we did not know the true identity of the pair involved: there is the usual recourse to the 'polyglot unconscious' (see above, p. 78 sq.), and the difficulty, by no means slight, that the young man too had forgotten the name of Castelvetrano! But the explanation becomes even more suspect when we learn[10] that the older man was Freud himself, and the younger was the faithful Ferenczi. Freud's self-analysis lacks all spontaneity because he had already been committed for a long time to a definite theory of the 'slip' (in that year, 1911, the theory was even more consolidated than at the time of the self-analysis of the forgetting of *Signorelli,* so that there was even less room for spontaneity). In reality, we have here one of those frequent cases of phonically similar names (Calatafimi, Caltanissetta, Castrogiovanni, Castelvetrano are all pentasyllabic, and all begin with *Ca-*), which share a semantic connexion (all four are Sicilian towns), and were linked in the minds of both Freud and Ferenczi since they visited these cities during a recent trip. This is a case, then, wholly analogous to that of *Signorelli–Botticelli,* which needs no supplementary 'Freudian' explanation. In fact, it is all the more similar in that Castelvetrano is certainly smaller and less well-known than the other two towns, if not also than Calatafimi (the two probably did not think of the expedition of Garibaldi's Thousand) – which means that it too is a *lectio difficilior.* All we need venture further is that Castrogiovanni probably helped Ferenczi to remember Castelvetrano, not because of the contrast *giovane-vecchio* (young-old), but because of the greater resemblance of the first element of the two words (which begin *Cast-*, rather than merely *Ca-*), and of their meaning (*castrum-castellum* – 'fortress', 'castle').

[10] See p. 19 note 2 in the *SE*. This episode, added to the 1912 edition of *The Psychopathology,* had already been recounted by Freud in an article of 1911 (in 'Zentralblatt für Psychoan.' I, p. 407), entitled *Ein Beitrag zum Vergessen von Eigennamen.* (The article is included in the fourth and all subsequent editions of *GW* IV 37 = *SE* VI 30).

Here are some more examples of 'slips' which we shall attempt to group into categories. For a start there are those – even if, as we have already said, they do not constitute the sole alternative to Freudian 'slips' – which are due to garbled pronunciation or confused writing. A strict observer of the Freudian faith would have to believe that every time one of us makes a mistake in the recitation of, e.g., 'Round the rugged rocks the ragged rascals ran' (or any other well-known tongue-twister), this is due to a trick played on him by his unconscious. For the error of pronunciation should be the index of the re-emergence of repressed psychic material. He would also have to believe that every linguistic innovation that involves an exchange between contiguous sounds such as *r/l*, every assimilation or dissimilation or metathesis, every anticipated or (more rarely) deferred insertion of sounds which recur in preceding or subsequent syllables of the same word – for example, the archaic Italian *strupo* from *stuprum*, *truono* from *tonitrus* via *tronus*; vulgar Latin *frustrum* for *frustum*; Italian *rosignolo* from *lusciniolus*, and so on – had their origin in an individual or collective 'slip' caused by repression rather than simply in their difficulties of pronunciation.

Is this a caricature? It would seem not, when an error of this very type, *Protragoras* for *Protagoras* (favoured by the fact that it concerns a little known foreign name), is explained by K. Abraham, with the approval of Freud (p. 92 note = 82 note), by the patient's fear of saying *Popotagoras*, a word that would have a 'disconcerting' allusion (*Popo* is the common German nursery term for 'bottom'). The patient is supposed to have displayed, so to speak, an excess of zeal: through fear of omitting the *r* in the first syllable, she inserts it in the second also. One's doubts multiply when one learns that the same patient was in the habit of saying *partrerre* instead of *parterre* (again a mistake that involves repetition of the *r* in contiguous syllables of a foreign word!) in order to avoid, according to Abraham and Freud, the word *pater* with its connotation of incest. If this were the correct explanation, we would expect to learn – and if it had happened, Abraham and Freud would certainly have told us – that the patient avoided saying the German word *Vater* in the first place, or garbled it in some way. In fact it would seem that the only taboo word for her was the Latin translation of

Vater – and this itself only when once it had first been rendered even more unfamiliar by its appearance, not in isolation and in its true form, but under cover of a distortion of *part* of a *French* word! Here we have yet another undue display of agility in translation on the part of the unconscious, analogous to that shown in the *Signorelli* and *Castelvetrano* cases. We need not doubt the patient's phobia about 'dirty' words. That she was indeed affected in this way is made perfectly clear from a few other examples of 'slips' cited by Abraham and Freud; moreover, she belonged to respectable circles that were anyway subject to fears of this kind. But the suggestive character of the psychoanalyst's questions, and the patient's actual speech difficulties, induced her to accept that two merely phonic 'slips' were also to be attributed to her phobia. We have only to glance at Hugo Schuchardt's classic work (*Der Vokalismus des Vulgärlateins*, Leipzig, 1866, p. 20 sq.) in order to find extremely numerous examples from the codices and inscriptions of late antiquity similar to *Protragoras*: e.g., *Trigridi, Euphratre, Grabriel,* and so on. In the *Aeneid* V 116, a 9th century copyist wrote *pristri* for *pistri* (see the critical apparatus in the editions of Sabbadini and Mario Geymonat). Just now, reading the proofs for an issue of 'Rivista critica di storia della filosofia', I found (and corrected, so it does not appear in the published text) *gregründet* for *gegründet*. Given the 'mass' character of similar errors, an individualizing explanation, as we have seen, loses credibility, above all when it is as contorted as that proposed by Abraham.

This is all the more the case when it is a question not, as we have seen, just of a particular type of error made by *different* individuals, but of one made directly by the *same* person, whom Freud describes (ibid.) as 'very likely to duplicate the first syllable of proper names by stammering'. Is it legitimate to select, from among all these instances of stammering, only those which best accommodate a phobic-sexual explanation, and to obscure or omit the others? It really does not seem so, for even if we admit that every patient constitutes a special case, our judgement of it must comprehend its entire symptomology, and not be based merely on an isolated symptom. This necessity is nearly always neglected by Freud. Apart from some very rare exceptions, *The Psychopathology* is a study of single 'parapraxes', not of individual personalities taken as a whole. Such a procedure is bound to give rise to falsification. Here I want to cite another example from my experience as a proof-reader. In the proofs of a work on ancient history I found the misprint 'ani' for 'anni'. A splendid example for a Freudian! – who will hasten to ascribe to the printer repressed homosexual tendencies or something of that sort. But note that two pages further on I found 'leterari' for 'letterari'. This alters the situation: what is indicated is a tendency on the part of the printer to 'conflate' double consonants – which is either the result of his dialect pronunciation (in this case, for example, he could have been Venetian) or represents an instance of the kind of overhastiness which leads to so-called haplography. So the notorious 'ani' loses any particular significance here.

The case I shall now quote seems to me to constitute a particularly instructive warning against the individualizing explanation of such 'slips'. In Italy, in the early 19th century, when Barthold Georg Niebuhr was beginning to acquire some fame for his audacious talent as a historian of ancient Rome, for his sojourn at Rome as Prussian Ambassador, and for his friendships and enmities with various local scholars, Italian intellectuals suddenly fell prey to a collective error, and wrote his name as *Niebhur*. The error displayed a remarkable capacity for survival, and examples of it can still be found today.[11] Louis de Sinner, the friend of Leopardi, who saw that even Prospero Viani had committed the 'slip' in the first edition of Leopardi's letters, jokingly advised Giampietro Vieusseux to correct this 'shocking' spelling or otherwise people would be saying 'que jamais Niebuhr n'a été chez une putain, *nie bei Hur*

[11] Piero Treves has also remarked on the phenomenon, *L'idea di Roma* (Milan–Naples, 1962), p. 125 note 26. The following are the titles of some of the very many works in which I have happened to notice the error: A. Mai in 'Giornale Arcadico' XI (1821), p. 362; A. Ranieri in the Le Monnier edition of the *Opere* of Leopardi, I, p. 28 (*Niebhurius*); Atto Vannucci in 'La Rivista', Florence, 27 May 1845 (no. 48), p. 205; Alberto Mario, *La camicia rossa*, Chap. V (I have not had access to the original edition of 1870; the Milan edition of 1925, p. 165 has the correct spelling; the subsequent Milan edition of 1954, p. 124, and the Bologna edition of 1968, p. 245 and note, have instead *Niebhur*; it could be, therefore, that the error was introduced later, but the case is still interesting); G. B. Carlo Giuliari, *La Capitolare biblioteca di Verona*, I, Verona 1888, p. 188 sq. But one also finds the same error, though not so frequently, in works on Leopardi in which Niebuhr is occasionally mentioned.

(*-e* ou *-en*)!'[12] ['Niebuhr has never been with a whor(e) or whor(es)'].
What for Sinner was a joke, a psychoanalyst might have taken in all
seriousness as a perfect example of 'Freudian negation'. The
garbled version of Niebuhr's name would have indicated that the
writer had said to himself without his realizing it: 'Never with a
whore!' and would thus have revealed his repressed desire to
consort with one at the earliest opportunity. But, unfortunately
for this ingenious interpretation, those who for a century and a
half have continued to commit this spelling mistake, have not
been Germans but rather Italians, the vast majority of whom,
beginning with Viani, were wholly ignorant of the German language, including the meaning of *Hure*. Consequently – unless the
current vogue for the 'innate' should persuade one to claim that
a person's Id can know German even if his Ego has never learnt
it – we shall have to resign ourselves to accepting one of those
'banal' explanations of Meringer and Mayer which Freud found so
displeasing. Precisely because the *h*, except in special cases, is
foreign to Italian spelling, and never occurs as a phoneme in spoken
Italian, an Italian writer is likely to be apprehensive, whenever he
starts to write the name *Niebuhr*, that he will miss out the *h*, and
will thus be led to anticipate it. Even this anticipation can, if you
like, be seen as a manifestation of anxiety; but it is an anxiety that
is entirely concerned with the fear of committing a spelling mistake,
and not connected to a 'deep' psychic force. Moreover, it is cured,
for the most part, by an improvement in one's knowledge of
German, even if this, unfortunately, is not accompanied by any
amelioration of one's neuroses. In the same way, Francesco de
Sanctis, despite his acquaintance – much greater than that of his
Italian contemporaries – with European culture, was continually
writing *Machbet* instead of *Macbeth*;[13] this, too, was a case of
anticipation of the *h* for fear of its omission.[14]

[12] See *Lettres inédites relatives à G. Leopardi* (Paris, 1913), p. 203.

[13] See Luigi Russo's philological note to his edition of the *Saggi critici* of
De Sanctis, III (Bari, 1963⁵), p. 338.

[14] The same thing very often occurs in cases where the writer is unfamiliar
with the letters or combinations contained in words of a foreign language.
Anticipation of the *y* (or the straightforward, simple substitution of the *y* for *i*)
is frequently found in mediaeval Latin codices: the spelling of the surname of
Jean Hyppolite (instead of Hippolyte) persists even today as an example of an

The '*Niebhur* case' provides a further confirmation of a methodological consideration on which we have already had reason to remark (p. 53, cf. p. 136). In Italy during the 19th and early 20th centuries, the rigidity of the social structure and its retarded sexual code was such that there were certainly very many who oscillated between the call of the brothel and the resolve to 'settle down' (i.e. to submit to the no less squalid confines of traditional bourgeois marriage). There were also many whose conscious purpose was not to find an alternative to this dichotomy, but who pursued liaisons with prostitutes with a mixture of attraction and guilt. So in all probability a 'psychoanalytic' diagnosis of the error would be perfectly applicable to the majority of those who by mistake wrote *Niebhur*. However (as is proved by their ignorance of the German language, and by the countless other analogous errors of the *Machbet* or *Hyppolite* type) there was not the slightest causal relationship between that mistake and their sexual frustrations. Once again, the 'connexion', the famous connexion which could 'be left' to Freud himself, may be wholly non-existent even when what it 'established' happens to be the case.[15]

An even more arbitrary explanation than that given for *Protragoras* and *partrerre* – arbitrary even in its result this time – is

---

error of this type, which was first made who knows how many centuries ago, by whoever gave a definitive form to the spelling of the name.

[15] A case involving the word *Hur(e)* is quoted in *The Psychopathology* as well (p. 49 sq. = 42 sq.). A group of male and female students 'were unable to produce' the title of the novel *Ben Hur* by Lewis Wallace: one of the women finally admits that she had forgotten the title 'because it contains an expression that I (like any other girl) do not care to use – especially in the company of young men' (*Ben Hur* sounds a little like *bin Hur*' – 'I am a whore'). But is this a case of genuine forgetting? It seems improbable, all the more so in that three of the young men present, despite their acquaintance with the book, remarked that 'strange to relate – they too were unable to produce the name'. It is much more likely that although the girl remembered the title very well, her prudishness made her reluctant to utter it (she resorted, instead, to other titles which more or less evoked the content of the novel – *Ecce Homo; Homo sum; Quo vadis?*), and that the young men, in order not to embarrass her, themselves also 'chivalrously' pretended to forget the name. The further hypothesis that the *homo* in the titles she substituted was an unconscious substitution for the neuter *Mensch* ('prostitute') that had come to her via the masculine *Mensch* ('man') is pure fantasy; yet another case of the 'polyglot unconscious', further complicated by a change in grammatical gender and in meaning.

expounded by Freud immediately prior to that case (p. 91 = 81, see p. 62 = 53 sq.). In Meringer and Mayer, Freud reads of someone who, instead of 'es war mir auf der Brust so schwer' ('it lay so heavily on my breast'), says 'es war mir auf der *Schwest*' (a non-existing word which is the result of an erroneous anticipation of *schwer* and its fusion with *Brust*), and then proceeds to correct himself. Freud is not happy with this: behind the confusion of sounds there must lie a deeper motive! Nor is he slow to find it: 'The idea can hardly be dismissed that the sounds making up "*schwe*" were further enabled to obtrude in this manner because of a special relation. That could only be the association *Schwester* (sister) – *Bruder* (brother); perhaps also *Brust der Schwester* (sister's breast), which leads one on to other groups of thoughts. It is this invisible helper behind the scenes which lends the otherwise innocent "*schwe*" the strength to produce a mistake in speaking.'

We should note here that, despite his *complete ignorance* of the person who made the 'slip' (as we have said, the example is taken from Meringer and Mayer, who give us no information on this score – we do not even know whether the person had a sister), Freud finds that the possibility that it was due to an incestuous thought can 'hardly' be excluded.[16] This combination of absolute certainty that there is something 'behind the scenes' which cannot be confessed, and of nonchalance, one might even say indifference, towards the specific explanation to be adopted of it, is typical of Freud's reasoning. (We have noted it in relation to the forgetting of *aliquis,* in Chapter 4.) Just as in that case Freud first claims to have discovered a cast-iron chain of connexions which lead back from the forgetting of *aliquis* to the thought of the unwanted pregnancy, and then declares that he is wholly disposed to accept a totally

[16] Shortly afterwards (p. 93 = 83) Freud retreats a little: 'I hope that readers will not overlook the difference in value between these interpretations, of which no proof is possible, and the examples that I have myself collected and explained by means of analysis'. But this admirable prudence is shortlived, since he immediately goes on to declare (in a passage we have already quoted) that he 'secretly' clings to the expectation that all 'slips' are to be explained by repression. Moreover, the confidence of his opinion of the *Schwest* mistake is inconsistent with his admission that errors of that type allow no proof. In any case, the difference in the degree of arbitrariness will not seem so great to anyone who has studied the way in which he analyses the 'slips' of the first chapters.

different route whose point of departure is no longer the omission of *aliquis* but the association *exoriare/Exorzismus* (which, as we have seen, itself has two distinct variations) – so in this case we read, on consecutive lines, first that the 'special relation (. . .) *could only be* . . .', and then, quite calmly, that '*perhaps also* . . .'. The important thing is to retain the idea of the incestuous thought – it matters little thereafter whether *Brust* remains *Brust* in the language of the unconscious or decomposes into *Bruder* and *Schwester*.[17]

To give another example (p. 134 = 122): 'A doctor had examined a child and was making out a prescription for it, which included the word "*alcohol*". While he was occupied in doing so the child's mother pestered him with stupid and unnecessary questions. He privately determined not to let this make him angry, and actually succeeded in keeping his temper, but made a "slip of the pen" in the course of the interruptions. Instead of *alcohol* the word *Achol* could be read on the prescription.' Here too, we have an extremely unlikely manifestation of the 'polyglot unconscious' – the determination not to become angry is supposed to have been expressed, no less, in a truncated form of the Greek adjective *acholos*. Yet more important, such an explanation is wholly superfluous. The episode, in fact, can perfectly well be explained by 'superficial psychology': a haplography (the omission of sounds which are duplicated) is one of those faults in writing (or in speech, in which case it is termed haplology) of the type we mentioned on p. 137, to which the most educated of men is subject even in the peace of his own study. In the present instance, the mother's questions could have

[17] A case on which it is not worth dwelling is given on p. 129 sq. = 117 sq. Freud had written *Buckrhard* in mistake for *Burckhard*. He immediately attributed the error to his dislike, not of that Burckhard, but of another of the same name who had 'annoyed me by an unintelligent review of my *Interpretation of Dreams*'. That 'distorting names is very often a form of insulting their owners' is a principle which is acceptable only in relation to *certain* distortions that are clearly insulting (in these cases, moreover, one will discover that the distortion is nearly always conscious, and therefore belongs to the category of jokes and not that of 'slips'. See above, p. 127). But simple cases of garbled pronunciation or confused writing do not have any demonstrable 'intentional' character, either conscious or unconscious; and even a German was particularly liable to submit a surname such as Burckhard, which contains only two vowels as against seven consonants (since it is a case of an error in writing, it is the letters not the phonemes which count), and in which the perilous *r* occurs twice, to a metathesis or anagram such as Freud made (on anagrams see p. 72 note 14).

further contributed to 'confuse' the doctor, despite his effort to maintain his professional dispassion and dedication.

We will be aware since our consideration of the forgetting of *aliquis* that a frequent cause of the omission or abbreviation of words is the tendency 'to dispense with the superfluous' (above, p. 36 sqq.). We should, then, I think, be ready to acknowledge an instance of this in an example provided by Jung (when he was still a close collaborator of Freud) and cited by Freud (p. 24 = 18). A man was trying to recite a well-known poem (Heine's *Lyrisches Intermezzo* XXXIII), which begins with the quatrain: 'Ein Fichtenbaum steht einsam / im Norden auf kahler Höh'. / Ihn schläfert; mit weisser Decke / umhüllen ihn Eis und Schnee' ('A fir-tree stands alone / in the North, on a barren height. / It slumbers: with a white sheet / Ice and snow cover it'.). But he cannot remember the end of the third line, 'mit weisser Decke'. It struck Jung as surprising that something 'in so familiar a verse' should be forgotten. I confess that I do not feel this at all. We shall come back to another aspect of the problem in the following chapter, where we discuss the difference between forgetting and pathological 'amnesia'. But for the moment, let us note that the sense and syntax remain unaffected even if the final phrase 'mit weisser Decke' ('with a white sheet') is omitted – so that these words would be particularly prone to be forgotten. What is more, this is one of the very few poems from the *Lyrisches Intermezzo* in which the separate lines of each quatrain do not rhyme – so that in this case the powerful aid which rhyme lends to memory is absent. I am less confident of a third possible factor, which may nonetheless have played a part: the ideas and images are not arranged in the most natural order, even granted the condensed form of a poem such as this which consists of only two quatrains. From 'Ihn schläfert' ('It *slumbers*') one wants to pass immediately to the beginning of the second quatrain, that is to what the fir-tree *dreams* ('Er träumt von einer Palme' ['It dreams of a palm'] and so on), but the intermediate phrase (from 'mit weisser Decke' to 'Schnee') tends to refer one back to the first two lines. Even this, admittedly slight, disturbance of the logic of the poem (which obviously does not necessarily detract from its lyrical merit) might have further interfered with the recitation. At the same time, the reciter's sense of rhythm would have made him realize that something was missing – which was why he broke off.

When subjected to a brief analysis by Jung ('I made him reproduce what occurred to him in connexion with "mit weisser Decke"'), the man said that the white sheet made him think of a shroud, and thus of an acquaintance who had recently died of a heart-attack, and this in turn of his fear that he himself might meet with the same death. Once again we must repeat that we do not want to doubt in the slightest that this fear was really present in the man's psyche and susceptible to arousal on any occasion. It is in the nature of obsessive thoughts (especially when they are not without foundation!) to be excited in this way – but precisely on *any occasion*. It is just this which deprives the forgetting of 'mit weisser Decke' of its force as a *specific* symptom of the repressed thought (which, in any case, was probably not so deeply repressed). Here too, if we take the trouble, as we did in the case of *aliquis,* we can by means of counter-examples establish that if our man had forgotten 'ihn schläfert', the transition from the image of sleep to that of death (the eternal sleep: *nox est perpetua una dormienda*) would have been very easily made; if he had forgotten 'Eis und Schnee', the coldness of the ice and snow would have brought to mind the chill of the corpse and tomb; and even the forgetting of 'steht einsam' would have allowed an association between the notion of solitude and that of death (the abandonment of 'customary, loving companionship' for the person who dies, a sense of aloneness for whoever remains).

Anyone who has practical experience of ancient texts, or of manuscripts or type-scripts or printers' proofs today, knows that one of the commonest of errors is dipthography – that is, the mistaken repetition of a part of a word, or still more often, of an entire word or of several consecutive words. In the case of copies of pre-existing writings, the error is very frequently produced at a moment in which the copyist or printer, on completing the transcription of a section of the text, looks back at the original and, instead of 'taking up' from the words he had reached, starts again at a point further back. In effect, this is a kind of retrospective *saut du même au même.* But it can very easily happen, even when writing original texts rather than transcriptions, that we commit errors of repetition, because our thoughts and their transmission do not always proceed at the same rate, and the writer can have the mistaken impression that he still has to write down something that he has in fact already written. Leopardi's *Zibaldone* offers numerous examples of these 'authorial dipthographies', which are obviously quite distinct from repetitions made deliberately for their stylistic effect.[18] When, therefore, Freud asserts (p. 142 = 128 sq.) that repetitions in writing and copying are 'likewise not without significance'; that 'if the writer repeats a word he has already written, this is probably an indication that it is not easy for him to get away from it: that he could have said more at that point but had omitted to do so'; that 'perseveration in copying seems to be a substitute for saying "I too" or "Just my case"'; he elevates to the level of a general rule cases which are *possibly* verifiable on some occasions (Freud gives no examples, but limits himself to a reference to medico-legal reports in which the dipthography *could* have been accounted for in this way), but which certainly constitute a negligible minority in comparison with the innumerable examples of purely 'mechanical' dipthography. Here too, a mania for psychologizing, a conviction that the most trivial error always answers to some 'intention', leads to the invention of a non-existent – or, what is the same, totally undemonstrable – essence at a level of reality which cannot be investigated.

What holds for dipthography also holds, subject to the necessary qualifications, for the 'perseverance at a remove' of certain memories. How many times have we sent a letter to an old address although we knew the new one: or put on the back of the envelope an old address of our *own*, often one that is several years out of date? If I say that the old address, which I have so frequently written, has made a more indelible 'imprint' on my mind than the new address, I shall be assailed for the crudity of this formulation,

[18] The critical edition of the *Zibaldone* is to be published shortly (see above p. 38 note 9). In the meantime, see the examples cited in the Flora edition (Milan, 1953), I, p. 1556. But Flora is wrong to see in these dipthographies 'those characteristic oversights made by anyone who copies from a preliminary draft or mere outline'.

despite the substantial truth of its message, which could be stated in more rigorously scientific terms. But when a Viennese woman commits a similar error (p. 138 sq. = 126), she is instantly taken to task by her psychoanalytically minded friend, who promptly supplies an explanation of its unconscious motive: she is envious of the large and spacious accommodation occupied by the recipient of her letter, and has repressed her desire that the latter should still be living in her cramped and less modern house. The woman who wrote the wrong address readily admits to the envy she feels for the recipient of the latter, who is in fact (the psychologist will hardly be indifferent to this particular) her sister. Here is a typical case of that phenomenon on which we commented before (p. 132), whereby psychoanalysis functions as a pastime for members of a neo-bourgeoisie who have come to accept it as a modern surrogate for an earlier confession of sins. The sins, for all that, are real enough – the woman will very probably have been jealous of her sister, because, particularly in certain social circles (but ultimately everywhere, so long as we have closed family relations and economic inequality), such envy is the rule rather than the exception. But if the sister had moved, not from a cramped to a spacious house, but because of financial straits from a palace to a hovel, and had the writer nonetheless addressed the letter incorrectly, this salon psychoanalysis would still have had its explanation ready: that she had written the old address instead of the new one would have been interpreted as an unconscious attempt to relieve herself of a guilt complex at no great expense – to re-accommodate her sister *ideally* in the splendid surroundings of her happier days, and thereby find a justification for not lifting a finger to help her escape *in reality* from her present impoverished condition. The traditional bourgeoisie which was hostile to Freud disdained to accept even the *confessio oris* ['confession of mouth']. The new bourgeoisie willingly submits not only to the *confessio oris* but even to a measure of *contritio cordis* ['contrition of heart'] – 'What a pity one's always so petty in such things!', exclaims the Viennese lady jealous of her sister – since it has understood that Freud is not asking for a *satisfactio operis* ['reparation of the deed'] which would be an actual negation of its own bourgeois existence and of the meanness which inevitably derives from it.

146

Again, one encounters from the third chapter of *The Psycho-pathology* onwards, errors of the *Signorelli–Botticelli* type: e.g., *Hartmann* for *Hitschmann* (p. 130=118 sq.), and *Lusitania* for *Mauretania* (p. 134=121 sq. – these were names of steamships). In these two cases, the 'slip' was facilitated by banalization in addition to phonic and conceptual similarity. Hitschmann was 'unknown' to A. J. Storfer, whom Freud cites as the author of the 'slip', whereas Hartmann was a 'well-known philosopher' who had also written a book on the unconscious (and the possibility of a 'slip' was made that much greater by the fact that the Christian name of both scholars was Eduard). The transatlantic steamer Lusitania, which was sunk in the war by a German submarine and thus became the subject of much emotion and hostility, was much better known than her sister-ship the Mauretania – all the more so in the case of the 'slip' cited by Freud, whose author was an American, since it was for the most part Americans who had perished in the disaster of the Lusitania. The lengthy investigation which we have already made of errors of this type (Chap. VI) allows us, I think, to dispense with detailed refutations of Freud's psychologistic explanations. Once again, however, their ethical and social interest is not cancelled by their scientific lack of substance. The environment which produced these 'slips' was one in which the man of science (Freud, perhaps, more than any other) was so obsessed by the need to justify his superiority over his own colleagues,[19] and the model husband was so little enamoured of

[19] For this aspect of Freud's psychology (which will remain a feature of all scholarship until a more egalitarian and cooperative attitude towards work is developed, though in Freud it was taken to a morbid extreme, which was accompanied by an 'absentminded' tendency to fail to acknowledge results appropriated from others), see again the works cit. by Fromm (*Sigmund Freud's Mission*, op. cit., Chap. IV), by Roazen (*Broth. Anim.*, pp. 88–93; 191–9; 193 note, and passim), and even that by the somewhat uncritical Freudian, Marthe Robert, p. 155 sqq. But perhaps most significant of all is Freud's exhortation to Groddeck in the first letter he wrote to him (5 June 1917, in *Letters of Sigmund Freud*, London, 1961, p. 322 sq.): 'While I should very much like to welcome your collaboration with open arms, there is one thing that bothers me: that you have evidently succeeded so little in conquering that banal ambition which hankers after originality and priority. . . . Besides, can you be so sure on this point? After all you must be 10 to 15, possibly 20 years younger than I (1856). Is it not possible that you absorbed the leading ideas of psychoanalysis in a cryptomnesic manner? Similar to the manner in which I was able to explain

his wife, that even the most trivial of 'slips' immediately issued in a trial of underlying intentions. 'Would that you might drown like the passengers of the Lusitania!' was apparently the affectionate thought that the husband's unconscious directed at his wife.

A very strong argument against the explanation of 'slips' by the 'association of ideas' seemed to Freud to be the existence of what in textual criticism are termed 'polar errors' – those which consist of the substitution of what would have been the correct word by its precise opposite. In the *Lectures* of 1915–16 he lends particular emphasis to this type of error, which he regards as a special confirmation of the Freudian theory of the 'slip': in its exposure of thoughts and feelings which are the opposite of those we want to display, the Id takes revenge on the Ego's lack of sincerity.[20]

In certain rare cases, this explanation is indeed probable. When the President of the Austrian Parliament solemnly announced at the beginning of a debate that since there was a quorum of members present, he herewith declared the sitting *closed* (instead of *open*), it must really have been a case of a vendetta on the part of his unconscious, since we know that he 'secretly *wished* he was already in a position to close the sitting, from which little good was to be expected' (p. 67 = 59). It is significant that this example, which Freud considered particularly instructive and quoted again several times in the *Lectures* (*GW* XI 27, 28, 33 sq., 40 = *Introd. Lect. Psych.,*

---

my own originality? Anyhow, what is the good of struggling for priority against an older generation?' In other words, even if it was you who first formulated certain ideas (the reference is to the concept of the Id, which for that matter owed its origin at least in part to Nietzsche, and to the extension of psychoanalysis to psychosomatic medicine – and here we might note that in his preceding letter Groddeck had expressed himself in the most humble and flattering of terms towards Freud), nevertheless I am the one who is or can be credited with their discovery, since I, by reason of my greater age, am likely to have communicated ideas of mine to you in some more or less mysterious form, even though they were never published. So forego these 'petty' triumphs, and cede to me the honour of being first – though I care nothing for it!

[20] See *GW* XI 33 sq. = *Introd. Lect. Psych., SE* XV 40 sq. Certain 'bungled' actions (in contrast to 'linguistic expressions') also display an oppositional relationship: see, for example, the episode referred to by Tausk in *The Psychopathology,* p. 252 sq. = 226 sq.).

SE XV 34, 35, 40 sq., 47), had first been pointed out, and already interpreted in a 'pre-Freudian' sense, by the much abused Meringer ('Neue freie Presse', 23 August 1900, cit. by Freud). This shows that even traditional psychology, for all its inadequacies, was not in fact so averse to invoking suppressed desire when an explanation in terms of it seemed reasonably probable.

But to look, as Freud does, for a repressed thought behind every polar 'slip' involves a failure to realize the commonest genesis of such errors. It appears that Freud could conceive of the notorious association of ideas only in terms of 'similarity' and not in terms of 'contrast' as well.[21] In order to demonstrate, in fact, how easily any term evokes its opposite, we need not trouble Heraclitus or Hegel; it is enough to reflect on the fact (as psychologists and linguists such as Meringer and Mayer had done) that polarity is included in the wider category of complementarity of images and concepts.

Let us take one of the most trivial of examples. The mythical brothers Castor and Pollux are renowned for their friendship; Eteocles and Polynices are brothers whose hatred of each other is no less legendary and proverbial. But from the point of view of complementarity – i.e. of the difficulty involved in speaking of the one without thinking, and even often speaking, of the other – the two pairs of names are identically situated. If, then, we want to be somewhat more precise, we must distinguish between two types of polar 'slip', neither of them Freudian. In the first, the influence of context is a determinant, or at least an auxiliary factor: if I speak or write about the contrast between Stalin and Trotsky in a context where I have already named each of them on several occasions, nothing is easier than to say or write the name of one instead of the other at a certain moment. Two factors combine to facilitate the error in this and other similar cases. One is conceptual complementarity (the thought of one evokes that of the other and,

---

[21] Freud foresees the second possibility in a passage from the *Lectures* (*GW* XI 27 = *Introd. Lect. Psych., SE* XV 34 sq.): 'instead we can appeal to the fact that contraries have a strong conceptual kinship with each other and stand in a particularly close psychological association with each other'. But there it is left, and one has the impression that Freud considered it more of a loop-hole than a genuine explanation, or, at all events, an insufficient explanation.

as a result of one of those displacements whereby words to be uttered immediately are anticipated by thoughts of what we shall say shortly, or of the whole trend of our argument, we lay ourselves open to a confusion of the two names); the other is acoustic persistance (the name which has just been spoken or written still 'resounds' in the mind; we already know that this occurs even when one is silently writing, since every piece of writing, like every piece of copying, is preceded/accompanied by 'internal dictation'). It goes without saying that the acoustic factor is reinforced whenever, as often happens, the antithetical words are phonically similar – one has only to think of all those pairs which are differentiated only by the presence or absence of a negative prefix (e.g. *direct – indirect*: a few years ago I wrote 'indirect tradition' instead of 'direct tradition' in an article in which I had already needed to use these two antithetical terms many times,[22] and it was not until Scevola Mariotti pointed it out that I realized the error, which I had overlooked even at the stage of proof correction). Polar 'slips' due to the influence of context, even between words which have no, or very slight, phonic similarity, are to be found very frequently in Marx's hand-written text of the *Grundrisse* – for example, *Produktion* instead of *Konsumtion* in a context in which he is continually speaking of production and consumption as complementary antitheses,[23] and so on.

In the majority of such cases, to expect the 'slip' to reveal evidence of a repressed thought – to seek, for example, to attribute a hidden Stalinism to someone of Trotskyist sympathies who said Stalin instead of Trotsky – would be merely fanciful, given the overriding number of cases which allow no such psychological explanation, but are nonetheless perfectly well explained along the lines we have mentioned.

In a second type of polar 'slip' the exchange is not influenced in any appreciable way by the context, but is due to a purely mental relationship between the opposing concepts. Meringer remarked on this second type in the passage quoted by Freud (p. 67= 59 sq., where he does not, however, distinguish it sufficiently clearly from

[22] See 'Maia' 22 (1970), p. 351, the penultimate line of the text. The article's specific concern was with *Alcuni casi controversi di tradizione indiretta*.

[23] See K. Marx, *Grundrisse* (Harmondsworth, 1973), p. 92, note 15.

what Freud was to call 'slips' due to repression): 'Now extensive observations have taught me that words with opposite meanings are, quite generally, very often interchanged; *they are already associated in our linguistic consciousness, they lie very close to each other and it is easy for the wrong one to be evoked.*' If we wish to indulge in the fashion for structuralist terminology, we could call the first type (influenced above all by context) the syntagmatic polar 'slip', and the second type (influenced only by the complementarity of the two opposing terms in our current conceptual-linguistic system) the paradigmatic polar 'slip'. I once chanced to write (in the 'Studi italiani di filologica classica' no. 23, 1949, p. 8 line 24, see the errata p. 235) 'omitted' instead of 'inserted'. Here the context exerted no direct influence – I had not had any reason to use the verb 'to omit', or any synonym of it, shortly before. But in the mind of any student of textual criticism – and this was the drift of my argument in the article – the omission of a word and its arbitrary insertion constitute a complementary pair of concepts, since they deal with two opposite types of corruption to which a text is subject: hence my 'slip'.

At other times, the distinction between the paradigmatic and the syntagmatic polar 'slip' is not so clear-cut, for the very reason that the 'slip', as we mentioned, is not due to a simple recurrence of opposite terms in a given context, but to the fact that – especially in polemical writing – whoever writes or speaks one word is thinking of the whole substance of the argument he intends to sustain. In the underground newspaper of the Committee for National Liberation of Tuscany, 'Il Combattente', 7 December 1943, in an article entitled *Attesismo* ['Waiting-ism'], we read (the emphases are mine): 'One hears it said quite frequently, even within our own ranks, that the struggle *against the Partisans* is not effective, in that for every German or Fascist killed the enemy can shoot several hostages. . . . It is not difficult to expose the error of this position: one has only to think of the political and military importance *absurd* by the struggle of the heroic Partisans of Yugo-slavia and the other Balkan states.'[24] There is no doubt that the

---

[24] The newspaper forms part of the collection of the library of the *Istituto storico della Resistenza in Toscana* at Florence.

phrase 'against the Partisans' is a polar 'slip' for 'against the Germans' or 'against the Nazi Fascists'. The author of the article (written and printed clandestinely, under constant threat of exposure which naturally increased the risk of such 'slips' occurring) was thinking of its dominant theme – the *Partisan* war and the necessity of its extension. The 'slip' resulted more from this basic thought than from the simple correlation between the two antithetical terms *Partisans* – *Fascists*. The other error, 'assurda' ['absurd'] for 'assurta' ['attained'] is not a polar error. It could be a mistake of dictation, facilitated by the relatively high-flown and non-colloquial nature of the verb 'assurgere' ['to rise' – to high office etc.]. But here too, it is probable (but by no means certain) that while the comrade was engaged in the writing or type-setting of that word, he was thinking of the idea which inspired the article as a whole: it is *absurd* of anyone to refuse to be committed to the struggle for fear of reprisals. Here, it is clear, we are indeed committed to a 'psychological textual criticism'; but the psychologism of which we do *not* feel the need in cases such as this, is precisely the Freudian type, which is bound up with the concept of repression.

That counterposition, for that matter, is nothing more than a particular case of complementarity, is shown by those 'slips' which one can still call 'polar' in a wide sense, though they relate to terms which are not genuinely opposites. Such is Pasquali's oversight, *lettore* ['reader'] for *autore* ['author'], which he himself recalls in *Storia della tradizione*,[2] 485, as pointed out to him by Carlo Ferdinando Russo. To anyone who keeps in mind the various forms which complementarity can assume, even the case which Freud narrates of the young doctor who 'had timidly and reverently introduced himself to the famous Virchow as Dr Virchow' (p. 95 = 85) will not seem strange. It is clear that here, much more than in the preceding cases cited, the young man's emotion on encountering the illustrious scientist played a decisive part: the thought that he had to present himself *to Virchow* was so uppermost that the mention of his own name was, as it were, submerged. All the same, this too, in its own way, is a polar error; the speaker and his interlocutor, that is, the sender and the receiver of the message, constitute a complementary pair not only from the standpoint of a third person (as in the case just now of Pasquali's 'slip': *lettore* for *autore*), but also from that of one of the two interested parties.[25]

Again Freud's comment is significant: 'I do not know how the ambitious young man justified the "slip of the tongue" he had made – whether he relied upon the flattering excuse that he felt himself so small beside the great name that his own could not fail to slip away from him, or whether he had the courage to admit that he hoped one day to become as great a man as Virchow, and to beg the Professor not to treat him so contemptuously on that account. One of these two thoughts – or perhaps both of them simultaneously – may have confused the young man while he was introducing himself.' What tortuous wisdom in so few lines! The more benevolent hypothesis (at least from Freud's point of view, and that of his epoch, which regarded *timor reverentialis* ['reverential fear'] before a Great Professor to be a duty and a virtue) is presented as a possibility in the last phrase 'One of these thoughts . . .' only to be immediately reduced ('or perhaps . . .') to the same level, in terms of causal significance, as that occupied by the more malevolent hypothesis – which represents yet another of the innumerable variations on the theme of the pupil's would-be identification with the Master-Father-Tyrant. Yet even this compromise solution (half fear, half suppressed ambition) is, in effect, ruled out by what is said before; for the student is unhesitatingly presented as 'the ambitious young man' (a description reminiscent of the young Jew who failed to remember *aliquis,* and his 'ambitious feelings . . .' – in both cases the German expression is identical, *der Ehrgeizige*), while the more benevolent hypothesis is presented

[25] We may note that this case has a certain similarity to another, quoted by Musatti (*Trattato,* p. 347): a patient comes to him who says he has been sent by Dr. Freud. Musatti's explanation (the patient's distrust of Musatti whom he considered too little known; an unconscious desire to increase the importance of his own case which led him to present himself as recommended by Freud in person) seems to me to be unnecessarily psychologistic. A more obvious explanation is that the 'slip' was due to the fact that the patient knew he was consulting a psychoanalyst who would cure him with a therapeutic method inspired by Freud. See, furthermore, a recent article by Musatti in 'Belfagor' (1974), p. 140, which claims that 'there is no elderly analyst who has not chanced on some occasion to hear himself addressed by one of his own patients as "Dr. Freud"'. It is precisely the frequency of this kind of 'slip' which, in my opinion, makes the 'individualizing' explanation less probable here than in the other, somewhat similar, case which Musatti cites in the *Trattato.*

as a piece of hypocrisy – 'a flattering excuse' is the euphemism –
even if it invites a smile of indulgence rather than anger. Although
he does not spell it out, Freud makes it very clear that for him the
other explanation is the correct one; his only doubt is whether the
student 'had the courage to admit' to his own desire to emulate
Virchow. Again, we should note that the picture Freud presents
of the university world, and of the medical faculty in particular,
with its omnipotent Professor and sullenly servile pupil who
dreams of the professorial chair, was, and still is, substantially true.
(I have no means of judging whether Virchow was an exception
in that world.) But the bitter psychologism which is its product is
unduly elevated to a general, absolute and eternal theory. The
result is often excessive accusations of intention even with regard
to a bourgeoisie which for its class responsibilities of a *quite different
order* (such as, in fact, were shared by Freud himself) indeed merited
accusation and dispossession.

There are many other 'slips' listed by Freud which we have not
examined, not only for reasons of space, but because the reader will
by now be able to imagine the kind of alternative explanations of
them (whether or not they are accepted) that we would provide.
We shall comment on certain other examples in the following
chapter, and on a few more in the last. Here I shall mention, rather,
an example found at the beginning of the third chapter of *The
Psychopathology* which is not, as Freud claims, 'typical' of the
mechanism of forgetting. In fact there is nothing to compare with
it either in the other cases cited by Freud or in the discoveries made
by students of textual criticism or linguistics. A 'younger colleague'
of Freud attempts to recite *Die Braut von Korinth* ('The Bride of
Corinth') by Goethe; but right from the start he introduces such
extensive alterations to the text that in effect it becomes another
poem, or, to put it in less drastic terms, a completely revised edition
of Goethe's version. For example, a line such as 'Wenn er teuer
nicht die Gunst erkauft' ['if he does not buy the favour dearly']
becomes (with complete change of meaning, and without any
respect for rhyme) 'Jetzt, wo jeder Tag was Neues bringt' ['Now
when every day brings something new']. His anguished thoughts
about his engagement to a woman older than himself (for which
Goethe's lines provided only a vague pretext) were so intense that

they caused him to invent entire lines. Here, indeed, we find ourselves confronted with an outright pathological symptom (that is to say, a manifestation of psychosis, rather than neurosis). The recitation of Goethe's poem was only the starting point for a species of delirious monologue. But, I repeat, in Freud's treatment of 'slips' this constitutes a wholly isolated case, and not a model to which we can make the other interpretations of 'slips' conform.

At the opposite extreme of such a 'reduction to the pathological', we find in *The Psychopathology* (p. 124 = 112 sq.) and in the *Lectures* (*GW* XI 32 = *Introd. Lect. Psych.*, *SE* XV 39) an example of one of the most banal 'slips' which is likewise considered by Freud to be typical, indeed as comprising virtually 'the whole theory of misreading'. However, one could say, on the contrary, that it agrees in every possible way with *our* explanation of the majority of 'slips', and not with Freud's. Freud quotes from the *Witzige und satirische Einfälle* of G. Ch. Lichtenberg: 'He perused Homer so much that he always read *Agamemnon* instead of *angenommen* ('supposed').' Is this a Freudian 'slip'? Does Lichtenberg's own explanation, to which Freud so readily consents, refer us to – let us not speak even of depth psychology – but some unpleasant or suppressed or 'semi-suppressed' thought (see the passage cited above, p. 131) which interfered with his discourse? No : it refers us only to a psychologico-cultural phenomenon that has its exact analogy in that erroneous correction of *translation* to *tradition* which Pasquali made because *for him* the second word was a *lectio facilior*. By way of comment on the passage, Freud remarks: 'in a very large number of cases it is the reader's preparedness that alters the text and reads into it something which he is expecting or with which he is occupied'. Quite correct; but everything which specifically distinguishes the Freudian theory is absent from this characterization of a (certain type of) 'slip'.

Slip and Error, Amnesia and Forgetting

What distinguishes the 'slip' from the error due to ignorance (to the fact that the object and the word for it were never known, or that they were confused, due to lack of education, with other words or concepts)? What distinguishes amnesia from mere forgetting? It seems at first sight that the distinction is obvious, and that Freud and the Freudians were well aware of it. Ernest Jones says in his assessment of *The Psychopathology of Everyday Life*:[1] 'The class of forgotten thoughts in everyday life to which this mechanism [i.e. that of 'slips' and psychopathological amnesias] mainly applies is, of course, that where the other causes of forgetting do not provide adequate explanations; in other words, it principally concerns matters that we should normally expect to remember. For instance, one would expect some hidden reason in the case of the name of a near relative or friend being forgotten much more readily than in the case of that of a casual acquaintance.' Freud himself, at the beginning of the second Lecture (*GW* XI 18 = *Introd. Lect. Psych.*, *SE* XV 25) underlines the *temporary* nature of amnesias and 'slips'. Musatti remarks[2] that amnesia raises the problem of a psychoanalytic explanation when 'one fails to recall something that it would, on the contrary, be normal to remember (and thus we expect to do so).' We could multiply quotations to this effect.

It would also be possible – and it would constitute no more than a reformulation of what Freud and the Freudians have themselves

---

[1] E. Jones, *Papers on Psychoanalysis* (London, 1938), p. 60.
[2] Preface to the Boringhieri edition of *The Psychopathology of Everyday Life*, p. viii.

observed – to say that error and forgetting involve a limited judgement that refers us, if not to the general level of education of the
persons concerned, at least to their specific knowledge in a given
field, or to the interest they show in the topic under discussion, or
to their general mnemonic ability. The 'slip' and the amnesia,
by contrast, involve a 'psychopathological' condition which has
nothing to do with the cultural level of the subject in question.
Every so often 'even Homer nods' . . . or represses! The 'patients'
whose 'slips' are recorded by Freud are all more or less (Freud is
himself, of course, the prime example) cultivated persons.

Up to this point, everything is straightforward. However, the
distinction between the two orders of phenomena, though very
clear in many cases, is not so in others. Freud too readily ignored it,
even in situations which called for further exploration and greater
methodological vigilance and caution.

In the first instance, from our survey so far, it transpires that
one and the same disturbance of discourse must, on different occasions, be regarded as an instance of a 'slip' or of an error or of
amnesia or of forgetting, depending on the subject's (particular or
general) degree of culture. No doubt we were right (above, p.68)
to consider Mussolini's *Anaxagoras* an error, a mark of his ignorance.
If, however, it happened to a student of the Pre-Socratics, or to
someone of a high general level of education, to say that according
to Anaxagoras man is the measure of all things, we would not for
this reason raise an outcry; from a formal point of view, in fact,
Anaxagoras for *Protagoras* has, as we have seen, all the characteristics
of a 'slip' of the *Signorelli–Botticelli* type. We would be rather
more puzzled if the Pre-Socratic scholar attributed the saying to
Thales, for example, or to Diogenes of Apollonia, because here the
phonic difference between the two names is too extreme, and the
'conceptual affinity' between the philosophers in question too
slight. (That they are all Pre-Socratic philosophers is too tenuous
and generic a bond.) The fact that it is impossible to explain the
substitution of Protagoras by Thales, or even more so, by Diogenes
of Apollonia, in terms of banalization and so on, would confront
us with one of two alternatives – either to make a drastic revision
of our judgement of the presumed 'expert' (who would then be
revealed as a complete ignoramus), or to postulate the forcible

interference of another thought that preoccupied the subject's mind at that moment (for example, while he was speaking or writing, he could have chanced to remember that he ought quickly to set to work on an article on Diogenes of Apollonia). The interference would have to be 'forcible' because the error would have been produced, quite untypically, without any 'enabling agency' in the form of phonic similarity or banalization.

The 'slip' could further be distinguished from the error on the basis of its temporary nature, on which we have just commented. This would constitute a different criterion from that based simply on a *personal* evaluation of the subject's degree of culture. We would then judge it to be a 'slip' when whoever had committed it went on to correct himself (either because the hearer's surprised reaction provided an intimation of his mistake or even without the assistance lent by such an external signal), or at least if, despite his failure to recover the correct word, he demonstrated his realization that the one he had uttered was incorrect. On the other hand, we would judge it an error when the subject displays no doubts about what he has said, and accepts (when he accepts it!) the correction communicated to him by others as something *new* in comparison to what he had up to that point believed, and not as an appeal to what he already knew. The distinction between amnesia and simple forgetting would be a little more complex. We shall have to take at least three cases into consideration: 1) where the subject, often to his own vexation,[3] fails to remember at that moment something

---

[3] On this vexation Freud insists more than once (in the article cit. above p. 63 note 1, and later, for example, in *The Psychopathology*, Chap. II and p. 99=90, and in the *Lectures, GW* XI 43 = *Introd. Lect. Psych., SE* XV 49), whether in regard to instances of forgetting or 'slips'. According to him, these manifestations of nervousness confirm that the patient was more or less unconsciously aware of the 'non-innocent' nature of his own forgetting or 'slip'. Now, in some cases the patient's agitation is to be explained by factors we have already described in Chapter 4 (the patient feels himself at the mercy of the analyst's scrutiny and prompting). In others, the vexation or anger are such as accompany any unexpected realization that one is 'not one's own master' – that one is not in a position to control one's own mind or body. Anyone suffering from arteriosclerotic amnesia is subject to a similar feeling; so too is someone who suddenly realizes that he cannot move a limb because of the onset of paralysis (which need not be hysterical, but could be due to a stroke), or someone who fails to hear what is said to him because of deafness. Freud tends towards a one-sided psychologization even of cases such as these.

which he maintains he knows, of which the memory will in fact come back to him shortly; 2) where the subject, in his quotation of a text (which need not necessarily be a literary work, but could be, for example, the rather lengthy title of a political party, or a proper name compounded of several names and surnames – for example, 'Popular Democratic Front for the Liberation of Palestine' or Anne-Louise-Germaine Necker, Baroness of Stäel-Holstein), omits one or more words, and does not realize the mistake because the overall sense is conveyed equally, or at least tolerably, well (see above, p. 35 sqq.); 3) where what is forgotten is not one element in the context remembered as a whole, but entire sets of ideas or branches of knowledge (we have only to think of how much we have forgotten as adults of what we learnt at school and lacked the interest to pursue thereafter), or else events in our own life, or more or less extended phases of it – here we are referring to personal knowledge or experience whose loss is inclined for the most part to arouse a general sense of regret ('I don't remember any of the mathematics I studied at grammar school!'), rather than any particular disappointment, in so far as such forgetting is rightly or wrongly considered 'natural', a kind of fading due either to the length of time elapsed or to the loss of interest, or to a combination of both.

All the same, there are still difficulties. If we proceed on the basis of the distinction we have just formulated approximately, we see that many cases which we ought to count as errors were *initially* cases of 'slips'. Anyone who declares that Anaxagoras considered man to be the measure of all things, and claims to be truly convinced of that, and even accuses anyone who hazards a correction of being ignorant, is guilty of an 'error' rather than a 'slip'. There must have been a moment, however – even if all of a decade beforehand – when he learnt, either from a teacher, or from a history of philosophy, or from some other piece of writing, whatever its subject-matter, of the correct name Protagoras. There must have also occurred another moment at which, as the result of one of the commonest *non-Freudian* 'slips' (see above, Chapters 6 and 7), Protagoras was substituted in his mind by Anaxagoras. Up to this point, the mental response of the uneducated or befuddled has been no different from that of the educated (who is also liable, as we have said, to commit 'slips' of this kind). The difference between them is revealed in what follows. Whoever is interested, if not directly in the history of ancient philosophy, at least in cultural problems whose scope might include the famous Protagorean principle, and who thus may have occasion to come in contact with Protagoras again either through subsequent reading or conversation, will very soon re-acquire the correct information, and his 'slip', even if here and there it may have passed unnoticed, will nonetheless have been of brief duration; and the longer such a man remains during the rest of his life in a state of 'cultural training', the more he will be on his guard against not just the recurrence of that, or an analogous 'slip', but also against the risk that the incorrect name becomes, so to speak, stuck in his memory. By contrast, the 'slip' will become consolidated once it has been registered and not immediately corrected, in the mind of anyone who no longer has reason to concern himself (even at a non-specialist level) with Protagoras and man's measure: so that a momentary accident issues in an erroneous conviction.

It is only if we suppose that the subject had received false information right from the start – if he had seen the maxim wrongly ascribed in a book, or heard a teacher attribute it to Anaxagoras, and had not subsequently had the desire or occasion to consult other authorities which would have disabused him – that we can allow that the erroneous conviction had its origin other than in a 'slip'. In the case of Mussolini, such a hypothesis is unlikely, since, as we have already mentioned, it is probable that his first source of information was the best history of Greek philosophy available at the time, a work that in many respects has not been superseded even today. This was Theodor Gomperz' *Griechische Denker* – in which, we can be sure, there is no confusion between Anaxagoras and Protagoras, whose doctrines are set forth with superb mastery. The 'slip', then, is to be attributed to Mussolini, and in all likelihood it did not make its debut in that grotesque speech of 1943, but was a veteran of some years, maybe even decades, and had already become consolidated as an error. But even on the hypothesis of an initial item of misinformation, we only transfer the problem to an earlier date: at the origin of the error there will always be a 'slip', committed in this case, not by the subject, but by his written or oral 'informant'.

We must, however, still make a further distinction, whose effect is to attenuate, though not completely obliterate, the demarcation between 'slip' and erroneous conviction. What we described as a 'consolidation' of the 'slip', whereby it is transformed into an erroneous conviction, is not a dubious privilege only of such cultural slatterns as Mussolini; one also encounters it in persons of wide education and high intelligence, if their gifts are accompanied, as often happens, by a certain nonchalance and excessive trust in their own memory. This type of person will certainly not fall victim to the consolidation as error of a 'slip' of the *Anaxagoras* type, from which he is likely to be preserved by the breadth of his acquaintance with the development of ancient Greek thought (in which Protagoras and Anaxagoras occupy positions too highly individual and important to be the subject of confusion) – and also by later reading and conversation, as we mentioned before. But the position is not so secure in the case of texts, for the most part poetry, quoted from memory. Where this is involved, even a literary critic of the utmost merit may chance, as a result of an early 'slip', to encumber himself for years and years with mistaken quotations. We have already remarked on the very numerous inexact quotations that one encounters in the essays and lectures of Francesco De Sanctis, for which he has been reproved by scholarly pedants. In the *Saggio sul Petrarca,* instead of Petrarch's phrase 'Sette e sett'anni' ['Seven and seven years'] De Sanctis writes 'Quattordici anni' ['fourteen years'] – the sum represents a banalization; instead of 'dopo le notti vaneggiando spese' ['after the nights spent in raving'], 'dopo le notti vanamente spese' ['after the nights spent in vain'] – this too is a kind of banalization, since the word possessed of greater power and pathos has been substituted by one that is more insipid and prosaic, and the whole line has taken on a more sing-song rhythm as a result; and so on.[4] In the *Saggio sul Leopardi,* Berchet's line: 'E quel sol gli rifulge più bello' ['And that sun shines more beautiful upon him'] is banalized by

---

[4] These examples are taken from Croce's preface to his edition of *Saggio sul Petrarca* (Naples, 1918), p. xx.

De Sanctis to 'E quel sole gli apparve più bello'⁵ ['and that sun seemed more beautiful to him']. Not to waste time on numerous other examples, let us ask whether it is not more probable that all, or nearly all, these cases were 'slips' that had for some time been fixed in De Sanctis' memory rather than momentary 'slips'. We cannot give any certain answer, but it seems to me that the first supposition is far more likely. Whoever has been involved in education, either as a student or as a teacher, and whose experience covers that period (let us hope it is now over) when it was the custom to set poems to be learnt by heart, is well aware that usually the 'slip' is produced in the process of learning itself, or very shortly afterwards; and once it has got a grip on one's memory, it is difficult to eradicate the incorrect version. This equally happens in the case of poems or passages of poetry which we have never *had to learn* by heart, but which we remember on the basis of frequent reading. Obviously my own experience (to which I also appealed above, p. 31 sq. in relation to a 'slip' that had been transformed into an error in my memory of a passage from Foscolo) is scarcely to be compared with that of a De Sanctis, not even in respect of a mental function such as memory, which may be said is 'subordinate'. All the same, I find it difficult to imagine that, given the number of inexact quotations to be found in De Sanctis, a large proportion of them do not consist of 'slips' that became consolidated over time. Certainly De Sanctis did not feel the need to consult the original texts, and hence was not aware that 'something was amiss'.

⁵ See F. De Sanctis, *La lett. ital. nel sec. XIX*, vol. III, *G. Leopardi*, edited by W. Binni (Bari, 1953), p. 140, and Binni's note, p. 319. The predication of the subject ('more beautiful') is rarer and bolder with a verb such as 'rifulge' ('shines') than with one such as 'apparve' ['appeared'] (where 'to appear' is a quasi-copula and 'more beautiful' a nominal quasi-predicate). The verb 'rifulgere' is also lexically rarer than the verb 'apparire'; and the simple past 'apparve' ['appeared'] is due to the attraction exerted by 'credé' ['believed' – the same past form] in the following line (which De Sanctis also quotes), while between 'shines' and 'believed' there is an inconsistency of tense. Besides, as Binni notes, in De Sanctis' incorrect version, the whole stylistic and rythmic progress of the line becomes more pedestrian and 'popular' – which is precisely in keeping with the opposition he wanted to establish between Berchet's 'popularity' and Leopardi's early style.

Much the same could be said, not of every kind of forgetting (we shall return to this shortly, but of that type of inaccurate quotation that consists in the omission of a word or parenthesis in a text that has been memorized. Here, too, one cannot rule out the possibility that the omitted words were already missing from the text which was our source of information; but usually it is our memory which, in accordance with the tendencies we have already described (p. 35 sqq.), has accidentally missed out a word or parenthesis. We have already said (above, p. 158, case 2) that the subject is normally not aware of these omissions, because the overall sense of the phrase is preserved. But if it is a question of poetical texts, and if the reciter has some sense of metre, or, more simply, is gifted with a certain 'ear', he will notice the lacuna. Such is the case with the omission of *aliquis* (above, Chapter 3) and the amnesia in the recitation of Heine's poem (above, Chapter 9). On neither occasion does Freud even ask whether it is a case of a momentary (or anyhow short-lived) amnesia, or whether it is a long-standing one that has by then become consolidated as 'forgetting'. He straightaway opts for the first solution, and in fact provides explanations in each instance which, were they correct, would presuppose a temporary amnesia. However, Freud's young Jewish interlocutor was not a Latinist, nor was the corpulent gentleman who was fearful of a heart attack a student of German literature (otherwise Jung and Freud would have told us). Virgil's lines for the one, as Heine's poetry for the other, were reminiscences dating from their schooldays. The hypothesis that the forgetting of *aliquis* and of *mit weisser Decke* went back years or decades at least deserved to be taken into consideration;[6] all the more so, given that in other cases – the most insistent of which is

---

[6] One might note that this hypothesis is relevant even to the conclusions reached by the explanations of these instances of forgetting: if the latter had occurred during a time when the young Jew or Jung's patient had still been going to school, the interpretations put forward in *The Psychopathology of Everyday Life* would *ipso facto* collapse, since the unpleasant thoughts which gave rise to them (the feared pregnancy of the Italian woman, in the first case, and the fear of heart attack, in the second) would have occurred much later, and therefore could not have been responsible for the forgettings. Freud seems never to have considered this possibility.

infantile amnesia based on repression, to which we will shortly allude – Freud certainly allows that events, emotions and fears had been forgotten many, many years prior to the analysis. At the start of Chapter III, Freud appears to make a further concession: 'We are not usually surprised, it is true, if a formula learnt by heart, or a poem, can be reproduced only inaccurately *some time later,* with alterations and omissions' (my emphasis). But this is his reply: 'Since, however, this forgetting does not have a uniform effect on what has been learnt as a whole but seems on the contrary to break off isolated portions of it, it may be worth the trouble to submit to analytic investigation a few instances of such faulty reproduction.'

Here again, while it is correct to insist (although the condition will perhaps never be fulfilled in all cases) on locating the cause of gaps in memory and of 'slips', it is misleading to present these phenomena as 'breaking off isolated portions' in detachment from 'what has been learnt as a whole'. If in the example of *aliquis* and in that of Heine's poem anything remains exempt from the disfunction of memory, it is precisely the overall quality, and that is how it is in the majority of cases; at other times, it is the phonic and rhythmical values, above all rhyme, or the beginning of the line, which are best retained in memory; but in each line there are also certain elements most likely to be forgotten or altered. The case of the 'breaking-off' produced by repressed psychic material which intervenes to disturb the discourse in the most unforeseeable manner, is by far the rarest.

Not even the Chapter which ought to have treated the problem of the relationship between 'slip' and error more specifically – that is, the tenth, whose title is precisely *Irrtümer,* 'Errors' – reaches satisfactory conclusions. On the contrary, in certain respects, it represents the most disconcerting chapter of *The Psychopathology of Everyday Life,* both because of its position (it comes after the discussion of parapraxes – which in the strict sense consist of *acts* rather than verbal 'slips' – but tends to hark back to the first chapters whose theme was 'slips' pertaining to linguistic expressions), and because of the confused, if not actually unintelligible formulations it contains. This is something exceptional for a writer of such exemplary clarity as Freud. For example, at the outset of the chapter we find: 'Errors of memory are distinguished from forgetting accompanied by paramnesia by the single feature that in the former the error (the paramnesia) is not recognized as such but finds credence. The use of the term "error", however, seems to depend on yet another condition. We speak of "being in error" rather than of "remembering wrongly" where we wish to emphasize the characteristic of objective reality in the psychical material which we are trying to reproduce – that is to say, where what we are trying to remember is something different from a fact of our own psychical life: something rather, that is open to confirmation or refutation by the memory of other people. The antithesis to an error of memory in this sense is ignorance'.

I must confess in all honesty that I cannot understand (and the difficulty is not the fault of the Italian translation) what the precise distinction is that Freud intends to establish between error of memory (*Irrtum des Gedächtnisses*) and paramnesia (*Fehlerinnern*) on the one hand, and between error of memory and ignorance (*Unwissenheit*), on the other. I have the impression that, to the extent to which Freud distinguishes 'error' from 'paramnesia', he precisely identifies it with 'ignorance', and to the extent to which he opposes it to ignorance, he identifies it with 'paramnesia' (the distinction in this last case would refer simply to the point of view adopted – to whether emphasis is given to the pathological process which induces the subject to 'remember badly', or to the objective difference between that remembrance and actual reality).

But even if the incomprehensibility of the passage is to be wholly attributed, as perhaps it should, to my own incapacity and not to Freud's confused presentation, the examples which immediately follow (for which Freud draws upon errors he had made himself in the first edition of *The Interpretation of Dreams*) reveal that in Freud's opinion there is only one type of error that is not pertinent to psychoanalysis: this is the error caused, as we have said above, by 'false information', or, as Freud calls it, 'ignorance' – that due, in other words, not to an impression having been forgotten, or confused with another, but to the fact that it *had never been learnt*. Let us see what he says on p. 246 = 220: 'These errors that derive from repression are to be sharply distinguished from others which are based on genuine ignorance. Thus, for example, it was ignorance which made me think during an excursion to the

Wachau that I had come to the home of Fischhof, the revolutionary leader. The two places merely have the same name: Fischhof's Emmersdorf is in Carinthia. I, however, knew no better'.

Any other error, that consists of an alteration to an already learnt impression, is for Freud not only a 'slip' (which in the last analysis is true – see the beginning of this chapter), but must be a 'slip' due to repression. The three errors cited before that of the two towns of Emmersdorf are: a claim that Marburg (instead of Marbach) was the town where Schiller was born; a reference to Hannibal's father as Hasdrubal (instead of Hamilcar) – Hasdrubal being the name of a cousin of Hannibal who was the Carthaginian commander before him during the interval between Hamilcar's death and his own, and also the name of one of Hannibal's brothers, famous for his death in the battle of Metaurus; finally, an assertion that Zeus had not only dispossessed Kronos, but also castrated him, whereas the most prevalent mythological tradition makes Kronos responsible for this mutilation of his own father, Uranus.

Philology has a ready explanation for all three errors. Marburg is phonically similar to Marbach, and furthermore, it is a *lectio facilior* because it is a larger city than Marbach and – as Freud himself remarks *en passant* – possesses a university; besides, Freud had been awakened from a dream 'by the guard [on the train] calling out the name of Marburg station', and thus a feature analogous to that of 'the influence of context' in transcription (above, p. 97) had further contributed to the dominance of Marburg over Marbach. Hasdrubal is phonically very similar to Hannibal, with which it is associated (even more than than with Hamilcar, for which it was erroneously substituted in Freud's text), and the confusion was facilitated by the fact that the Hasdrubal who was Hannibal's cousin had been his *immediate* predecessor in the command of the Carthaginian army in Spain; while Hamilcar can be considered to have been his predecessor in the more general and proper sense (since Hasdrubal's command, as we have said, was an interlude of little importance): thus a confusion arose between Hannibal's father – who in effect was also his predecessor and created the preconditions of the war later fought by his son – and the truly immediate predecessor, who was also one of his more elderly relatives. The fact that Freud (as he himself reminds us here and elsewhere)[7] had from his boyhood cherished a particular admiration for Hannibal and for the house of Barca in general, and that he knew their history very well, presents no problem, since the 'slip', as we have already established, can affect material in which we are extremely well versed. It could even be that the emotion aroused in Freud by the memory of Hannibal and his family assisted in the confusion. Nor is there any difficulty, as any author of books or articles is aware, in the fact that Freud, once he had committed the 'slip' 'overlooked it in three sets of proofs' (p. 243 = 218). We all know that an author is the worst corrector of his own proofs precisely because he is the most interested in his own writing, of which he already has an intimate knowledge, and is thus the least inclined to read the proofs word by word. I have already cited examples of errors that have escaped notice despite repeated proof reading (pp. 149–50), and it would be easy for me to give others (in an early article I failed to notice a glaring misprint, *causale* ['causal'] for *casuale* ['casual'], which recurred twice in succession a short distance apart, and which, of course, altered the sense of the entire discourse).[8] Finally, the confusion between Kronos and Uranus – even admitting that Freud only knew later of the existence of another version of the myth, according to which it was Kronos himself who had been castrated by Zeus[9] – is perfectly explicable given that the two cases each concern the dispossession of the father by his son; while for Freud, who had by that time developed the theory of the Oedipus complex, castration is considered the hostile act that every child, on the basis of his identification with his father, expects of the latter . . . and which every father, in preventive defence, inevitably effects or projects in more or less symbolic fashion on his own son.[10]

[7] Since all his biographers mention it, we need hardly recall Freud's long-standing obsession with the character of Hannibal, which attained the proportions of a veritable identification and for long prevented him from setting foot in Rome.

[8] See 'Studi ital. di filol. classica' n.s. 23 (1949), p. 33 line 11 from the bottom of the page and p. 51 line 17.

[9] This other version of the myth is mentioned by Freud himself, (p. 243 note = 218 note), but he does not say whether he only became aware of it later, although this seems to be the case.

[10] Roazen (*Broth. Anim.*, p. 112): 'While a son may hate a father surrogate, it is equally likely for an older man to be jealous of a younger one. The Oedipus

But precisely because in Freud's doctrine, between the error that results from lack of information, and the error derived from repression, *tertium non datur* ['there is no third way'], he is obliged to supply a psychoanalytic explanation of all three 'slips' – which are then presented as 'unconscious vendettas' whose motives are so intimate that in an account of what are his own dreams, Freud prefers to keep them concealed. The explanations, especially the second and third, are as usual so contorted as to arouse the most justified suspicions of an '*a posteriori* psychologization'. Here too, moreover, a series of counter-examples would be eminently possible. *The Interpretation of Dreams* is a book that *abounds* with narratives that stop short, or have been emended in order not to violate professional secrecy, or to prevent the exposure of Freud's own sentiments and experiences. If it had to be supposed that every one of these innocent insincerities had its corresponding 'slip' (Freud declares a little later in *The Psychopathology*, p. 247 = 221, that he is 'scarcely able to tell lies any more. (. . .) As often as I try to distort something I succumb to an error or some other parapraxis'), not only *The Interpretation of Dreams*, but all Freud's other writings which refer to individual episodes of neurosis would be laden with 'slips'.

But the limitations of Freud's doctrine are even more visible in his theory of forgetting than in his theory of 'slips' – with which, for that matter, it is strictly connected. Here, as we know, he had an illustrious precursor in Nietzsche, even if a relationship of direct descent between the two would seem to be excluded. Nietzsche, in fact, lacks any truly specific theory of forgetting in terms of repression. On the one hand, he warns against the illusion that we have any real knowledge, simply by virtue of the fact that we have given it a name ('forgetting', 'oblivion'), of a process of which we are nearly entirely ignorant – even of whether it at times amounts to a genuine cancellation of what we once knew or

---

complex should not be presented only from the point of view of the son. How does a father react to murderous hate?' A little further on (p. 113): 'Freud's male pupils wanted his love, but he gave it only if they came close to castrating themselves as creative individuals.' See also G. Devereux's altogether convincing remarks, which are taken up and developed by M. Schatzman (*Soul Murder*, London, 1973, pp. 99–103, 107 sq.) on the 'Laius complex'.

experienced, or whether it always consists simply in a suspension of this. On the other hand, he interprets oblivion not as a merely passive fact but as an active force, comparable to the process of digestion and assimilation of food, whose effect is to nourish the organism and enable subsequent replenishment.[11] Freud's theory concurs with Nietzsche's in its refusal to consider forgetting as something obvious and in its interpretation of it as an active process. But in addition (although a first intimation of this too is to be found in Nietzsche)[12] Freud develops a specific theory of forgetting as a mechanism of repression, which now and then allows for the existence, as we have seen, of another type of forgetting due to inattention – but whose overall tendency is to reduce to the minimum, or directly deny, the importance of the latter.

It is always a progress, of course, to see a problem in what common sense regards as 'natural' and in need of no explanation. But emphasis on the problematic nature of the phenomenon, and the need for investigation of it, must hold good as much for remembering (and all other mental processes) as it does for forgetting. Oddly enough, however, Freud tends, even more than Nietzsche, to regard 'remembering' as obvious and only sees forgetting as 'problematic', whereas in fact each process demands equal explanation. Moreover, however displeasing it may be not only to Freudians but also to left-wing psychologists (anti-Freudian for social and political reasons which, as I have said, I share, though I do not believe an assessment of Freud's work can be reduced to such terms), any such account must necessarily have recourse to neurophysiology – even if it cannot be exclusively neurophysiological. If we maintain, as Freud does – and within certain limits legitimately, since psychology or any other human science can only achieve the maximum of scientificity and materialism possible at any given stage of cultural development, and cannot

[11] See F. Nietzsche, *Werke*, Krit. Gesamtausgabe herausg. von G. Colli und M. Montinari, 5. Abteil., I. (Berlin 1971), p. 115 (= *Dawn of Day*, London and Edinburgh, 1911, aphorism 126); and, more fully, 6. Abteil., II (Berlin, 1968), p. 307 (= *Genealogy of Morals*, London and Edinburgh, 1911, beginning of Chap. II). I owe these and other Nietzschean references to my friend Mazzino Montinari.

[12] Ed. cit., 6. Abteil., II (Berlin, 1968), p. 86 (= *Beyond Good and Evil*, aphorism 68): the passage is cited by Freud, p. 162 = 146 sq. in a note added in 1910.

passively await an ultimate and perfect fusion with the natural sciences – that psychology has a provisional and relative level of autonomy from its neurophysiological base, we can see how many of Freud's ideas on the problem of forgetting are even at this level arbitrary 'postulates', uncontrolled by either observation or experiment. To say that forgetting is an active force and not a *vis inertiae* is absolutely right given we want to polemicize against the idea that forgetting is a cancellation of memory due simply to the effect of time – in other words, if we want to stress that any account of forgetting cannot abstract from the subject's interest in any particular recollection. But this applies *equally to his interest and to his disinterest*. By far the greater proportion of what we forget takes the form of 'mental waste' which, in accordance with a principle of economy (our brain's capacity to store memories is not unlimited), is eliminated by our mind in order to make space for fresh remembrances. That is not to say, of course, that among the dismissed memories there are not some which it would have been very useful to retain; it means only that during a certain phase of my psychic (and social and cultural) life, I had little interest in certain thoughts and experiences as I lived them. If the 'active force' of forgetting also, and above all, designates this capacity to 'eliminate the superfluous', we would accept it; if it is taken only to designate repression, our concept of forgetting will be quite incomplete (since one recalls and does not forget what is unpleasant much more often then Freud is disposed to allow!)[13] and we will be condemned to invent illusory explanations of the type we have cited many times, for nearly all instances of forgetting.

The Freudian theory of infantile amnesia is the prime example of this at the macroscopic level. 'We take the fact of infantile amnesia – the loss, that is, of the memories of the first years of life – much too easily; and we fail to look upon it as a strange riddle. We forget how high are the intellectual achievements and how complicated the emotional impulses of which a child of some four years is

---

[13] Freud never asserted that the tendency to repress unpleasant thoughts always prevails (see for example p. $163 = 147$); but, confronted with the need to explain an instance of forgetting, he never assumed an initially unprejudiced position but always tried to attribute it to repression. Repression is therefore given a statistically false and 'inflated' status in his account.

capable, and we ought to be positively astonished that the memory of later years has as a rule preserved so little of these mental processes.' (p. 54 = 46) I am well aware that any really serious discussion of this 'marvel' as Freud sees it, and of which he has a ready rationale, would involve a consideration of the entire Freudian theory of infantile sexuality. But in the meantime, we may legitimately ourselves marvel at the confidence with which Freud postulates a synchronic development of all the child's mental and psychical faculties, and excludes, for no plausible motive, the possibility that the development of intelligence, affectivity and memory could proceed at significantly different rates – as is the case with the various faculties which are broadly grouped together under the title of 'intelligence';[14] or with the development of the diverse mechanisms and systems of the child's body, and their differing functions in relation to the outside world; or again with the process of senile decay, which also occurs at anything but a 'uniform' rate. We are also entitled to ask how it is that a child forgets not only his own 'Oedipal' emotions and experiences, which are unpleasant and thus destined to be repressed, but also his pleasant experiences (my friend Giuseppe Giordani has remarked on this to me). I am not oblivious to the banal and 'irritating' nature of these objections. But unless one is to resort to a specialist refusal to discuss with laymen, one must be able – if possible without sophisms – to reply to vexing queries of this sort.

What of everything that we learnt at school, and have forgotten (sometimes very rapidly – for example, immediately after an examination) due to lack of interest and disuse? If we extend the concept of repression – and it may be legitimate to do so – to include, among unpleasant psychic material, that which we were *forced* to learn, and which even at the time had no interest for us whatsoever, then we may quite tenably consider such instances of forgetting as amnesias derived from repression. But Freud does

[14] It is well known that the work of Jean Piaget and his followers represents a decisive progress in this field of research. This started after the First World War – in other words, it post-dates the first phase of Freud's thinking. But even before Piaget, Freud's 'astonishment' at the fact of infantile amnesia, and the explanations by which he sought to account for it, could not but encounter objections at the level of common sense.

not seem content with this. He relates the case of an examinee, who in answer to a question about representatives of Epicurean philosophy in modern times, mentioned the name of Gassendi and was congratulated by his teacher, who passed him *summa cum laude*. In reality, the student had been lucky: two days before, in a café, he had heard someone speak of Gassendi's epicureanism, whereas up to that point he had been ignorant even of his existence. 'The result of this (. . .) was a subsequent obstinate tendency to forget the name Gassendi. My guilty conscience is, I think, to blame for my inability to remember the name in spite of all my efforts; for I really ought not to have known it on that occasion either.' (p. 33 = 27)

The student thus confesses a 'guilty conscience' and therewith provides Freud with his proof (see above, Chapter 5). But how many sins – especially if they consist not in evil deeds but in wicked thoughts, together with their respective scruples and remorses – have been, not revealed, but *created* by the Catholic institution of confession! Freud's argument that 'the reader would have to know the high value he [the student, now graduated], sets on his doctorate and for how many other things it has to serve as a substitute' cuts two ways. It might help us to understand the reason for the exaggerated importance the student attached to his 'guilt' for a success that had been merely fortuitous – this is Freud's interpretation. But it might also make us suspect that this student was given to 'self-torture' of a kind that would induce him to see his relatively innocent amnesia as a guilt complex. From time immemorial, items of information which we hardly can be said to know, but which 'stick' in the mind under the impulse of examination conditions, are 'forgotten overnight'.

For that matter, we tend to forget even what we have learnt voluntarily, once this ceases to be an object of constant or recurrent interest. Freud is so bent on enlarging the field of application of a very specialized type of forgetting that he minimizes, on the one hand, this 'physiological' forgetting, and, on the other hand, the pathological forgetting which is due to organic illnesses such as arteriosclerosis.

Some Provisional
Conclusions

What may well most irk readers of this little book – not only more or less orthodox Freudians, but also opponents of Freud – is its insistence on the sophistry with which Freud accommodates his explanations to the facts. Of the three objections to psychoanalysis which I outlined in the first chapter, could I not have chosen to develop the first, which was most directly concerned with the political and social limits of Freudianism? The second objection – that psychoanalysis is insufficiently materialist and unduly removed from neurophysiology – is certain to incite the reserve of readers on the left, for whom this book is primarily intended. Yet I fear the third order of objections on which we have just remarked may leave them even more indifferent or hostile. Many will see it as no more than a façade behind which we have pursued a petty hunt for errors of the sort that we solemnly declared at the outset of this work we precisely wanted to avoid. Above all, they will detect here the ideal of a neutral and objectively true science, which they consider to be one of the most dangerous mystifications of bourgeois culture.

Now, a critique of Freudianism as an ideology has been assayed in the course of this work, above all in Chapter 8. It has been directed, not so much at Freud's work as a whole (on which there is an abundant literature that is in little need of repetition), as in particular at *The Psychopathology of Everyday Life,* which hitherto has been too little examined from this standpoint. I shall have something more to say on it in these last pages. But at the outset of the first chapter, I declared my commitment – and have later re-emphasized it – to that small number of Western Marxists or aspirant Marxists (especially few on the militant and anti-institutional left, which is where I would like this to find a hearing) who refuse to make a gift of scientific objectivity to the bourgeois and the reformist, and to identify knowledge simply with practice – thereby abandoning materialism and unwittingly regressing to 19th century trends of bourgeois activism or pre-Marxist utopian socialism, instead of developing the *'scientific* socialism' which Marx and Engels wanted and hoped to found.

Scientific socialism involves at once dissociation from utopian socialism, and rejection of a bourgeois science which functions merely as an apology for the established order. There were good reasons for the reappearance of utopianism in the 60's, when Marxism re-emerged in the West as a revolutionary force (although still a minority one). The fundamental cause of this phenomenon has been the tragic delay of a proletarian revolution in the industrialized West, and the capacity for 'self-immunization' and survival displayed by late capitalism. Disillusion with the various 'socialisms in one country' has been another, related determinant. No Marxist today can limit himself to a mere perusal of the 'sacred texts'. Nor is an attempt to recover the work of Marx alone, from the supposed falsifications of Engels and Lenin, an adequate political solution – even if it were not historiographically invalid. The truth is that there is a need (an urgent one) for a profound revision of the kind of which Lenin spoke, which has nothing to do with 'revisionism' in the sense in which that word is commonly used. But this revision should be a refoundation of *revolutionary-scientific* communism. We cannot dispense with either of these two terms. The first is essential because capitalism cannot be 'reformed' except in keeping with its *own* laws of development, which lead to the ever greater alienation of man, and ultimately to the barbarization and annihilation of all humanity. The second is imperative because a polemic against science (as distinct from false science or capitalist use of science) is a counsel of despair.

A scientific communism also signifies a non-simplistic relationship to bourgeois science. The latter (as Marx, Engels, Lenin and Trotsky always correctly argued) is not totally ideological, but has a genuinely scientific content which reveals an objective reality, that as such is in a certain sense always 'neutral' – even if the practical need which motivates any given programme of research is anything but neutral, as is not only the use made of scientific knowledge (by ourselves or the bourgeoisie), but also the organization of scientific research itself, and the participation or exclusion of 'non-specialists' in it.

Nor can we even say that the relationship between science and ideology has remained, or is destined to remain, invariant within bourgeois culture. The less the bourgeoisie has to combat the 'enemies on its right' against which it had to struggle during its historical ascent, the more conservative it becomes as a class (innovatory only in the interests of survival), and the more its science loses the democratic and humanitarian spirit of its better days – even then inherently contradictory, but not a mere 'fraud'. Scientific progress continues to be made today, but it is increasingly the work of highly specialized elites, in the best of cases dedicated to an illusory ideal of 'pure research', and in the worst conscious servants of capitalist industry. Once its 'enemies on the right' ceased to exist, or were reduced to vestiges of the past, the bourgeoisie had exhausted its historical function. Today it deserves to perish: it survives only because its loss of any progressive function has not been accompanied by a sufficient maturation of the working class in the advanced industrial countries – of a proletariat capable of resisting the alternative of reformism or fascism, and of forging its own antagonistic vision of society as a whole, with an entirely distinct system of needs and values.

Since the turn of this century, the bourgeoisie has known and felt that it deserved to die. At times it reacts to this knowledge with intoxicated violence and brutal activism, with a parade of jingoistic and anti-decadent mythologies, with rabid invective not only against the proletariat but also any fraction of its own class which yields to 'defeatism', even resorting to demagogic propaganda that what is 'bourgeois' is not capitalism and its repressive apparatus, but particular forms of intellectual refinement. At other times, on the contrary, it has made dolorous or ironic confession of its own infirmity and iniquity. Thus on the one hand there have been fascist trends in bourgeois society, vaunting a crude 'health' and bestial myths of blood and race, and on the other hand, there have been bourgeois trends of a refined decadence.

We are not concerned here with the former. It may, however, be said that Stalinism, although it played an essential role in the political and military defeat of fascism, nevertheless promoted a culture that was not entirely antagonistic to that of the latter, but *in part* competitive with it. It exalted an abstract and false image of a docilely content proletariat, heir to the whole tradition of bourgeois moralism and its work and family ethic. The result was eventually, with the crisis of Stalinism, to shift many intellectuals on the left, even in Eastern Europe, towards a no less uncritical allegiance to the ideologies of that *other* bourgeois culture – ranging from neopositivism to psychoanalysis or structuralism – and towards a confusion of avant-garde art, even in its most exhibitionist and insufferable forms, with avant-garde politics.

By comparison with this 'healthy' (in reality, all too frustrated and repressed) fascist and clerical type of bourgeoisie, it scarcely needs to be said how much more worthy of respect is the type of intelligentsia we have characterized as refined-decadent – indeed worthy of admiration in the person of its best representatives, even from militant opponents of the bourgeoisie. Psychoanalysis is an essential component of the ideology of this intelligentsia.[1] It is more

[1] The relationship between these two trends of 20th century bourgeois thought needs an extended treatment that is not possible here. We shall content ourselves with a very schematic comment on a single aspect of it, which is certainly no novelty, but is useful to remember. However intense the antagonism between these two sectors of the bourgeoisie has been in certain periods, in the great majority of cases the 'refined' bourgeoisie has joined forces with the crude and chauvinist bourgeoisie, whenever the latter has allowed it, in defence of the nation and suppression of the proletariat. One has only to think of its interventionism during the First World War (here I refer, of course, not just to Italy but to all the states in the conflict) and of its tolerance of Fascism and Nazism. For the most part, it has been the philistine-nationalistic bourgeoisie which has broken with this alliance whenever it felt strong enough 'to go it alone', and extended its persecution of the proletariat to conspicuous groups within the 'refined' bourgeoisie – now considered 'defeatist' or even (wrongly) complicit with communists. Yet even when confronted with the first unambiguous signs of a rupture in the alliance, the 'refined' bourgeoisie has very often continued to regard the proletariat as its principal enemy, and to delude itself that the former entente, or at least mutual tolerance, could be re-established with the nationalist bourgeoisie. Not even Freud, nor the majority of his followers, were immune to this blindness. For too long they remained convinced that it was enough to ostracize and eventually banish the communist Reich from the ranks of psychoanalysis, in order to evade Nazi persecution. In this respect, see: *Reich Speaks of Freud,* pp. 155 (where Freud's shameful footnote to Reich's article of 1932 is

interesting and difficult to establish a comparison between its capacity for knowledge of objective reality, or its relationship to science and ideology, and those of e.g. the mid- 19th century or 18th century phases of bourgeois culture itself. Consciousness of belonging to a class in crisis *can* confer on its most gifted members the benefits of cognitive insight that loss of self-idealization affords. It may permit a disenchanted and demythicized view of one's own class. The great bourgeois writers of the 20th century have been examples, and Freud was another. In their works, in different yet related ways, the misery and perfidy of the bourgeoisie found its most impious critics within its own ranks.

On the other hand, however, a self-criticism which does not conclude in an alignment with the oppressed class, in the end inevitably becomes in some sort a self-justification. However 'disenchanted', such a self-criticism contaminates itself anew with ideology. The refined-decadent type of bourgeoisie is right in its rejection of a certain expedient optimism characteristic of its progressive 19th century forefathers. It is also right in its acknow-ledgment of a 'human unhappiness in general' from which (so far as we can see) not even communism will be wholly able to liberate us. But it then ideologically conflates this general unhap-piness with the specific unhappiness which is historically and socially determined. Indeed, for the most part it does not see even unhappiness in general with the lucid materialist consciousness of a Leopardi, as the effect of man's biological frailty and the oppres-sion exercised over him by nature, but interprets it in a romantic-existentialist register of a more Schopenhauerian than Leopardian type. The result is often a complete reversal of perspective in which individual sufferers become 'elect souls', who nearly always belong to the upper classes. For Freud himself, neurosis is an illness more or less confined to the bourgeoisie, and psychoanalysis a method designed for the therapeutic needs of that class (with the addition, at the most, of certain 'particularly deserving' members of the proletariat)[2] – not only because of the unavoidable costliness of

---

reproduced), 158 sq., 161 sq., 164 sq. and passim. This does not, of course, in any way mitigate the moral odium and intellectual obtuseness of the persecutors of psychoanalysis, as of every other movement of 'refined' bourgeois thought.

[2] See above, Chapter 8, note 12.

the cure, but also because it demands patients of considerable culture and psychological nicety. If at the beginning of his studies every pupil of psychoanalysis has to become a patient of an analyst, every patient has to become to some extent a pupil.

Moreover, the dual refusal to see to what extent human un-happiness – not only in work relations, but also in customs, in family and sexual morality – is determined by the division of society into classes, and to what extent it is also due to the oppression that nature[3] exercises over man, leads to a search for something 'unavowable' behind every form of human behaviour which is or appears to be abnormal, behind every manifestation of individual discontent – which can be ascertained only by psycho-logy. While the accusation of pansexuality often levelled at psychoanalysis is largely wide of the mark, the charge of psycho-logism is, I believe, much more accurate. The preferred explanation is always the most tortuous and complicated, and thus the most 'misanthropic'. Even in this respect, Freud displays the temper of his time – a period in which psychologism reigned supreme throughout European bourgeois culture and literature. Thus, up to a point, he interprets a psychological complexity that is really existent in his patients; but beyond that point he 'over-interprets'[4] them. We have already considered quite enough examples of this over-interpretation. I should like to cite just one more, this too taken from *The Psychopathology of Everyday Life*, because in its brevity and apparent simplicity, it epitomizes the completely arbitrary nature of so many of the cases. 'A young father presented himself before the registrar of births to give notice of the birth of his second daughter. When asked what the child's name was to be, he answered "Hanna", and had to be told by the official that he already had a child of that name. We may conclude that the second daughter was not quite so welcome as the first had been.' (p. 249—224)

[3] For Freud's underestimation of this aspect (though he did not deny it), see above, p. 114 sq.

[4] I am using the term 'over-interpretation' in its philological sense (of an over-subtle and contorted interpretation which reads more into the text than is actually present in it). The same term (in German *Uberdeutung*) acquired a different meaning in psychoanalysis: see Laplanche-Pontalis, *The Language of Psycho-analysis*, cit. p. 293 sq.

From what can we 'conclude' this? From the fact that by giving the name of his first-born he indicated a preference for her, and thus annoyance at the birth of the second child? But would it not be just as legitimate and no less arbitrary to argue that the repetition of the name suggested that he held the two children in equal affection? The one explanation is worth the other, and neither of them is worth much. The least arbitrary explanation is in terms of the persistance of habit. The father had already uttered the name of his first child a thousand times, and had already said, in reply to innumerable queries, that she was called 'Hanna'. A moment of distraction or emotion served to activate a conditioned reflex – he was not yet accustomed (after all it was the first time that it was needed!) to give a different answer to the question 'What is the little girl called?' That is probably all there is to it. But an explanation of this kind does not expose any – even relatively innocent – 'hidden quirk' of the human mind, and thus it does not recommend itself to depth psychologists.

It is this hyper-psychological bias which is, I think, the principal cause of the arbitrary interpretations to which Freud subjects the 'slip', the dream, and everything we do. It is the effort to penetrate *at all times* to an underlying, unpleasant reality arrived at only by dint of a victory over the subject's resistances, which makes him opt in the majority of cases for the interpretation which is most intriguing – and most improbable. We have seen that this hyper-trophy of psychologism corresponds on the one hand to a refusal to acknowledge the class division of society and the unhappiness it produces, and on the other to a dissociation of psychology from neurophysiology (and thus to an at least potential anti-materialism). We may now conclude that the sophisms and forced interpretations which we initially characterized as generically anti-scientific, can themselves be said to form (if only indirectly) the 'ideological' limit of psychoanalysis. If scientists like Darwin and Pavlov did not feel any tormenting pressure to load the dice, this cannot simply be attributed to their greater 'scientific honesty' – subjectively, Freud was equally honest.[5] The cause is rather to be sought in the fact

[5] I am prepared to concede this, though I must confess that I am not entirely convinced of it. It seems difficult to attribute Freud's reticence on certain matters of extreme importance – for example in the account of 'little Hans' and that of

that Darwin still shared the faith of a bourgeoisie that saw its mission as the progress and advancement of knowledge. In Pavlov's case, the transition from a traditional bourgeois background to the new reality of the Soviet Union had no major impact;[6] it was not that he was indifferent to the change in his environment, but thanks in part to the freedom of research allowed him under Stalinism, he was spared the experience of its worst devastations. It was not a question of any difference in 'temperament', therefore – of a more or less tranquil or neurotic individual disposition. Pavlov and Darwin (even more so) experienced neurosis, and paid the price in terms of diminished personal happiness;[7] but they were not surrounded by an environment that was collectively neurotic and inducive of neurosis. They were yet further removed from the peculiarly intensive neurotic atmosphere of the micro-society experienced by Freud, who lived through the late 19th and early 20th century crisis of Central Europe – a bourgeois in a bourgeois society which discriminated against him as a Jew, and a denizen of the hallucinating ambience of the Psychoanalytic Society.

There is no doubt as to the major relevance – one that many Freudians admit was on the whole retrogressive – of the change in direction that was marked by the foundation of the journal *Imago* and became accentuated in the war, after the war and during the

---

Schreber, whose effect is to allow certain serious difficulties in the adaptation of his theory to these cases to pass unobserved–to unconscious 'repression' on the part of Freud himself: see M. Schatzman, *Soul Murder,* op. cit., p. 93 sqq. Moreover, certain of the most forced interpretations of 'slips' and dreams appear to be located in, so to speak, an intermediate zone between an unconscious tendency to manipulate the data to the greater benefit of the theory, and a conscious falsification. But the problem does not have any very great importance: Freud could always consider such arbitrary interpretations as provisional hypotheses whose confirmation would be the task of subsequent developments in psychoanalysis. In any case, what is at issue is not vulgar bad faith, but Freud's undue attachment to a theory to which he had dedicated his existence.

[6] Felice Persanti provides an excellent account in his profile of Pavlov ('I protagonisti della storia universale' 54, Milan, CEI, 1965, especially p. 438 sqq.) and in his introduction to Pavlov, *I mercoledì* (Florence, 1970).

[7] So far as Darwin is concerned, one has only to recall what he himself says in his *Autobiography* about his hyper-emotionality, his reluctance to appear in public, indeed his pathological need for a tranquil and secluded life. For Pavlov, see the description he himself gives of his phobias in *I mercoledì* (cit. in the preceding note), pp. 322–4.

period of Freud's illness, when a predominant interest in the theory of sexuality and the cure of neurosis gave way to an increasing bias towards theories of 'civilization' in general and the Death Instinct was introduced to accompany Eros. However, we do not subscribe to the common view that it was only in this later phase that Freud abandoned scientificity for apriorism. (Indeed, we should admire his heroic struggle against a mortal disease and his effort to respond, even if from within a bourgeois perspective, to the clamorous problems posed by the barbarism of the war and its aftermath.) On the contrary, there are already very strong anti-scientific tendencies in Freud's early work. The difference lies in the fact that these do not assume the form of the great 'collective myths' which first appear in *Totem and Taboo* and achieve their final development in *Moses and Monotheism,* but rather of arbitrary and forced interpretations of dreams, 'slips' and neurotic symptoms. It is Freud the interpreter who must first of all be criticized. To judge from the title, we might have expected that Paul Ricoeur would have made this topic his priority in *De l'Interpretation.* But on reading the book, one realizes that, apart from some isolated insights, Ricoeur has an altogether different aim in mind – to compound a strange brew of Freudianism and religion, in which the more imbued with mystery an interpretation, the better it pleases. It is certainly commendable that Ricoeur opts for Freud rather than Jung;[8] however, one has the impression that this choice is often the product of a misunderstanding and that Ricoeur approves of Freud precisely to the extent that his work anticipates or emulates that of Jung.

We too prefer the early Freud. But for his scientific papers, not for his books of interpretation. His masterpiece remains the *Three Essays on the Theory of Sexuality.* Even in the *Lectures* of 1915–16 the best pages are those in which he takes up and summarizes the themes of the *Three Essays.* Can one legitimately distinguish these works from *The Interpretation of Dreams* and *The Psychopathology*

[8] P. Ricoeur, *Freud and Philosophy, an essay on interpretation* (New Haven and London, 1970 – original French edition, 1965), p. 176: 'I must admit that this firmness and rigour makes me prefer Freud to Jung. With Freud I know where I am and where I am going; with Jung everything risks being confused: the psychism, the soul, the archetypes, the sacred.'

of Everyday Life? Certainly not in any absolute way: Freud would have replied that without the 'royal road' provided by the interpretation of dreams, and in a lesser way by that of 'slips' and other parapraxes, it would not have been possible either for him to have made the discoveries expounded in the *Three Essays,* or for others to have accepted these.[9] All the same, such a claim is really only relevant to the weakest and most contestable aspects of the Three Essays (fear of castration, which in fact is scarcely mentioned in the work, and infantile amnesia) – whereas the essential nucleus of the work, which is sufficient alone to guarantee Freud's greatness, consists of the distinction between 'sexuality' in the wide sense and 'genitality', and hence the explanation of the so-called perversions as infantile erotic tendencies and the theorization of the child as 'polymorphously perverse'. All of this is wholly acceptable or can be taken as the basis for further discussion and development even by someone who has grave reservations about the analytic method and its all-purpose symbolism.

It is also significant that in the *Three Essays* Freud reveals an exceptional sensitivity to the problematic nature of his material, and an intense awareness (to be found elsewhere only in a few writings of this period, and in nearly all his later works increasingly reduced to a mere token) of the insufficiency of a theory of sexuality that was as yet without an adequate basis in physiology and biochemistry.[10] The ostentatious confidence and dogmatism of the works of 'interpretation', on the other hand, although these for the most part pre-date the *Three Essays,* directly reflect the weakness of their solutions. Furthermore, the *Three Essays,* together with some of his writings on the sexual education of children

---

[9] Freud presents the case of *Little Hans* (1909) = *Analysis of a Phobia in a Five-Year-Old Boy, SE* X 3 sqq., right from the first pages as a direct experimental verification – obtained by means of the analysis of a child – of results at which he had previously arrived, in the *Three Essays,* from the analysis of neurotic adults.

[10] See the end of *Drei Abhandlungen zur Sexualtheorie, GW* V 145 = *Three Essays on the Theory of Sexuality, SE* VII 243: 'The unsatisfactory conclusion, however, that emerges from these investigations of the disturbances of sexual life is that we know far too little of the biological processes constituting the essence of sexuality to be able to construct from our fragmentary information a theory adequate to the understanding alike of normal and of pathological conditions.'

published shortly afterwards, mark the moment at which Freud appears most convinced of the necessity of a prophylaxis of infantile neurosis by means of a more liberal sexual formation.[11] The accent is here put on sexual repression as the outcome of a false civilization, rather than the inevitable price of any civilization; and despite the inevitable absence of any emphasis on the class divisions of society, or more generally on the relations of *power* that obtain in every hierarchical society and the part they play in the creation of neurosis, there is at least the idea that a reform of infantile sexual up-bringing would involve a reform of society as a whole, even if only in the sense of its radical laicization.[12] It was from the *Three Essays* – and related writings of the same period – that Reich later took his inspiration. He was right to give priority to these studies, though he was careful to point out what he considered to be their limitations.[13]

One of the fundamental contrasts to be noted in Freud's work, as soon as he abandoned his very early neurophysiological studies, is between a materialist scientific formation, which may be traced primarily if indirectly back to Helmholtz, and a general cultural formation in the 'humanities', in which literature and the visual arts feature largely (Freud frequently appeals to the latter, with a certain anti-academic coquetry, as 'documents' that confirm psychoanalytic theory), and powerful anti-materialist and anti-Enlightenment impulses predominate. A contrast of this kind

[11] The letter to M. Fürst on *The Sexual Enlightenment of Children* (1907, in *GW* VII 19 sqq. = *SE* IX 131 sqq.) and the paper on *'Civilised' Sexual Morality and Modern Nervous Illness* (1908, in *GW* VII 143 sqq. = *SE* IX 179 sqq.), are particularly important from this standpoint.

[12] See the end of the first of the two writings cited in the preceding note.

[13] See the letters of 1935 to Lotte Liebeck, in *Reich Speaks of Freud,* op. cit., pp. 205 sq., 212 sq.; and Reich's positive evaluation of Freud's work on *'Civilised' Sexual Morality* (cited above, note 11), in *Sexual Revolution* (London, 1969), p. 10 sq. In one respect, however, Freud and Reich alike maintained a traditionalist attitude: their justification of 'polymorphism' was that it was a necessary transitional stage prior to the attainment of genitality (in the strict sense) as the 'norm' for an adult. But once the autonomous value of sexual hedonism has been accepted (not inevitably bound to reproduction), there is no reason to restrict polymorphism to the infantile stage. This is not, of course, in any way to reduce the communist idea of 'happiness' merely to sexuality, even in its widest sense – which would constitute an immense improverishment of the term. Besides the hints of this to be found in Marcuse, see e.g. Shulamith Firestone, *The Dialectic of Sex* (London, 1972), p. 221, sqq.

already existed, and still persists in the culture of very many scientists, especially doctors, who are materialist – often vulgar materialist – in what relates directly to their science, yet 'humanist' or even fideist (and hence politically conservative or naively reformist) in their overall vision of reality. Lenin was acutely aware of this contradiction, and predicted that the anti-materialist shift within European bourgeois culture towards the end of the 19th century would ultimately exacerbate this dichotomy within the culture of scientists as well. In a man possessed of Freud's exceptional breadth of culture and interests, this tension would obviously assume a much more subtle form than in many of his contemporaries, however celebrated as scientists. We must never forget his 'determinism', which no debate on the concept of causality (a scientifically legitimate and necessary debate, yet all too often liable to regressive philosophical disquisitions) ever managed to shake; nor his atheism. These aspects of his cultural personality, which go well beyond his specialist work, preclude any definition of Freud as a 'guilty materialist' (Lenin's pertinent formula for the scientists he was attacking), or as an idealist who more or less unconsciously adopted a materialist method for pragmatic purposes within the confines of his own science.

The contradiction, rather, is *internal* to all these aspects of Freud's thought. What we have termed his general cultural 'humanism' is not just a characteristic – as with other scientists – of extra-scientific or vulgarly popular writings (which, in any case, form no part of Freud's work – not even his late anthropological and sociological essays can be dismissed so peremptorily), but affects the core of psychoanalysis itself, which is simultaneously a doctrine that never entirely abandoned certain materialist principles, *and* a metaphysical and even mythological construction.

The contradiction is rendered more complex by the fact that Freud combined what can only be termed a philosophical vocation (at times he explicitly acknowledged its nature as such) with a strange and ambivalent hostility towards philosophy.[14] It might be

[14] The main passages are quoted for example by P. Roazen, *Freud: Pol. and Soc.*, pp. 101–8. Although this book is very useful as a collection of material and evidence, it is greatly inferior to Roazen's work on Tausk and Freud (*Brother Animal*) to which we have referred frequently. In his biography of Freud

thought from many of his pronouncements that the latter was simply a case of the largely justified distrust of a man involved in experimental science for the grand speculative 'systems', the *Weltanschauungen* with all their apriorism and immunity to proof.[15] However, the philosophies to which he was most attracted, as he became more or less directly familiar with them, were precisely those which were most 'poetical', and richest in myth and fantasy – in short, the most anti-scientific. It is no accident that he was to acknowledge Nietzsche and later Schopenhauer as the thinkers who were most akin to him, his 'precursors' – even if he always scrupulously insisted that he had arrived at conclusions similar to theirs before he had read their works, and by purely scientific means. For its part, the literature of European decadence could scarcely have found so much inspiration in psychoanalysis, if this had really been a doctrine of materialist enlightenment.

Students of Freud, especially those who – with the best intentions – have argued for the materialist and enlightened nature of his work, do not seem to have paid sufficient attention to this paradox. It is certainly true that if we liberate the genuine Nietzsche from ultra-irrationalist and even pre-fascist interpretations of his work, we find a potent critic – even if an 'internal' critic – of the hypocrisy and false moralism of the bourgeois Christian ethic; and in his vitalism there are undoubtedly materialist and hedonist elements. But the aphoristic and contradictory character of Nietzsche's thought is such that it can instil materialism only in someone who has already become a materialist by another route (and not merely by pragmatic adaptation in a particular discipline). Certain of Nietzsche's professions are also genuinely enlightened – one need

---

and his pupils, Roazen succeeds much better in being at once affectionate and irreverent than either Jones (apologetics under the guise of objectivity) or Sachs (sympathetically, but irrationally laudatory). But in his exposition and criticism of Freud's political and social ideas, Roazen fails to take any account of their historical context, or to refer to the political forces and personalities at work at the time. His remarks on Marxism are incredibly superficial – if I am not mistaken, neither Reich nor Marcuse are so much as named!

[15] In addition to the passages cited by Roazen (see the preceding note), see the last Lecture of the second series (*GW* XV 170 sqq. = *New Introd. Lect. Psych.*, *SE* XXII 158 sqq.).

only recall, among others, the *Aurora* aphorism (197). But this is an enlightenment that is nearly entirely consumed in a polemic against a certain type of romanticism, and therewith remains within the limits of an exasperated aristocratism.[16] In the case of Schopenhauer – whose influence is in any case essentially restricted to Freud's late work – there is no need even for the niceties of distinction that Nietzsche allows us to make.

Compared with Germany, a more direct contact with the culture of the 18th century Enlightenment was relatively easy in Austria in the late 19th century, where a historian of classical thought who was also possessed of theoretical interests, such as Theodor Gomperz, could be formed by English philosophy (in which, as is known, the influence of the Enlightenment, uninterrupted by the wave of Romanticism in continental Europe, persisted late into the 19th century). In particular, Gomperz had admired John Stuart Mill, and promoted a translation of his works. Freud was responsible, under a commission from Gomperz (to whom he had been recommended by Franz Brentano), for the translation in 1880 of Volume 12 of this German edition of Mill.[17] Later, when the wife of Gomperz became a patient of Freud, she embarked on what proved an unsuccessful attempt to overcome the hostility of the Viennese university world towards Freud;[18] and in 1907, in answer to a query as to the 'ten best books' he had read, Freud included Gomperz's *Griechische Denker*.[19] However, neither Gomperz – whose works contain a vindication of naturalism, hedonism, and of the Sophist school, in contrast with the 'Platonocentric'

[16] This emerges more clearly than ever, I would say, from Thomas Mann's defence of Nietzsche's 'enlightenment' in the lecture of 1929 on *Freud's position in the history of Modern Thought* ('Criterion' 49, July, 1933), p. 549 sqq. Mazzino Montinari is, of course, right to object to Lukács's simplistic condemnation of Nietzsche (see his recent contribution to the collection by various authors, *Il caso Nietzsche*, Cremona, 1973). But the remarks made by Cesare Cases on Nietzsche ('Quaderni Piacentini' 50, July 1973, p. 136) remain valid – whose context makes it evident that the 'enlightenment' which Cases acknowledges in Nietzsche is to be understood in a very limited sense. See also D. Lanza, *Il suddito e la scienza,* in 'Belfagor' 29 (1974), p. 1 sqq., and esp. p. 14 sq.

[17] See Jones, *Life*, I, p. 61–2; P. Merlan, in 'Journ. of History of Ideas' 6 (1945), p. 375 sqq.

[18] Jones, *Life*, I, p. 373–4.

[19] Jones, *Life*, III, p. 453.

interpretation hitherto predominant in the study of Greek philosophy – nor his juvenile and perhaps (as Jones himself admits)
somewhat indifferent and literal translation of Mill, left any visible
traces on Freud's intellectual formation. Certainly he had his
reasons to be distrustful of the agnostic aspects of empirio-criticism
and later Viennese neopositivism – indeed in general of any revival
of subjectivist idealism.[20] But these were scarcely the hall-marks of
the 18th century Enlightenment! Yet Freud showed no interest in
either the materialist hedonism or the political and ethical amelior-
ism of its greatest thinkers. It has been claimed that there are
significant similarities between Freud's psychology and that of
Herbart,[21] between the Freudian collective unconscious and the
Kantian transcendental, between the Super-Ego and the Categorical
Imperative.[22] But these comparisons too do not appertain to the
materialism of the Enlightenment, for such analogies certainly do
not refer to the specifically enlightened dimension of Kant's
philosophy.

The apparent absence of any influence on Freud of such vulgar
materialists as Büchner, Moleschott or Vogt might be considered
evidence of his scientific rigour. But even Ernest Jones, who is
inclined to rationalize every aspect of Freud's life and ideas, and to

[20] See his acerbic anti-methodological remark (against Viennese logical
positivism) which Roazen, *Freud: Pol. and Soc.*, p. 109, cites from T. Reik's
memoirs: 'those critics who limit their studies to methodological investigations
remind me of people who are always polishing their glasses instead of putting
them on and seeing with them'. Note also, in the last Lecture of the second
series (*New Introd. Lect. Psych.*, *SE* XXII 175 sq.) his attack on philosophers
who deny external reality, whom he terms 'anarchists' or 'nihilist intellectuals' –
thereby ingenuously assimilating anarchism to socio-political nihilism. This was
in a way the obverse error to that of the idealist-revolutionary Marxism of the
early Lukács and Korsch, who assimilated acknowledgment of the objectivity
of the external world to a mystifying bourgeois 'reification'.

[21] See Jones, *Life*, I, p. 407 sqq. The analogies are, in fact, too striking to be
accidental; but Jones argues convincingly that the influence was *indirect*.

[22] Freud himself points to the similarities at several points. See especially
GW X 270 = the paper on *The Unconscious* (1915), *SE* XIV 162, and *GW* XIII
380 = *The Economic Problem of Masochism* (1924), *SE* XIX 167. See also the
conversation recorded by Marie Bonaparte, *Eros, Thanatos, Chronos* (Florence,
1973), pp. 160–3. Despite her existentialist leanings and her confusionism,
Marie Bonaparte proved herself, with regard to this single problem, as more of
a realist and potentially more of a materialist than Freud in his last years. She
dared to oppose the pro-Kantianism of the master with arguments that, although
somewhat naive, were essentially correct.

justify his work as a correct and coherent whole, considers it a 'baffling problem in the study of the development of (his) ideas, and also in that of his youthful personality' that Freud – despite his claim in *An Autobiographical Study* that he owed his first impulse towards scientific research to a reading of Darwin – always remained a convinced Lamarckian,[23] not a Darwinian, and un-critically believed in the hereditary nature of acquired charac-teristics. Among such inherited characteristics, he privileged psychic traits – indeed even specific thoughts, memories and regrets, starting with the killing of the Father by the primitive horde. The effect of this psychological Lamarckianism was to lend antiquated notions that had little to do with science, and a lot to do with the doctrine of Original Sin, an appearance of scientific respectability. The principle postulated by Haeckel, according to which the ontogenetic recapitulates the phylogenetic (a principle which any biologist today would accept at best as a crude approximation in need of very extensive qualification), becomes – especially from *Totem and Taboo* onwards – a device to enable Freud to attribute his speculative constructions to 'phylogenetic heredity'.[24] Virtually any contemporary Freudian would be quick to pronounce the harshest judgement on the 'vulgar materialist' Haeckel, with considerable reason. But he would also be prompt to minimize Freud's inheritance from Haeckel (which was neo-Lamarckian and mystico-vitalist rather than truly materialist) and to ignore the fact that it deteriorated yet further when Freud transposed it from

[23] Jones, *Life*, III, p. 332 sqq.

[24] P. Ricoeur (cited above, note 8), p. 188 sq., is correct to object to this un-controlled use of the concept of phylogenetic heredity. His criticism, however, is made from the 'right': he does not want to substitute Freudian myths by a more scientific explanation of the genesis of particular social institutions and collective psychological characteristics, but to dissolve the problem of temporal and historical genesis into that of a 'foundation', an ideal genesis. Thus his criticism of Freud ultimately comes to resemble that which Croce made of Vico. Marcuse, in Chapter 3 of *Eros and Civilization,* for his part tends to dismiss the science-fiction aspects of Freud's phylogenesis too expediently as irrelevant, treating them merely as a symbolic representation of repressive civilization. But one cannot, after Marx and after Engels, regress to a pure and simple meta-physical catastrophism. Marcuse's book does not altogether represent this, nor, as we know, is *Eros and Civilization* his last word on the subject. All the same, a lack of materialism is noticeable throughout his work, though less so than in that of the other members of the Frankfurt School.

the domain of biology to psychology and thence directly to society and culture.[25]

But in the late 19th and early 20th centuries, to call oneself a materialist – in any but the narrowly confined pragmatic or scientistic sense – necessarily involved some kind of serious, even if polemical, contact with Marxism. Now, what is astonishing about Freud is not his opposition to communism, for which in a sense we should be prepared, but his total lack of interest in Marxism. The form of 'communism' that took shape in Russia after Lenin's death, and later during the Stalinist epoch, was such as to justify many of Freud's reservations. For although it was his membership of the bourgeoisie that primarily accounted for these, this cannot, in all honesty, be said to have been their only motive. But what is really scandalous is that Freud, whose main interest lay in the problems of the genesis of civilization and the family, never felt any need to make a serious reckoning with Engels's *Origin of the Family* and in all probability was not even curious to read it; that he thought it possible to dismiss the whole of Marx's thought as 'not even materialist' but merely Hegelian, while at the same time on his own (damning) admission, he knew scarcely anything

[25] G. Jervis is correct in his negative judgement here (in the introduction to the Italian translation of *Eros and Civilization* – *Eros e civiltà*, Turin, 1964, p. 14). He refers to Le Bon's doctrine of 'the collective mind of the masses' (cited by Freud himself in *Group Psychology and the Analysis of the Ego*) and to Lamarck as antecedents for this theory of Freud's. But it should be emphasized that Freud's Lamarckianism, as is proved by the very use of the terms ontogenesis and phylogenesis, was mediated through Haeckel (see a note by A. Kardiner in Hook, p. 92 and, more superficially, Rapaport, *Structure*, p. 22). This was a damaging mediation, because the mystic vitalism which was always combined, though never truly fused, with the crude materialism in Haeckel, left its traces on Freud, even more detrimentally on Groddeck, and unfortunately on the later Reich too. Jones himself informs us (*Life*, III, p. 335 sqq.) that it was Freud's belief that this neo-Lamarckianism could reinforce the so-called principle of the 'omnipotence of thought' (not of course in the sense that a Fichte or a Gentile would have given to this scarcely reassuring expression, but in the sense of the determination exercised by unconscious psychic processes on the human body). It was a similar conception that made possible the growth of psychosomatic medicine, an important area of scientific study which is still capable of major developments. But it also provided the rationale in Groddeck's work, and to some extent in that of the late Reich, for the abandonment of materialism in favour of a confused 'animism'. Freud was more circumspect in this matter; but there are undeniable Groddeckian elements to be found in his work; see below, p. 199.

of Marxism; that he complacently asserted, in his attack on this Marxism, of which he was ignorant, that the origin of class society lay in racial differences;[26] and that he managed to spend his entire life in Austria yet remained unaware of the proletarianization of artisans and peasants, and of the growth of large-scale industry, when hundreds of members of the bourgeoisie less intelligent than he, and more interested in the preservation of their own class, knew only too well that these were not matters of 'race' nor even purely of technology. Yet it is perhaps most significant of all that, contrary to what we might have expected, Freud in his later period was rather more hostile to Marxism than to the USSR. Despite the aversion to communist 'fanaticism'[27] inspired in him by the

[26] See the whole of the final section of the last Lecture of 1932, *GW* XV 191 sqq. = *New Introd. Lect. Psych.*, *SE* XXII 176 sqq., and esp. p. 176: 'Social distinctions, so I thought, were originally distinctions between clans or races.' This biologistic assertion is immediately followed by technologistic pronouncements: class division, which is originally due to race, is later subject to changes that are an effect of scientific discovery and technological invention (not that Freud had the slightest inkling of the connexion between forces of production and relations of production). Some of Freud's hypotheses are grotesque: the 'present economic crisis' (of 1929), which succeeded the First World War, is seen as the necessary price of 'our latest tremendous victory over nature, the conquest of the air'. With such formulations we lose what glimmers of insight Freud had displayed in the second paragraph of *The Future of an Illusion*, where he had acknowledged that the discontents of bourgeois civilization (or civilization as it had existed until then) were not equally experienced by all its members, for that society had 'not got beyond a point at which the satisfaction of one portion of its participants depends upon the suppression of another'. For this, see G. Jervis, 'Quaderni Piacentini' 42, November 1970, p. 97 note 10, which refers to an observation by F. Gantheret. The whole of Jervis' article is important for the problem of the relations of psychoanalysis and Marxism; it also contains one of the most perceptive and balanced evaluations of Reich's personality and work. Another 'glimmer' of truth on social relations is pointed out by Francesco Orlando (*Per una teoria freudiana della letteratura*, cit., p. 48 sq.) in a passage from *Jokes and their Relation to the Unconscious*, which belongs to Freud's early works (*GW* VI 120 sq. = *SE* VIII 196 sq.). All the same, it should not be forgotten that these were occasional moments of lucidity in a vision of society which as a whole remained conservative and unaware of classes (which means that its class standpoint was that of the dominant class).

[27] See *GW* XV 195 = *New Introd. Lect. Psych.*, *SE* XXII 180. In Russia 'the writings of Marx have taken the place of the Bible and the Koran as a source of revelation, though they would seem to be no more free from contradictions and obscurities than those older sacred books'. This statement, be it noted, contains not only a condemnation (which would in large part be justified) of the dogmatization of Marxism, but also – in the phrase 'though they would

new reality of Stalinist Russia, and his fears that the Psycho-analytical Society might itself be suspected of communism[28] along with a host of other crimes, his attitude towards those very qualities of iron will that Stalinism displayed – towards that renaissance, so to speak, of the barbaric spirit that always awakens a certain envy on the part of a bourgeoisie ailing from too much civilization – was tinged with a benevolent expectancy and admiration. Granted that Marxism had perhaps become a religion in the USSR, he never-theless always regarded such a secular faith as preferable to the restoration of Christianity predicted by so many intellectual and political or para-political movements in the West.[29] It was towards Marxism as science (and thus as a rival to psychoanalysis!) that he was not prepared to make concessions; or, at least, the 'reform' that he demanded of Marxism before he could grant it the seal of scientificity was a positivist *mélange* not unlike a theory of social development and conflict in terms of their diverse 'factors', that Antonio Labriola in his day had attacked so effectively.[30]

---

seem' – an evaluation of Marx's works themselves as *no less* contradictory and anti-scientific than the ancient 'sacred books'. Nor is there, in this last Lecture which surveys obscurantist or falsely progressive 'world views', a single word against the Fascism that held sway in Italy and Hungary, against the clerical Fascism of Seipel and Dollfuss in Austria, or the Nazism which was about to triumph in Germany. We can understand that Freud was constrained to silence in the interests of his own personal safety, and that of his pupils. No one would have had the right to demand that Freud, who was by then old and mortally ill, should have waged a political battle in which many others, for all their youth and strength, were disinclined to engage. But, *accompanied by an attack on Marxism,* this silence shifted his whole political and cultural presentation in a reactionary direction. This was not motivated by personal fear, but by something either better or worse – a dogged hope that psychoanalysis might be able to establish a *modus vivendi* even under the blackest and most racist bourgeois dictatorship. See above, p. 177 note 1.

[28] See above, p. 177 note 1. Reich, as is proved in passages from his letters which we cited there, was perfectly well aware that his expulsion would not have the slightest effect in protecting psychoanalysis from Nazi or Fascist persecution.

[29] *GW* XV 196 = *New Introd. Lect. Psych., SE* XXII 181: 'At a time when the great nations announce that they expect salvation only from the maintenance of Christian piety, the revolution in Russia – in spite of all its disagreeable details – seems nonetheless like the message of a better future.' But what follows immediately afterwards puts the admission in a significantly different perspective.

[30] The problem of the unity and distinction of the 'biological' and the 'social', and of the irreducibility of the one directly to the other, is still an unsolved

Freud, then, was a 'materialist' and a 'man of enlightenment', of whose general non-specialist culture it can be said that it was wholly exempt from materialism and enlightenment, but on the contrary was strongly imbued with irrationalism and decadence. The importance of Schopenhauer and of Nietzsche for Freud has already been emphasized. Thomas Mann, when he sought out Freud's precursors besides Nietzsche, cited Novalis and the whole of the German romantic tradition, with its irrationalism that was so often paraded in scientific metaphors (*Naturphilosophie* of Schelling's type).[31] He then commented on Freud's work: 'Measured by its methods and its aims, it may be said to tend to enlightenment, but of a kind too disciplined to be open to any charges of blithe superficiality';[32] but it also was of a kind 'too disciplined' for us to be able to consider it enlightened.[33]

Even the briefest examination of certain fundamental elements of psychoanalytic theory makes it clear, I think, that in every instance an initially materialist and hedonist inspiration was, so to speak, 'smothered' by a social and cultural conditioning which then produced an idealist regression. The concept of the unconscious is a prime example. This is not the appropriate occasion to study its tortuous formation and involution in Freud's thought. But it may be noted that Freud from the outset vacillated between a biological-instinctual interpretation, in which the unconscious

---

question within Marxist theory. But one cannot fail to note the awkwardness, even of terminology, and the underlying a-critical 'ethnicism' of Freud's approach (*GW* XV 194 = *New Introd. Lect. Psych., SE* XXII 179). Reich, in his better period, had posed the problem with the utmost clarity in the introduction to *Sexuality in the Cultural Struggle* (in Italian translation in the work by Reich and others, *Contro la morale borghese,* Rome, 1972, p. 90 sq.).

[31] T. Mann (cit. above, note 16), pp. 557, 568.

[32] Idem p. 570.

[33] Although Wilhelm Wundt's criticisms of psychoanalysis (*Grundzüge der physiologischen Psychologie,* III⁶, Leipzig, 1911, p. 636 sqq.), and in particular of the Freudian theory of dreams, predictably reveal an inadequate understanding of the new problems posed by Freud, his remark that Freudianism appeared to be a 'modernized' reversion to traditional philosophies of nature of Schelling's type, was not without foundation. We have commented on the nature and significance of Freud's Lamarckianism, and will shortly say something of the influence of E. von Hartmann on him. Wundt's critique was the more acute in that when it was written this aspect of Freudianism had not yet emerged into the light of day, as it was to do in the writings of the post-war years.

represented the 'voice of Nature' that has been rejected and silenced by a repressive civilization, but continues, as Lucretius would have said, *latrare* ('to make vehement demands'),[34] in an unsuppressible need for happiness; and an interpretation which prevails in Freud's later work, in which it becomes – with the development of the notion of the collective unconscious – the depository of an arcane wisdom, akin to a Kantian transcendental knowledge revisited through Schopenhauer and Eduard von Hartmann.[35] This ambiguity is not fortuitous, nor is it restricted to Freud. Whenever we encounter the limitations of a purely rationalistic conception of man's psychic activity as one confined entirely to his fully conscious experience – and thus confront the problem of the extent to which it contains much that is pre-logical – there are two solutions available to us. They lie in opposite directions but are easily confounded. The one acknowledges the biological nature of man, his 'untamed' origins and the ineradicably 'animal' quality (with a by no means purely negative connotation of the word) that survives even in social and civilized man. The other exalts the existence of a-logical activities within the human psyche (sentiment, intuition, art, religion) as the domain of a privileged experience which discloses a truth that is loftier and more esoteric than those attained by mere intellect. The history of philosophy and culture provides many examples of a partial or total 'religious' deflection of materialist or hedonist demands. The philosophy of Vico and Rousseau and much of what has been termed pre-Romanticism represent in differing ways and with varying degrees of insight, examples of an 'unstable equilibrium' of the two. It was not until the advent of Romanticism that the scales tipped decisively towards spiritualism (even then there was still an enormous variety in the positions adopted which it would be

---

34 Lucretius *De rerum natura*, II 17. ['Nonne videre/nil aliud sibi naturam latrare, nisi utqui/corpore seiunctus dolor absit, mente fruatur/iucundu sensu cura semota metuque?' 'Do you not see that nature vehemently demands but two things only, a body free from pain, and a mind released from anxiety and fear for the enjoyment of pleasurable sensations?']

35 There is no need to dwell on the influence of Schopenhauer, especially with regard to the Death Instinct (in any case, see Lecture XXXII). On the influence of *Philosophie des Unbewussten* (1869) by the disciple of Schelling and Schopenhauer, Eduard von Hartmann, see Jones, *Life*, I, p. 414.

simplistic to ignore). The psychoanalytic movement had its spokes-
man for an explicitly mystical and metaphysical conception of the
unconscious in Jung. Freud, by contrast, never renounced the
claims of rationalism altogether. Yet I think it is difficult to deny
that the less Freud remained true to his original materialist-hedonist
inspiration, the more he paved the way for the follies of Jung, and
that his last works represent a need he in some sense felt to emulate –
rather than merely combat – the latter.

I would nevertheless say that the involution of the Freudian
concept of the unconscious cannot be adequately assessed by the
single criterion of its dissociation from biology. Freud was never
a subjective idealist of the gnoseological type: he never denied the
existence of the external world. It was not without reason that the
Italian idealists despised and ignored him, since this was anyway
their attitude towards everything touching on psychology – a
discipline which no amount of zeal on the part of those who
sought to distance it from physiology could convince them was not
contaminated by 'naturalism'. Freud never rejected biology.
Indeed, a Marxist would have good reason to accuse his social
theory of biologism. It was rather in his conception of biology
itself – in his choice, that is to say, of a vitalistic biology – that he
displayed his 'idealism'. We have already remarked on his Lamarckian leanings. Now, neo-Lamarckianism (here our intention is
not to pass a historical judgement on Lamarck, who was in his day
a very great scientist and thinker) was, as we have already pointed
out, one of the forms assumed by the revival of biological vitalism
in the early 20th century. But Freud's refusal to identify 'drives'
with 'instincts', his one-sided conception of the unconscious as
pure activity pursuing its own purposes with its own language, and
not *also* as mechanical passivity, his undervaluation of all those
animal and human psychic processes which formed the object of
Pavlov's remarkable studies – these already reveal a germ, and
possibly more than a germ, of vitalism.

Whoever takes the trouble to compare our explanations of 'slips'
and instances of forgetting with those of Freud, will easily see that
the difference between them does not consist in the presence or
absence of an appeal to the unconscious. Our explanations, too,
nearly always presuppose the existence of unconscious psychological

or socio-psychological mechanisms. Banalization, the elimination of the superfluous, and so on, to which these explanations have so frequently referred, are scarcely ever registered by the speaker or writer responsible for them. Moreover, leaving aside the philosophical antecedents of the Freudian unconscious, it could be said that linguistics – a discipline which has always, especially since the mid to late 19th century, had much contact and exchange with textual criticism – has always considered a large proportion of changes in language to be unconscious processes. Even if we restrict ourselves to the 19th century, the Romantic linguists, Schleicher and the new grammarians – though in dispute over any number of other important problems – were in complete agreement on this. The substance of the difference lies elsewhere. Our explanations of 'slips' and instances of forgetting – like explanations of linguistic change – presuppose an unconscious in which 'mechanical' processes of a kind that are consistent with Pavlovian psychology have a large part to play; whereas Freud's explanations depend, as we have seen, on the re-emergence of repressed psychic material which is regarded as unpleasant or unavoidable by the conscious Ego, but which the unconscious *wishes* to express and expresses in its own particular language in a form more or less distorted by the resistances still opposed to it by the Ego.

We shall not repeat here the very many examples of these alternative types of explanation that we have already provided. I shall restrict myself to two further cases of forgetting 'due to lack of interest' (see the end of the last chapter) which Freud interprets as cases of amnesia derived from repression. Picture to yourself, says Freud in the third *Lecture* (*GW* XI 47 = *Introd. Lect. Psych.*, *SE* XV 53) 'a young man confessing to his fiancée that he had forgotten to keep their last rendezvous. He will certainly not confess it; he will prefer to invent on the spur of the moment the most improbable obstacles which prevented his appearing at the time and afterwards made it impossible for him to let her know. We all know too that in military affairs the excuse of having forgotten something is of no help and is no protection against punishment, and we must all feel that that is justified. Here all at once everyone is united in thinking that a particular parapraxis has a sense and in knowing what that sense is. Why are they not consistent enough to extend this knowledge to the other parapraxes and to admit them fully? There is of course an answer to this question too.'

We have already noted on other occasions[36] that the founder of depth psychology was a bad psychologist of elementary and superficial behaviour; and that the 'judicial' comparisons that Freud so often invokes are particularly unfortunate and retrograde. Here we have another pair of fine examples. Why does the parapraxis of the young man's failure to keep his appointment with the woman he loves insult the latter, so that he feels constrained to invent false excuses? Presumably because his beloved may think that his forgetting signifies a loss of interest (of amorous passion) on his part. Here we confront an instance of one of those forgettings which, even if we do not want to call them cases of 'inertia' lest we incur the posthumous reproaches of Nietzsche, we may still regard as an example of the way in which we eliminate or attenuate memories that have become less important to us for others that are felt to be more significant and essential. The erstwhile flame of passion is spent, or at least burns much less ardently! But Freud's explanation – not stated explicitly, but unambiguous in the overall context of the passage – is much more 'sinister'. He treats it as a case of amnesia derived from repression: the young man's sentiments towards the woman are not mere indifference but actual hatred, and the thought of the impending appointment with her was so unpleasant that his Ego submerged it in his unconscious. This was not then, strictly speaking, an instance of forgetting due to neglect or omission; there was a definite intention to evade the encounter. However, it was left to the (more maleficent and more authentic) Id to realize an intention that the Ego had not dared to act upon. Very well, then: admitted that the young man's feelings towards the woman were of this nature, would it not be more probable that this was a case of a *consciously* missed appointment? Or, if we really want to be circumspect, we should take all three hypotheses into consideration. One might note that Freud does not cite the case in reference to a particular young man with whose sentimental liaisons he has some acquaintance, but as a general example. There is therefore no justification for the certainty with which he opts for one of the three possible explanations.

Even worse is Freud's analogy from 'military life'. The latter is subject in all countries to harsher and more oppressive rules of conduct than in so-called civilian life, on the grounds that even a slight departure from them represents a much greater danger; it is this which necessitates what we might term a 'juridical state of emergency' whereby all distinction between wilful and unintentional or unpremeditated crimes is greatly reduced or altogether abolished. The effect is, of course, to increase the risk (a militarist would say that this was a necessary evil) of condemning the innocent. Freud, however, tries to tell us that a penal code which is more oppressive and inhuman, and more peremptory in its verdicts and condemnations, is psychologically better founded because every case of forgetting is revealed, on close inspection, to be intentional.[37]

It might be said that these aberrant applications of Freud's theory of the unconscious do not cancel the fact that its great superiority and fecundity lies precisely in its dynamic character. The unconscious is seen not as a sedimentation of dead material, but as an active force which has its own specific structure, speaks in its own language and disturbs the fragile rationality of the Ego. There is some truth in this objection; and so long as the 'finalism' or 'intentionality' of the unconscious of which Freud speaks means, as it often does, that instinctive tendency possessed by every human being to assert his own need for happiness against every form of oppression, there is no real cause to suspect Freud of 'teleologism' in the metaphysical sense. But in the course of its development, Freud's thought shifts towards an ever greater 'personalization' of the unconscious, which ultimately becomes a

---

[37] Naturally, the distinction between premeditated and unpremeditated guilt is a problem not only for philosophers but also for jurists of the left; but in the opposite sense to that which preoccupied Freud, since for them even a deliberate crime has its (social) determinants. In any case, between a sentry who falls asleep because of fatigue and one who does so because of indifference to the fate of his company or who even treacherously feigns sleep, there is a significant difference even for the staunchest opponents of free will (within, that is, a repressive institution such as an army, whose existence a Marxist may justify as an unhappy transitional necessity only in the case of revolutionary war).

sort of secondary personality common to us all – one immune to
the insincerities and self-deceptions of the conscious Ego, and
immanent to that collective unconscious which, as we have said,
becomes very similar to a Kantian-Schopenhauerian *a priori*. This
also produces – in contradiction with Freud's repeated allusions to
the provisional nature of the distance between psychology and
neurophysiology – wholly antithetical claims, not only as to the
permanence of this distance but as to the actual 'priority' of the
psychic over the physiological. Such claims, which become increasingly common in Freud's post-war work (though they were
not wholly absent before), elicit exclamations of satisfaction not
only from Freudians of existentialist and christianizing inclination,
but even from that most balanced of scientists, Ernest Jones.[38] This
was not a question – as we have already noted – of any conversion
of Freud to idealism *tout court,* but of his rejection of a physiology
which was necessarily too 'mechanistic' (and rightly so!) to provide
a foundation for Freud's vitalist psychology. Moreover, there can
clearly be detected in Freud's assertion of the 'priority' of the
psychic, and in his conception of the unconscious as 'intentional',
the influence of Franz Brentano – yet another thinker who was far
from materialist, indeed derived his psychology from distant
Thomist origins.[39]

Freudian 'determinism' underwent a similar metaphysical trans-
figuration. On the one hand, Freud's profession of determination
appears to be, and is in fact, too bound to a 19th century epistemology which even in its prime was subject to repeated crises,[40] that

[38] Jones, *Life,* II, p. 241: 'There was now [in the essay of 1913, *The claims of
Psychoanalysis to Scientific Interest,* in *GW* VIII 389 sqq. = *SE* XIII 165 sqq.]
even a note of triumph over the way in which psychoanalysis had "restricted the
physiological mode of thinking", a striking contrast from the days of twenty
years before when physiology was to him Science *par excellence* and when he had
made desperate attempts to describe the mental processes in physiological – more
strictly, in physical – language.' See above, note 25 and elsewhere.

[39] Rapaport, *Structure,* p. 13; P. Merlan, in 'Journ. of History of Ideas' 6 (1945),
p. 375 sqq. and 10 (1949), p. 451. Freud attended Brentano's lectures from
1874 to 1876; this was the only university course for which he registered which
was not under the auspices of the Medical Faculty.

[40] Enrico Bellone has shown their frequency in *Note sulla revoluzione scientifica
nella prima metà dell'Ottocento,* in 'Critica marxista' 6, *Sul marxismo e le scienze,*
(1972), p. 153 sqq.

were to intensify in our own century. On the other hand, we have already seen how a belief in determinism that is not controlled by adequate experimental verification may even be compatible with magic (above, Chapter 7). The last chapter of *The Psychopathology of Everyday Life* ('Determinism and Superstition'), which is where Freud most emphasizes his determinism, is also where we find a marked tendency – despite cautious qualifications – to admit to the existence, not only of telepathic, but also of occult 'phenomena'. It is well known that Freud was always drawn to such notions (why, after all, should the unconscious which was so powerful and still so unexplored, not prove capable of this as of so much else?),[41] and that this aspect of his thought later found a bizarre development in George Groddeck's strange compound of insight, naive philanthropy and unintentional charlatanry.

A determinist standpoint – or any more up to date conception of causality which, while acknowledging the inadequacy of the old determinism, does not deny causality itself nor confer on human thought and will the divine power of being 'uncaused causes' – necessarily involves an uncompromising rejection of so-called free will and of any ethics that is contaminated by voluntarism or moralism: *non ridere, non lugere neque detestari, sed intellegere!* ('neither ridicule, nor grief, nor hatred, but understanding!') The study of neurosis, in particular, ought powerfully to aid us to understand that it is not possible to apply the notion of 'guilt' in the traditional moral sense to neurotic behaviour, even in its most anti-social forms. This does not mean that we abandon the struggle against all agents of oppression or tenants of privilege of whatever kind, starting with the capitalist class and its watchdogs; or that we can abstain from anger or passionate hostility towards them. But such anger is only the emotional reaction to the extraordinary improbability, if not impossibility, of persuading them to retire voluntarily from the defence of an iniquitous social order, and to the painful necessity, once an attempt of that kind has failed, of countering reactionary violence with revolutionary violence. It is also a reaction to the difficulty of initiating any revolutionary action – whether because of the strength of the dominant class or

---

[41] Roazen, *Freud: Pol. and Soc.* pp. 110–17.

the acquiescence of the oppressed class (an important element in which is the more or less compelling temptation that each of us experiences to comply with the status quo). Anger of this kind does not involve any mythological belief that there is a range of 'free choice' for the oppressor, who might have elected to play the role of altruist and benefactor but opted instead, who knows why, for that of overlord.

Though the connexion between morality and class situation lay beyond his horizon, Freud often declared himself in principle to be convinced of the non-existence of 'free will'; and it must be stated that psychoanalysis dealt its own particular blow to moralism and voluntarism. Thus if it were merely a question of establishing that many aspects of Freud's practice, taken in isolation, were in contradiction with the ethics which psychoanalysis ought to have dictated, the matter would have minimal importance. However, here again, the contradiction was not simply a case of Freud 'not practising what he preached', but was intrinsic to his theory itself, or at least to many of its applications at the scientific non-practical level. If an ethical system is to be genuinely free of anti-scientific moralism (and from equally anti-scientific and exhibitionist displays of immoralism, which are merely the 'other side of the coin' of the ethics of class oppression, just as saccharine pseudo-democracy and fascist brutality are merely the two modes of domination of the bourgeoisie over the proletariat), it needs to do more than proclaim its commitment to determinism and its disbelief in free will. It must also emancipate itself from psychologism. Yet the inquisitorial technique of analysis itself – in which the 'good' patient is one who ultimately lets his resistances be overcome, and so to speak signs the confession which the analyst has preordained and suggested to him – allows the moralism it has chased out of the door to come back in through the window. Freud's extremely misanthropic view of humanity – which sees a desire for the death of the father, brothers, sons and all of those whom we might in any way identify with them, as the necessary price not of an authoritarian society to be overthrown, but of 'civilization' in general – also tends in the same direction. A Leopardian pessimism escapes this fate because, in a first movement, it opposes a good nature to a corrupt civilization, and then in a second movement, it identifies nature as the enemy of man and founds a new morality on the solidarity of men in their struggle against it. This does not mean that it forgets the evils conjoined to natural calamities by a false and corrupt civilization, by an oppressive morality which fights against 'nature's' demands for vitality and happiness rather than against the ways in which nature thwarts their satisfaction. Leopardi thus had every right to affirm, in a passage from the *Zibaldone* (2 January 1829) which anticipates the *Ginestra,* that his pessimistic philosophy 'not only does not lead to misanthropy . . . but of its nature excludes the possibility of it', because 'it makes nature to blame for everything, and in its total exoneration of men, it redirects hatred, or at least grief, against a higher principle, the true origin of the evils of life'. Freudianism, notwithstanding its theory of nature as hostile to man, which considered in isolation has, as we have noted, a Leopardian resonance, really interprets inhumanity as consubstantial with civilization – and therefore at the most only mitigable by psychoanalysis or a somewhat more permissive morality, and a somewhat less severe Super-Ego. A return to nature in a Rousseauesque sense, or in that of the early Leopardi, is ruled out by Freud. So too is a civilization which at least eliminates the unhappiness caused by economic and social conditions and their norms of behaviour. *Die Kultur geht vor* ('Culture takes precedence') was Freud's reply to Reich:[42] the claims of happiness must be subordinated to the unhappy exigencies of civilization. But while traditional Christian ethics promised the felicity of the next world in exchange for the sacrifices imposed in this, and secular ascetic philosophies held that the renunciation of pleasure was recompensed by a 'good conscience', by the higher joys derived from an improved moral condition, Freudianism rightly dispensed with such false consolations – but retained their moralism. 'Civilization' makes you more wicked and more un-happy, yet must be defended at all costs. The truth in Freud's ethics was that of its hedonistic formation; but his hedonism – like his materialism, and his 'determinism' – was stifled by the superimposi-tion of idealist tendencies which ultimately functioned to preserve the existing social order.[43]

[42] *Reich Speaks of Freud,* p. 45.
[43] Writing of Freud's relations to Marxism (on which we commented a little

In my opinion, among the innumerable analogies between Freudianism and other interpretations of human reality, one of the more interesting, despite the fact that it has probably been made before, is with Epicureanism. The Epicureans too advocated, as is well-known, an oddly renunciatory hedonism: they started by energetically proclaiming the primacy of pleasure (indeed, with deliberately provocative vulgarity, the 'pleasures of the stomach'),[44] but then very quickly modulated this to be absence of pain and anxiety, *aponia* and *atarassia*. In Freudian terms one might say that Epicureanism effected a transition from the 'pleasure principle' to the 'reality principle' (it is known that Freud entertained the idea of such a transition long before he explicitly theorized it in the famous essay of 1920).[45] The result was that a Stoic like Seneca could perceptively note the severity and sadness of Epicurus's ethics, not dissimilar to the morality of his Stoic adversaries.[46] Here again, it was not so much the individual character of its founder which was reflected in the paradox of Epicureanism, but rather the refusal of his school of thought to pose itself as a revolutionary philosophy or even to urge a radical reform of social mores, and its restriction to the provision of an alternative justification of conventional morality. However, the history of Epicureanism over the centuries, above all from the epoch of Humanism to that of the Enlightenment, was to demonstrate that it could be a powerful subversive force within science and morality. This is undeniably true of Freudianism too. For the most part, Epicurus no more intended this to be the case than did Freud. Yet

---

earlier), Jones, *Life*, III, p. 368, is beatifically naive: 'His humanism made him dislike the violence and cruelty apparently inseparable from it, and his realistic sense made him profoundly distrust its idealism.' Which means: he had a 'humanistic' abhorrence of revolutionary violence and a 'realistic' conviction that bourgeois violence and repression were destined to persist eternally.

[44] Epicurus, fr. 409 Usener.

[45] See Jones, *Life*, III, p. 290–1. E. Fromm, *The Mission of Sigmund Freud*, cit., p. 36 sqq. Freud as early as 1833 was writing to his fiancée that 'our striving is more concerned with avoiding pain than with creating enjoyment' (*our* refers here to the practice in cultivated circles, by contrast to the direct inclination to enjoyment among the vulgar masses, as Freud himself explains in his letter).

[46] Seneca, *De vita beata*, 12, I; 4. See E. Bignone, *L'Aristotele perduto e la formazione filosofica di Epicuro* (Florence, 1973²), II, p. 220 sq.

it must be admitted, I think, that the former was even in his own day the greater and more original thinker.

In order to avoid further digressions, of which there have already perhaps been too many, we shall here merely mention one other respect – related in fact, to that just noted – in which Freudianism is reminiscent of Epicureanism and Hellenistic philosophies in general. This is their convergence in a form of psychotherapy which is neither strictly speaking medical (since they have recourse neither to drugs nor to physiotherapy, nor to any other type of directly somatic intervention on the patient), nor political or social in character. Such a therapy aims to achieve a cure by 'raising the consciousness' of the patient, in an awakening that is seen not merely as preliminary to practical action, but as itself healing and liberating. (By contrast, consciousness of its exploitation is only a precondition of the class struggle of the proletariat; without the latter the former would merely render the misery of the working class equally or more intense – with the meagre consolation of now being a Pascalian 'thinking reed'.[47]) I am fully aware that Freud himself was not slow to realize the inefficacy of his initial rationalist method of treatment: the patient, 'informed' of the origin of his disturbances, even if he assented intellectually to the analyst's explanations, nonetheless remained neurotic.[48] Indeed, explanations that were too hastily provided could even lead to an actual deterioration of his condition. But Freud's corrective to this over-simple rationalism was a sort of 'waking hypnosis'. Once conscious acknowledgment of his ills by the patient proved insufficient, the new solution was for him to 're-live' the traumatic experiences of his infancy. Hence the interminability of the cure, which was to assume the proportions of *another*, substitute neurosis – one that in the majority of cases proved not curative. This is admitted today

---

[47] See B. Pascal, *Pensées*, 113, 114, for the notion of the *'roseau pensant'*, in relation to which Pascal writes: 'La grandeur de l'homme est grande en ce qu'il se connaît misérable; un arbre ne se connaît pas misérable. S'est donc être misérable que de (se) connaître misérable, mais c'est être grand que de connaître qu'on est misérable'. ('Man's greatness lies in the fact that he knows his own misery. A tree does not know that it is miserable. To know one's misery, then, is to be miserable, but to know that one is miserable is to be great'). Trans.

[48] See, for example, *GW* VIII 124 and 475 = *Observations on 'wild' psycho-analysis, SE* XI 226 and *On Beginning the Treatment, SE* XII 168 sq.

by many psychiatrists on the 'left', and no longer merely on the 'right'. Obviously, further discussion of the therapeutic possibilities of psychoanalysis, and of the important variations that even ortho-dox Freudians have introduced into psychoanalytic treatment since Freud's day, is a matter for psychiatrists themselves, rather than for those who have never had any training in psychoanalysis. (In this case, as in others where it is a question of specific technical knowledge and practical experience, the distinction between the specialist and the non-specialist cannot be suppressed entirely – or at least, not for a long time.) The layman may only wonder whether certain therapeutic difficulties are not due at least in part to a concept of therapy that remains too pre-scientific, too closely related to the old tradition of 'healing souls'.

This conception of psychoanalysis has been accompanied by the confidence that Freud himself possessed in its capacity (superior to that of Marxism, which he saw as a narrow-minded economism) to improve the moral condition of mankind. Freud, as we have seen, declared that, thanks to psychoanalysis, he had become virtually incapable of lying (p. 167). Ernest Jones, in the assessment of *The Psychopathology* to which we referred,[49] asks what social advantages ensue from the analysis and self-analysis of 'slips' and other para-praxes. His answer is that if we remain in ignorance of such acts 'both intellectual and moral dishonesty is facilitated to an extra-ordinary degree' and innumerable acts of unconscious deceit become possible. An example of such an act? – 'the impecunious man who forgets to pay his bill because he doesn't really want to'. Jones immediately goes on: 'At the same time, the line between the two types of dishonesty is nowhere a sharp one, and in many cases one can only conclude that the subject could with a very little effort recognize the suppressed motive, which is more than half-conscious'. It would obviously be redundant to ask Jones (who, after all, was not Freud, and though more prudent and less para-doxical than his master, was altogether more complacent in his bourgeois existence, and scarcely affected by the 'discontents of civilization') whether it might not be preferable to act to eliminate poverty, rather than to persuade the poor by psychoanalysis to

<hr />

49 E. Jones, *Papers on Psychoanalysis,* op. cit., p. 112; see Chap. I, note 3.

pay their bills or else, in the event of extreme destitution, to die an honest death of starvation; or to ask him which was greater – and thus more in need of psychoanalysis – the dishonesty of he who accepts the gulf between the rich and the poor, or the dishonesty of he who in his poverty is constrained to forget (i.e. to pretend to forget) to pay his bill? But rather than belabour Jones posthumously with supernumerary and by now all too obvious objections, it is more interesting to dwell for a moment on his admission that between conscious and unconscious dishonesty 'the line . . . is nowhere a sharp one'. The process we have described as the personalization of the unconscious in effect makes it ever more difficult to demarcate the two, so that the best examples of parapraxes are, as we have noted (p. 127), those which are voluntary, such as jokes. Despite Freud's excursions into pre-history and persistent attempts at biological rationales (such as the use of the ontogenetic-phylogenetic argument, or of a Schopenhauerian death instinct which becomes the tendency of living matter to return to the quiescence of the inorganic), the Id and Ego are the two facets of bourgeois man. The Id is his corruption, his egoism, his incapacity for love without hatred. The Ego is the superficial veneer of respectability which conceals this brutality – the way in which bourgeois man strains to preserve appearances to himself and to others, though he is never really ignorant of his own true nature. (Naturally, the bourgeois then projects the personality of the proletarian in his own image, with a certain extra severity in his moral judgement: how well bourgeois society would function if all paupers were 'honest men' and paid their bills!)[50] The Super-Ego is the strict ethical ideal of 'duty', accepted not as a painful but temporary necessity, but as a permanent repression of hedonistic impulses which, in their turn, are permanently irrepressible. These

[50] Without in any way seeking to attribute to Freud the pachydermic bourgeois self-satisfaction of Jones (we commented a little earlier on the difference between the two), it must be said that the example of the poor man who forgets to pay his bill finds its counterpart (not its source of inspiration, since one is dealing with a passage that Freud wrote in 1919, after the publication of Jones's essay) in the episode in *The Psychopathology* (p. 223 = 200), of the waiter whose 'parapraxis' consists in his unintentional confession that he charged the client a higher price than was owed: in all probability this was a case of a wholly chance parapraxis of the sort we considered earlier.

hedonistic impulses, for their part, are very different from 18th century aspirations to 'happiness'. For once aggression is interpreted not as the consequence of oppression and frustration, but as equally 'primordial' as Eros itself, such impulses encompass not only sexual desire, but the drive to kill one's fellow men, to overwhelm them in every possible manner. When Freud calls for a somewhat less severe Super-Ego, he is pleading not only for a relaxation of moralistic constraints which are futile, or useful only to the dominant class, but also for greater leniency towards the 'sincerity' of the behaviour demonstrated in war.[51] After the defeat of the Central Powers, Freud became more pacifist, yet the only timid alternative to this uncontrolled aggression that he could find was the ingenuous paternalism of his reply to Einstein in 1932: 'One instance of the innate and ineradicable inequality of men is their tendency to fall into the two classes of leaders and followers. This suggests that more care should be taken than hitherto to educate an upper stratum of men with independent minds, not open to intimidation and eager in the pursuit of truth, whose business it would be to give direction to the dependent masses.'[52]

Trotsky's judgement on psychoanalysis in an article of 1927[53] is

[51] See the last part of *Thoughts for the Times on War and Death*, SE XIV 273 sqq., on which we have already commented, p. 115 note 15.

[52] *Warum Krieg?*, GW XVI 25 = *Why War?*, SE XXII 212.

[53] L. Trotsky, in an article on *Culture and Socialism* ('Novy Mir', January 1927), in English translation in *Problems of Everyday Life* (New York, 1973), p. 233 sq. The same ideas, though their general tenor is more pro-Pavlovian, are expressed by Trotsky in a letter to Pavlov of September 1923, in Italian translation in *Marxismo e scienza* (Rome, 1969), p. 51 sq. (the article and letter are also in French translation in *Littérature et révolution*, Paris, 1964). Among other things, Trotsky writes in the latter that 'during my stay in Vienna [1907–1912] I was in fairly close contact with the Freudians'. Other comments on Freud are to be found in *Literature and Revolution* (New York, 1960), pp. 42, where Trotsky notes that 'the most paradoxical exaggerations of Freud' are nonetheless 'significant and fertile ideas' and speaks again of Freud, Jung and Adler as members of a single 'school', 198 and 220 (where he argues that psychoanalysis can be reconciled with materialism, which was also the opinion of Radek). Another text of interest included in the 1923 Russian edition was *Eros and Death* (it dates from 1908), though it does not comment explicitly on Freudianism. After his final exile from the USSR, Trotsky had a further occasion to refer to Freud – still in tones of esteem, even if very fleetingly – in his lecture given in Copenhagen in 1932 (see the memoirs of his wife, Natalya Sedova, in V. Serge, *Vie et mort de Trotsky*, Paris, 1957) and in one of the polemical writings of his Mexican period (*In Defence of Marxism*, New York, 1973, p. 24). See also Trotsky, *My Life*

notable for its equanimity and insight: 'The idealists tell us that the psyche is an independent entity, that the soul is an unfathomable well. Pavlov and Freud both think that its foundation is physiological. But Pavlov descends, like a diver, right to the bottom, and carefully rummages about the well, working from the depths upwards; whereas Freud stands over the well with a piercing gaze, in an effort to penetrate below its perpetually moving and turbulent waters, and to grasp or catch a glimpse of the images of the things which lie at the bottom. Pavlov's method is that of experiment; Freud's that of conjecture. It is too simple, or rather simplistic, to want to declare psychoanalysis "incompatible" with Marxism, and to turn one's back on Freudianism. There is no warrant for this, since in Freudianism we have an instance of a working hypothesis which can, and indubitably does, allow for the development of deductions and conjectures along the lines of a materialist psychology. Experimental methods will in due course submit these conjectures to verification. But we have no motive or right to proscribe the other procedure, which, even if it may appear less valid, after all seeks to anticipate conclusions towards which experimental methods are at present advancing only very slowly.'

In this very interesting text, two positions are adopted, each of them correct, although situated at different levels. One of them is political and cultural in character. At a time when there was already a tendency (which reached its height during the epoch of Stalinism proper) to dogmatize all culture and assert a single 'official' line – to the exclusion of all others – in every domain (scientific, philosophical or artistic), Trotsky was absolutely right to warn of the

(Harmondsworth, 1975) pp. 227–8: 'Through Joffe [who was being psychoanalyzed by Alfred Adler] I became acquainted with the problems of psychoanalysis, which fascinated me, although much in this field is still vague and unstable and opens the way for fanciful and arbitrary ideas'; see I. Deutscher, *The Prophet Armed Trotsky 1879–1921*: (Oxford, 1954), p. 191. A note on 'Wittels' book about Freud (a bad book by an envious pupil)' is to be found in Trotsky's *Diary in Exile* (Cambridge, Mass., 1935), entry for 16 May 1935: the reference is to Franz Wittels, *S. Freud: his personality, his Teaching, his School* (New York, 1924). This does not pretend to be a complete documentation of Trotsky's judgements on psychoanalysis, and is very probably not so; but it may supplement the very deficient anthology published under anonymous editorship in *Psyche* 10, 1955, p. 481 sq. (L. Trotsky, *Opinions sur Freud et la psychanalyse*).

danger of such a fossilization and of the evil effects it would have not only on culture in the USSR, but also on the entire political climate of the country. He felt that the elevation of Pavlovianism to the status of sole psychology compatible with Marxist materialism was, notwithstanding Pavlov's great merits, an act of political and cultural tyranny, which would in the long run prove detrimental to the work of Pavlov itself. So indeed it was to prove. To this day Pavlov's work is treated with a completely unjustified suspicion and hostility by Marxists in the West, not merely because of their own tenacious anti-materialism, but also because of the monopoly which Pavlovianism has for too long possessed in the USSR. If this was the main danger, Trotsky also appears (if one reads the entire article) to be warning of another – that a too wholesale rejection of bourgeois science as totally invalid and ideological would inevitably result in a summary dismissal of Freudianism (ignoring the fact that Pavlovianism itself, although it had a materialist character, did not have one that was properly speaking Marxist). There was, in effect, at the time when Trotsky was writing, the risk that a certain naive 'ultra-leftism' would provide fuel for the imposition of Stalinism, only to be subsequently liquidated by it.

Trotsky's other stance was more specifically epistemological; it was concerned with what we should mean and claim when we speak of a materialist orientation in the sciences, particularly in the human sciences. Trotsky realized the dangers inherent in the abandonment of entire fields of knowledge simply because they do not yet permit a rigorously materialist study. It is better, he argues, to accept a tendential materialism – that gradually subtracts those areas of investigation from the dualism of 'mind' and 'body' or the reduction of all human reality to that of the spirit – than to reject *sine die* all research that cannot be founded on secure biological bases. We shall have to wait some time before Pavlov surfaces 'from the bottom of the well' – that is, before he can explain all human psychic facts in neurophysiological terms; in the meantime, we cannot reject what Freud may be able to tell us – which even if it has not been altogether experimentally confirmed, permits further experimental control and 'confrontation' with the findings of Pavlovian research.

Trotsky's demands still remain valid today. I think, however, that they need to be made more specific in two respects. Culturally and politically the main danger today, for Marxism in Western Europe, and – sooner or later – for Marxism in Eastern Europe too, is not a dogmatic declaration of the 'incompatibility' of Marxism with various bourgeois currents in the sciences, but irresponsible pastiches of Marxism with psychoanalysis, structuralism, or phenomenology; for what is always sacrificed in such unions is materialism. We have already said that the correct reaction to such tendencies cannot be a sterile defence of orthodoxy. What is needed is rather a renewal of theory that takes the form of a critical reflection on historical events that have occurred in the world since the time of Marx and Lenin, and on certain aspects of human reality that have been somewhat neglected by Marx and Marxists – and not in the spirit of a zealous adjustment to the latest fashions of bourgeois culture.

So far as an assessment of Freudianism is concerned, Trotsky had remarked – a few lines before those we quoted – on the 'excessive' importance that Freud attributed to sexuality, though he commented that this was a dispute within a common framework of materialism. He also noted the frequently 'fantastic' character of Freud's conjectures. In 1923 he wrote in a letter that the Freudians were combining a 'physiological realism' with a 'virtually literary analysis of psychic phenomena' and were constructing 'a whole series of ingenious and interesting hypotheses, which are nonetheless arbitrary from the scientific point of view'.

However, it seems to me that Trotsky perhaps conceded too much to Freud's 'materialism'. He was correct in thinking that Freud's initial postulates, if that is the term for them, were materialistic, but he tended to overlook the negative character of the idealist transvaluation that very quickly occurred with psychoanalysis, which rendered an encounter between Freud and Pavlov, and also between Freud and Marx and Engels, ever more problematic. All the same, we must not forget that the Freudian theory to which Trotsky was referring was that developed during the years Trotsky spent in Vienna before the World War, and before *Totem and Taboo*. He apparently remained in ignorance of Freud's speculations on 'civilization', at least throughout the time before his expulsion from the Soviet Union.

If, despite this, even serious Marxists continue to feel a need for a Freudian Marxism so insistently, it is because a real and inescapable problem lies behind their concern – the animality of man, the relationship between man and nature, the existence of unhappiness beyond exclusively social and historical conditions. There is also the need for a Marxist psychology, on which Lucien Sève has been right to insist (however one judges his attempt to satisfy it). Here Marx and Engels provided only starting points; but without such a psychology, our very comprehension of political and social facts will always remain incomplete.

But the development of these themes necessitates a reformulation of the materialist foundation of Marxism, and a deeper understanding of its relationship to hedonism. Psychologists and psychiatrists of the far left have long been lucidly aware of the extent to which capitalist society and all class societies induce neuroses. In this sense it is true that the best prophylaxis (indeed the only really decisive one) for the greater part of the neuroses and psychoses lies in the overthrow of capitalism and the establishment of a transitional society that genuinely progresses towards communism, rather than stagnating and regressing towards a pseudo-socialist and bureaucratic society. All the same, it will be of little avail to pursue this path, and the proletariat will not be helped in its overall struggle for communism, if it is forgotten that the location of neurotic disease is the nervous system, and that psychiatry and neurology have a specific part to play in the battle which all of us have a duty to wage against capitalism. Their task is to cure, by all means at their disposal, neuroses and psychoses, once these have taken form, and to discover new, more efficacious remedies against them. Their aim should certainly not be to adapt the patient to the capitalist system, but to regain him for the struggle against it – since neurosis and madness are a serious obstacle to his participation in the struggle. To think that the struggle is in itself the therapy is for the most part (though not always) a voluntaristic illusion, as it would be with regard to any other social disease. There can be no doubt that capitalism is responsible for silicosis; but we could scarcely imagine (save in exceptional cases of heroic behaviour) a partisan army, or even simply an efficiently organized opposition, whose members were not as yet 'soldiers' though already highly politicized and subversive of the capitalist system, that was composed entirely of comrades suffering from serious forms of silicosis. The discovery of a more effective remedy for this disease than those at present known, *might* serve to reconcile the workers to the form of organization of the glass industry which suits their bosses – who are quite prepared to sacrifice the health of the proletariat for the sake of maximum profits. But its effect might also be to render these workers once more capable of a fight against capitalism when they would otherwise have had to resign themselves to being 'unfit' for service (as is said in medical military parlance). If this is how things stand, it is not only at the cognitive level – which, of course, Marxism can never afford to neglect if it is to become a progressively more scientific and secular vision of the world – but also at the practical level that there is a need to restore the relationship between psychology-psychiatry and neurophysiology, for whose dissolution psychoanalysis has to a large extent been responsible. This naturally means that the entire Freudian theory of the neuroses, from slips to maladies, must be submitted to scientific controls, however pedantic and mundane the task may appear to be.

It will also be necessary to explore the problem of Freudian 'pessimism'. It would be wrong to accuse Freud generally of pessimism – an error which was to some extent common to the so-called 'Freudian revisionists' (Fromm, Horney, Sullivan) and to Reich; although the revolutionary optimism of Reich in his better period was not only more sympathetic but also much less facile than the reformist optimism of the Freudian revisionists, while even among the latter Fromm had some justification in claiming an individual position of his own[54] against Marcuse's sweeping criticisms. It is not pessimism as such which is debatable, but the Freudian *type* of it. The Romantic and Schopenhauerian

[54] See Fromm's reply to Marcuse – which is not lacking in sound arguments – in the work of various authors, *Contro la morale borghese* (cited above, note 30), p. 113 sqq. Lenin is eccentrically presented by Fromm as a man 'insensible' to ethical and political problems, who was the legitimate father of Stalinism. Unfortunately, it is not only Marxist Freudians who are responsible for such nonsense, but also a significant proportion of the revolutionary left in Europe and America.

derivation of the latter merits a much more comprehensive study than has been possible here. The problem it poses is not merely one of acceptance or rejection of Thanatos alongside Eros. It encompasses the object of pessimism itself (is Nature man's enemy in the Leopardian sense, or is 'human nature' evil?), and our attitude towards this objective reality (do we affirm man's irrepressible right to happiness, and thus fight against the biological as well as historical and social limits to it, or do we opt for 'sublimation' and a prudent accommodation to a society and a nature that inflict unhappiness on us?). It is their refusal of the second alternative that Marxism and the materialist pessimism of Giacomo Leopardi have in common – though we must never forget the great differences in their background, their interests, and their perspectives. But here we encounter a far wider set of problems, some partial aspects of which we have sought to discuss in recent years, but which we cannot develop here.

Postscript

Rather than provide a preface to this book – which would not have amounted to much more than a repetition of the short statements made in the first chapter – I have chosen to append this postscript. Its aim is two-fold: to thank friends who read the type-script of my work for their comments and suggestions on bibliographic material, and to clarify further (in the light, moreover, of certain works which I came to read only when this book was already in proof) a number of themes which are especially likely to cause perplexity, or even a direct rejection of the entire work.

I first discussed the subject of this book years ago with Carlo Ginzburg; we did not find ourselves in complete agreement, but it was he who stimulated me to proceed with the study. More recently, various objections and contributions have been made to me by Franco Belgrado, Luigi Blasucci, Alessandro Ferace, Carlo Alberto Madrignani, Francesco Orlando, Vanna Raffuzzi, Michele Ranchetti, Aldo Rossi, Vittorio Rossi, Ennio Scalet and Sabina de Waal (who are all primarily interested in psychoanalysis as one of the 'human sciences', and in particular in its relations with Marxism). I am also indebted to two friends, Francesco Dessí, who is a biologist, and Giuseppe Giordani, who is a doctor. I have had to cite only those with whom discussions were most prolonged and committed; the list would have been much lengthier if I had recorded all those friends with whom I have had briefer, though highly valuable, exchanges of ideas.

It is customary for the author, after he has expressed his gratitude in this way, to add that the responsibility for the ideas contained in the work, and above all for its errors, is entirely his own. In this case, such a declaration, which is often a pure formality, must be given especial weight. I have a duty, in fact, to make it clear that to a greater or lesser extent the majority of the colleagues I have named dissent, at times from the overall judgement on psycho-analysis expressed in the book, at times from the particular criticisms of the Freudian explanations of 'slips' and instances of forgetting, at times from the often 'pamphleteering' tone of their formulation. There is also a minority who are in agreement, or whose disagreement relates only to isolated points. I have not listed these latter separately lest it appear that I was clumsily seeking to recompense their assent with a sort of 'honourable mention'. I am indebted as much to the former as to these latter, and I shall be even more so if they, and other eventual readers, are moved to express their opinions publicly, with the candour and even vigour that cannot damage genuine friendships, and which in any case is likely to be provoked by the polemical tone of my work.

One theme to which I feel I should return is the 'unfalsifiability' and thus the non-scientificity of the Freudian method of interpretation of 'slips', dreams and neurotic symptoms (see above, p. 47 sq.; 77, and elsewhere). I must emphasize that, for my own part, a commitment to this line of criticism does not imply any profession of a specifically 'Popperian' faith, nor more generally any adherence to logical empiricism – of which I know too little, but to which I am in any case a stranger by intellectual background and by politico-cultural orientation. I also believe that it would be entirely wrong to measure psychoanalysis (and by implication, the other human sciences, or those whose object falls between the 'natural' and the socio-historical) against any ideal of absolute scientific rigour, and to use that as the criterion for pronouncing it non-scientific. Up to this point, I find myself in complete agreement with an important article by Michel Legrand (*Le statut scientifique de la psychanalyse,* in 'Topique', October 1973, pp. 137–57), which Carlo Alberto Madrignani brought to my notice. Legrand studies two antagonistic conceptions of science currently championed today – the one empiricist or empirio-criticist (of which 'verificationism' and 'falsificationism', for all the disputes between their respective advocates, constitute only two sub-species), the other 'theoreticist'. Legrand's disatisfaction with each is wholly justified, even if a certain equivocation results from his assumption that Louis Althusser is the principal representative of the 'theoreticists'. This is not because Althusser cannot rightly be criticized as a 'theoreticist', but because Legrand seems to concede that theoreticism is a legitimate (if not the only possible) form of Marxism. In reality, this theoreticism owes nothing to Marx or Engels or Lenin, but derives in Althusser from 'Platonizing' conceptions of science which emerged (or re-emerged) much later – in the epistemological climate associated particularly with mathematical logic, which then passed into structural linguistics (especially the Danish school) and thereafter to non-linguistic structuralism (Lévi-Strauss). Althusser's merit lies in his reassertion, against erroneous interpretations of Marxism, of the distinction between science and ideology; but it is precisely his theoreticist conception of science which is responsible for his unqualified identification of ideology with the immediacy of common sense, with the 'empirical' and 'lived' – whereas for Marxism, it also includes metaphysics, religion and Platonic idealism. Legrand's criticism of empiricism (p. 241 sq.) is still too Althusserian, while he believes it to be Marxist; or rather, it is a juxtaposition of an Althusserian critique and a polemic (in itself just) against the 'false neutrality' of bourgeois science, exemplified by so-called psychometric tests. Certainly the 'measuring of intelligence' is an outright fraud, since it presents inequalities which are the outcome of the class division of society as 'natural'. But bourgeois ideology is culpable *jointly and severally* for this pseudo-scientific fabrication; it would be difficult to blame it merely on empiricists rather than theoreticists, or vice versa. Legrand is absolutely right to seek a conception of science which could surpass the one-sidedness of empiricism on the one hand, and of theoreticism on the other. But it is doubtful whether this can be attained by any appeal to Bachelard, who was certainly a notable figure in French philosophy during the 30's, but remained trapped in a contradiction between theoreticism and odd intuitionist and aestheticist tendencies, and whose influence precisely on Lévi-Strauss and Althusser was to be far from beneficial. I believe that to attain Legrand's proposed objective, the route signalled by Ludovic Geymonat and pursued in his own work and that of his pupils (see above, the works cited, p. 47, note 5, p. 198, note 40 –

besides many others) has proved itself to be much more fruitful and much more authentically materialist and Marxist. However, Legrand arrives independently at one of the important conditions upon which Geymonat insists: that due emphasis should be given to the history of science, not in order to dissolve science into history (which would constitute a new form of idealism) but in order to rehabilitate the objectivity of scientific knowledge while at the same time rejecting any dogmatic absolutization of it.

Here we reach the problem which interests us, and on which Legrand's article converges: the scientificity of psychoanalysis. Can a science dispense with even a minimum condition of 'falsifiability'? Must it entertain the possibility that some experience might confound it? Is the objection of Nagel and Hook (see above, p. 48 note 6) against psychoanalysis – that it is precisely so contrived as to render it immune to any control – to be rejected along with Popper's (definitely 'ideological'!) ideas about the 'open society' and his attack on what he calls historicism, or Hook's arguments against Marxism? I think not. For one thing, it should be remembered that this minimum condition (of 'proof' and 'disproof') has a history that pre-dates both Austro-British logical positivism and Dewey's pragmatism: it was present during the entire evolution of modern science, and biologists and students of medicine before Freud were keenly aware of it. One has only to think of Claude Bernard's masterpiece, which in many respects is yet to be surpassed, *An Introduction to the Study of Experimental Medicine;* or of the concept of *differential* diagnosis itself, which is essential to the scientific status of medicine and does not have its counterpart in psychoanalytic practice.

Legrand's reply to Hook and Nagel is, in my opinion, evasive and unconvincing. He is correct to remark, with an acute sense of history, that 'scientificity' is not inherited by any science, fully formed, as its birth-right, but is always a gradual conquest. All sciences are born 'inexact', by the labour of researchers whose first commitment is to science (with such merely provisional epistemology as this involves) and not to epistemology for its own sake. Again, he is right to observe that when the 'systematization' of concepts and their rigorous formulation becomes predominant, this is often the final phase of a science – a phase of completion, but also of senility, or at least of temporary sterility – in which there is a tendency 'to self-conservation of the theories rather than their creative advancement'. (p. 248). Though I concur with this statement, it cannot but remind me of the risks now run by linguistics, despite an extraordinary success which would seem to create a mockery of them. Here is a subject, which is increasingly tending (fortunately there are also some counter-tendencies) to contract into a 'philosophy of itself', to reformulate in a more rigorous manner the discoveries of the 19th and early 20th centuries, rather than to acquire new knowledge. I am also reminded of the analogous dangers which beset many sectors of Marxism today, and which include the risk of subordination to an imported epistemology derived from quite other currents of thought: from phenomenology, structuralism, or psychoanalysis itself (we cited a little earlier the example of Althusser in this respect).

So far, so good; but Legrand's more specific argument against Hook and Nagel seems to me to be primarily vitiated by a certain confusion between 'falsified' and 'falsifiable'. Science, says Legrand – in part reiterating comments in T. S. Kuhn's work – 'even in the course of its normal activity, is always concerned with problems which it is not in a position immediately to resolve; it is continually confronted by recalcitrant facts which cast it into doubt. To use a somewhat colloquial but apt expression, one could say that in science things are always somewhat out of joint. . . . If we were obliged to abandon a theory every time the facts failed to fit it, we would have to abandon every theory all the time' (p. 245). This formulation is too drastic, for between the alternatives of a model of science as a set of truths established once and for all, of which there can only be confirmation *per omnia saecula saeculorum*, and the opposite model of a science constantly belied by a succession of new experiences, there is fortunately a third possibility: that of a theory which emerges in part corrected from its confrontation with new facts, and in part 'relocated' – that is to say, confined to a more restricted field of application and contained within a more general theory. This indeed is the most normal pattern in the development of a science. However, if we discount its polemical extremism, Legrand's formulation can otherwise be accepted. If psychoanalysis had hitherto proceeded and were now proceeding in keeping with it, its scientificity would be guaranteed. But the flaw in the Freudian method of interpretation, and in the theories which Freud constructed from it, is not that these have in part been refuted by new experimental data which they have been able to accommodate only through modification of their initial postulates, but in something quite different – their immunity to falsifiability as such. Would that we had seen Freud forced more often to admit that a dream did not comply with his theory that all dreams are wish-fulfilments! The theory would have lost its absolute claims, but would have remained an extremely important moment in the history of psychology, now limited but not annulled. By contrast, the actual non-scientificity of the theory resides precisely in its capacity to elude (by way of sophistry) every possibility of falsification. Does someone have an anxiety dream about the death of a beloved person? Have no fear; this too is a wish-fulfilment, for it represents a resurgence of archaic psychic material which reveals that at some point in the infantile life of the dreamer the death of that person was indeed desired. The anxiety dream is concerned with the dreamer's *own* death? Another case of a wish – this time for self-punishment because of a guilt complex. Thus, just as Hook relates the futility of his search for a psychiatrist who could inform him what a child who had not been subject to the Oedipus complex would be like, we might ask with equal justification what characteristics a dream would have to possess in order not to be a wish-fulfillment. I am aware that in the final stage of his thought Freud admitted certain exceptions to this theory; but these were only in 'extreme' cases of persons who had undergone some very severe shock due, for example, to a train crash or grave injury suffered in war, and who regularly dreamed every night of a recurrence of the same accident. Moreover, more Freudian than Freud himself on this point, Jones attempts to maintain (see *Life*, III, p. 290) that even these dreams could be expressions of wishes. In fact, it is clear that on the contrary, the exceptions allowed for by Freud are too few and marginal: their number would be correspondingly greater and more notable (to the point where they could no longer be counted as 'exceptions') were one to forego the sophistical procedures employed by Freud. The very notion of 'archaic' (ontogenetic and phylogenetic) dream material, of the kind brought to light by 'slips' and neurotic symptoms, would assume a quite altered dimension.

Further on (p. 249) Legrand makes another objection to Hook and Nagel. The facts that refute a theory, he says, cannot be thought up 'in the study', but reveal themselves spontaneously when the theory enters into crisis as the result of the inauguration of new experimental techniques and new epistemological principles. Here too there is a confusion between falsification and falsifiability, though transferred to a different level. Legrand's earlier objection presumed a theory in continuous process of reassessment and correction in confrontation with new experimental data; this objection, by contrast, presupposes a relatively 'epochal' stability of a theory, which lasts until a revolution in science proclaims its death sentence. But even in the first formulation of a theory – its 'youth' – the scientist cannot help but submit it to controls. It is not true that such controls cannot be constructed: any scientific proposition, to the extent that it affirms a specific connexion between events, excludes other connexions and thereby declares certain phenomena 'forbidden' or 'impossible'. If, however – like the Freudian theory of dreams – it is devised in such a way that every possible refutation, given appropriate manipulation, is revealed as only apparent, then the theory is non-scientific from the *moment of its conception.*

What may however be contested, is the admissability of the counter-examples of the type that I employed on p. 44 sq. and on p. 143, in considering the free association that ensued from the forgetting of *aliquis* or a passage from Heine's poem. One could argue (and Franco Belgrado, Francesco Orlando and, with particular pertinence, Luigi Blasucci have done so) that it is precisely the fact that these episodes form 'individual histories' – comparable to the longer and more complex histories contributed by cases of real and actual neurosis and their treatment by the method of free association – that makes counter-examples irrelevant. The other associative chains that I have imagined (*ultor-Eltern* and so on) would then only be abstract possibilities; nothing would guarantee that if, instead of *aliquis*, Freud's young interlocutor had forgotten *ultor*, he would have followed the sequence *ultor-Eltern* or one similar to it. Certainly the diachronic disciplines, in which one cannot repeat the same experiments, or vary only one factor in them without alteration to any of the others, do not allow for absolutely rigorous counter-examples. Yet the associative chains, precisely because Freud considers them to be governed by the most stringent determinism, must indeed present some uniform typology, be obedient to the same 'logic' (which might be the logic of the unconscious, and other than that of the conscious Ego, but one still subject to its own rules). If in truth the forgetting of *aliquis* had been the product of that particular unpleasant repressed thought, the associative chain which led back to it from *aliquis,* and which would be the only 'true' one, should possess the privilege of a greater verisimilitude than the others I have imagined, which lead back to the same thought but start from some other word in Virgil's line. To argue the absolute invalidity of these (perhaps imperfect) counter-examples, one would have to pay a high price: one would have to assert the total individuality and non-repeatability of each 'history' of every neurotic. This would be to make psychoanalysis a 'historicist' doctrine in the pejorative, irrationalist and intuitionist sense which is incompatible with the very idea of a science.[1]

---

[1] See above, Chapter 7. There are, moreover, other demonstrations in the present volume of the 'unfalsifiability' of Freudian explanations, to which the objections above are not applicable: see, for example, pp.118; 133 sq.; 135 sq.; 137-9; 146. I should also like to say that our knowledge of the mechanism of 'slips' due to repression would be better verified if Freud and Jung themselves, who had before them, alive and talking (necessarily not the case with us), the young Austrian who had forgotten *aliquis,* and the elderly man who failed to recall the whole line in Heine's verses, had not contented themselves with the 'success' of their analyses, but had invited their interlocutors to abandon themselves to free associations starting from a word other than the one in fact forgotten in Virgil's line, or from another hemestich in Heine's poem. This would have provided much more rigorous counter-examples than the necessarily hypothetical ones to which I have been obliged to resort myself. If such associations, which started from words different to those in fact forgotten, had come to nothing (i.e. they did not permit the exposure of a repressed thought), Freudian theory would have been vindicated. If instead, as I personally believe to be likely, they had arrived at the same result, this would have confirmed the thesis I developed above (p. 53): any other 'parapraxis' would have functioned equally well in order to bring to light an anxious thought which was pressing in the pre-conscious and waiting for *any* occasion to surface (always admitted that one can speak of a pre-conscious thought rather than one already present to consciousness right

Today, especially since Lacan, there is much talk of the unconscious as a language. It is a matter for wonder that, for all the talk so little – if any – progress has been made in the formulation of the rules which must then govern the logic, grammar and lexis of the unconscious. It would obviously be absurd to expect a kind of standardized grammar of the unconscious of the Port-Royal type, in which everything was rational and relied on a one-to-one correspondence between signifier and signified. Given that the historico-natural languages which we speak while awake and conscious have innumerable homonyms, synonyms, redundancies and lacunae (to the point where, if one compared them with the artificial language of mathematical logic, one could refuse them the very status of languages); while poetical language, for its part – to increase its powers of expression even at the cost of its function as communication – takes liberties that are unknown or much less known to ordinary language (its far wider use of simile, metaphor, figures of speech of every kind, its recourse to archaisms or expressions in dialect which have stylistic value, and so on), we should expect the language of the unconscious to enjoy even greater figurative, associative and symbolic licence.[2] But however unencumbered and free-ranging, this language must still have its code. Otherwise, not even the analyst would be able to interpret (except by way of some mystical telepathy) the messages transmitted by it. So that whatever the extent of its freedom, it must also possess *restrictions*: what constitutes a signifier is not only that it denotes one or more signifieds, but that it does *not* denote an infinite number of others. The same can be said of the relationship between symptom and disease; only in this case, as we have seen, the situation is further exacerbated by the fact that Freud nearly always expounds and interprets single 'slips', and not an entire symptomology p.136). This is a procedure which any doctor would regard as

----

from the outset of the analysis, see p. 52). My purpose in this note is not so much to deplore what Freud and Jung failed to do in their own day (though it certainly demonstrates the insufficient rigour of their enquiries) but rather to invite contemporary analysts today to explore similar counter-examples.

[2] The subject is extremely well treated, and given a much more exact and articulated exposition than is to be found in my brief comment, by F. Orlando, *Per una teoria freudiana della letteratura,* op. cit., especially Chap. IV.

ridiculous, since one can practically never construct a diagnosis from an isolated symptom.

The paradox – and it is aggravated by those Freudians who have insisted even more than Freud on the nature of the unconscious as a language – is that Freud deciphered the language of the unconscious on innumerable occasions (and it continues to be interpreted by those of his disciples who fortunately are still alive), but never specified its code. The great merit of a recent book by Gemma Jappe (*Über Wort und Sprache in der Psychanalyse*, Frankfurt a M., 1971), which Sabina de Waal was kind enough to bring to my notice, is that it keeps well away from Lacan's obfuscations – but it still does not directly perform the task that its title invites one to expect. The idea of the 'predominance [*primauté*] of the signifier', which Lacan has singled out as characteristic of the language and the logic of the unconscious (that is, the tendency to make associations based not on conceptual affinity but on the phonic similarity of words), is one that is not without interest. Francesco Orlando[3] has encouraged me to reflect upon it. But – here, I know, he is not in agreement with me, and I await his reply to my comments – there are included among the Freudian associations not only many based on the phonic similarities of the signifiers, but also many that are founded on similarities (or oppositions) of the signifieds. We need only think of all the associations based on the names of saints in the case of the *aliquis* episode (above, p. 29 sqq.), or of the association between Bosnia and Herzegovina in the Signorelli case; or of that between the 'white mantle' (of snow) and the shroud in the case of the gentleman analyzed by Jung (above, p. 142 sq.); and the list could be greatly extended. Moreover, all the cases of translation, where we spoke somewhat facetiously of a 'polyglot unconscious' (pp. 43 sq.; 78–81; 139 note 15), rely not on a simple

[3] J. Lacan, *Ecrits* (Paris, 1966), p. 467 and elsewhere (see the *Index raisonné*, p. 895, under *La suprématie du signifiant sur la signifié*); Orlando, *Per una teoria*, op. cit., p. 52 and elsewhere. But Lacan (not Orlando) tends to conceive this preponderance or supremacy of the signifier as an essential characteristic of *every* language (not just that of the unconscious), on the basis of a forced interpretation of the Saussurian concept of the 'sign', which is consistent with the whole anti-objectivist tendency of current semiology for which the perfect sign is one which signifies nothing (see my comments in *On Materialism*, pp. 151–8; 183–5).

glissade from one signifier to another, but on a two-way process: from signifier to signified, and from the latter to the signifier with which another language expresses the same concept. One might further point to the use of symbology: can one ever be certain of an interpretation in a language in which a concept, especially one of a sexual nature, can disguise itself in a practically unlimited number of symbols, and in which the interpreter is therefore permitted to translate symbols into concepts, once again, without restrictions?

The failure hitherto to develop a logic and grammar of the unconscious is a particular, if conspicuous, case of a more general phenomenon. Though it is thirty-five years since the death of Freud, and thirty since the end of the persecution and ostracism of Freudian doctrine (if we except particularly reactionary ambiences against which we must always be vigilant, but which for the moment have not managed to obstruct the success of psychoanalysis in Europe, and more than ever in America), psychoanalysis has made very little secure progress as a science, if any at all. The image – shared by many, including Legrand – of a youthful science, whose impetuous advance excuses a certain deficiency of rigour and methodological refinement, is in contradiction to this fact, which is not easily gainsaid. I have said that psychoanalysis *as a science* is virtually at a standstill. By contrast it has, as we all know, achieved – and will continue to achieve – an immense success among writers, literary critics, philosophers, sociologists and cultural anthropologists. This triumph is not the result of a mechanical transposition of a doctrine created to cure neurosis into heterogeneous fields of study. For the extension of its application has corresponded to a real transformation of the theory itself. This transformation started with Freud himself, when an increase in the number of therapeutic failures and a decrease in his original interest in neurophysiology caused him to present psychoanalysis ever more as a general theory of humanity and civilization; and it has continued since Freud's death. Doctrines which started as more or less imaginative 'metaphysics' and later became sciences are common enough (it is enough to cite evolutionary theory in biology). Psychoanalysis has pursued the opposite path: though its aspirations were seriously scientific at its birth, from the outset it contained an admixture of speculative tendencies and then increasingly regressed from a science to a myth within a declining European culture. Today we observe the paradox that while psychoanalysis as a therapy records ever more failures, psychoanalysis as a theory finds its most ardent advocates among literary critics and philosophers. To note this is not to detract from the central importance of Freud for bourgeois culture during this century; but it does incline one to locate it on a different level. There can be no doubt that Freud greatly enriched contemporary man's knowledge of himself; but more in the sense that Proust, Kafka, Joyce, Musil have done so, than in the sense in which Darwin, Marx, Engels, Lenin or Einstein have done so. This is not a distinction between natural and human sciences, which merely assigns psychoanalysis to the latter (such an allocation would anyway be inexact, since Freud's ideas on man, civilization and society are fraught with a dire Lamarckian-Haeckelian biologism, as we have seen). It is an assertion that with the exception of some inspired but fairly restricted scientific conquests, psychoanalysis is neither a natural nor a human science, but a self-confession by the bourgeoisie of its own misery and perfidy, which blends the bitter insight and ideological blindness of a class in decline.

All the same, if I may allow myself to express a wish for the debates to which I hope this book will give rise, I would not want these to focus just on the problem of a general option for or against psychoanalysis, or for or against its compatibility with Marxism; I would want them also to confront specific problems. Is it legitimate, for example, to postulate a 'Freudian' motive for all or nearly all 'slips' and instances of forgetting, or are the majority of these psychic disturbances indeed related to unconscious factors, but to a much more mechanical-instinctual unconscious, and thus one much less connected with the individual history of the person who committed the 'slip'? Does there, in addition to the forgetting derived from repression, exist a 'physiological' forgetting (of far more frequent occurrence) due to loss of interest or the intervention of other preoccupations which demand for themselves our not unlimited mnemonic capacities? Must such processes as banalization, the influence of context, the 'polar' error and so forth, content themselves with the subsidiary role allocated to them by Freud of

Begünstigungen to the 'slip', or are they to be allowed in the majority of cases to be considered as 'causes' of the 'slip' itself? Before one attributes an instance of forgetting or a 'slip' to a relatively recent repression, ought one not to ask whether the 'slip' (if by now consolidated as 'error') or the forgetting arose a long time before the actual or presumed repression (see p. 162 note 6)? Finally, how is it that even among those 'slips' that are due to repression, we do not encounter any that relate to class antagonism or to fear of 'physical harm' (disease, death, see pp. 114–19)? Is this the effect of a censorship of such menacing issues by Freud or does it have some other plausible explanation? These I believe to be problems that merit discussion, even – indeed especially – by those who consider my solutions to them to be mistaken.

Index of Names and Themes

Abel, K., 115n
Abraham, Karl, 135, 136
acceptance of the analyst's interpretation by the patient, 53–60
Adler, Alfred, 117n, 206n
Albini, Giuseppe, 33n
Albini, Umberto, 37n
Alfieri, Vittorio, 27
Althusser, Louis, 88n, 90n, 215, 217
amnesia (see also 'lapsus'), 155–6, 162–4, 167–71; Freud's theory of a. caused by repression, 41–5, 167–71 and passim; infantile a., 169–70; similarity of Freud's theory with that of Nietzsche, 167–8; alternative explanations, 29–32 (see also forgetting and 'elimination of the superfluous'); stabilization of a. and its transformation into forgetting, 162; feigned a., 139n.; vexation of someone who is affected by a., 157n

anagrammatic, errors, 72n, 141n
analysis: 'at a distance', 50n, 140; suggestive intervention by the the analyst, 50–53; general suggestive atmosphere, 51–3
Andreas-Salomé, Lou, 116n, 117n
Andrieu, Jean, 21n, 25

Andocides, 37
Arlow, Jacob A., 15n
association (free) in psychoanalytic technique, 41–7, 49–56, 60, 77–81, 220; a. by translation from one language into another, 43f., 78–81, 138n, 139n
Athenaios, 74–5
Austro-Hungarian society, 107–9 and passim
Aristophanes, 22
Avesani, Rino, 20n

Bachelard, Gaston, 215
banalization, 30–5, 39, 63, 72n, 157; b. as contributory cause for substitutions of phonically similar words, 65–7, 146–7, syntactic b., 31n, 32–5; b. in word-order, 39; explanation of the phenomenon, 92f.; countervailing tendencies to b., 99–100
Barabino, Giuseppina, 20n
Barbieri, Orazio, 72n
Bassin, F. V., 48n
Becker, Felix, 85n
Begünstigungen (circumstances favouring a slip or an instance of forgetting without being its cause), v. lapsus
Belgrado, Franco, 213, 219
Bellone, Enrico, 198n

Rossi, Luigi Enrico, 28
Rossi, Vittorio, 213
Rousseau, Jean-Jacques, 193
Russo, Carlo Ferdinando, 138n,
157

Sabbadini, Remigio, 136
Sachs, Hanns, 79n, 184n
Salust: *lectio difficilior* drawn from
a recent edition, 39n
Samonà, Giuseppe Paolo, 101
Saussure, Ferdinand de, 91, 94,
222
Scalet, Ennio, 213
Schatzmann, M., 167n, 179n
Schelling, Friedrich Wilhelm
Joseph, 192, 193n
Schiller, Friedrich, 33, 94n, 104
Schleicher, August, 195
Schlimmbesserung
('disimprovement'), 71–6
Schopenhauer, Arthur, 13, 177,
185–6, 192–3, 198, 205, 211
Schuchardt, Hugo, 136
Schreber, Daniel Paul, 179n
Schulze, Wilhelm, 72n
Schwartz, Eduard, 25
science: 'neutrality' of s., 17,
173–5; s. and ideology in bour-
geois culture, 174–7, 208, 215
Sciesa, Amatore, 99
Sedova, Natalya Ivanovna,
(Trotsky's wife), 206n
Seipel, Ignaz, 190n
Seneca, 202
Septimius, Lucius, 73n
Serge, Victor, 206n
Servius (ancient commentator of
Virgil), 32–4
Sève, Lucien, 88n, 89, 90n, 210
sexuality (in broad sense) and
genitality, 182, 183n
Shakespeare, William, 104n
Sinner, Louis de, 104n

slip, *passim*; does Freud allow the
existence of non-'Freudian' s.?
128–32, 224–5; 'causes' of the s.
and *Begünstigungen*, 83–4, 92,
96f., 131n; individual and
collective s., 70, 71ff., 91f., 101,
122; individual non-'Freudian'
s., 101, 122; cases where the
Freudian explanation is
plausible, 122f., 147–8; gaffes,
104–5, 127; absence of class
conflict and fear of death in
Freud's explanation, 110–9;
Freudian critique of previous
theories of the s., 83–5; s. and
'errors', 155–67; failure to relate
theory of the s. to successive
conceptions of the Unconscious,
81; significance of the vexation
felt by someone making a s.
157n; the single s. and sympto-
matology, 221–2; s. provoked
by suggestion or auto-
suggestion, 94, 151; s.
attributable to banalization, see
banalization; s. of substitution
of a phonically similar word,
22n, 63–73, 95, 134f., 146, 165;
s. of garbled pronunciation or
writing, 130, 135–42; s. due to
influence of the context, 97f.;
'polar' s., 148–53; s. of
repetition, 143–4; s. consisting
in the 'perseverance at a remove'
of memories, 144–5; see also
amnesia
Somenzi, Vittorio, 95n
Spinoza, Baruch, 96
Stalin, Josef Vissarionovich, 109,
148, 149; Stalinism, 176, 191
Stärcke, J., 106n
Statius, 66
Stoll, Jakob, 24n, 37n
Storfer, A. J., 146
Strachey, James, 15n

Index of Slips

The slips and other parapraxes referred to by Freud are marked with an asterisk

*ab for *ex*, 39n
*Achol for *Alcohol*, 78n, 141
Adrasto for *Alcasto*, 65–6
*Agamemnon for *angenommen*, 154
against the partisans for *against the Germans and the fascists*, 150–1
Ἀγησίλαος for Ἀκουσίλαος, 65, 70
*aliquis, omitted, 29–35, 39–40, 43–7, 49, 55–6, 78, 85, 89, 94, 103, 109, 118, 140–1, 162
Anaxagoras for *Protagoras*, 68–9, 156, 158–60
Anticlea for *Euryclea*, 22, 65
Armida for *Alcina*, 68
assurda ('absurd') for *assurta* ('attained'), 151
autonomisti for *atomisti*, 101, 124

*Ben Hur, forgotten (or intentionally not said out of prudery?), 139n
*Boltraffio (from *Botticelli*) for *Signorelli*, 63, 70–1, 75–7, 85, 89, 100
*Botticelli for *Signorelli*, 63–5, 69–70, 75–8, 85, 89, 94, 100, 103, 109
*Buckrhard for *Burckhard*, 141n

*Calatafimi (*Caltanissetta*) for *Castelvetrano*, 133–4

*charging a higher price than is owed, 205n
Charmadam (later 'corrected' to *Carneadam*) for *Charmidam*, 73–4
Cinzia for *Trivia*, 67
*closed for *open*, 147

De Gasperi for *De Gregori*, 123–4

Emilio for *Emidio*, 99
Eupolis for *Aristophanes*, 22
*ex nostris ossibus for *nostris ex ossibus*, 39–40
*exoriare remembered with special clarity, 46

*forgetting to pay the bill, 204–5
Freud (patients who state they have been sent by Freud, or who call their own analyst Freud), 152n

*Gassendi, forgotten, 170–1
Gattopardiani for *Gottorpiani*, 101, 125

*Hanna, name of the first daughter given incorrectly instead of that of the second, 178–9
*Hartmann for *Hitschmann*, 146
*Hasdrubal for *Hamilcar*, 165–6
husband for *brother* (feigned slip), 127n

Radical Thinkers